The Poetic Workmanship of
ALEXANDER POPE

The Poetic Workmanship of

ALEXANDER POPE

by

REBECCA PRICE PARKIN

1966

OCTAGON BOOKS, INC.

New York

Reprinted 1966
by special arrangement with University of Minnesota Press

OCTAGON BOOKS, INC.
175 FIFTH AVENUE
NEW YORK, N. Y. 10010

LIBRARY OF CONGRESS CATALOG CARD NUMBER: 66-29334

Printed in U.S.A. by
NOBLE OFFSET PRINTERS, INC.
NEW YORK 3, N. Y.

Preface

ALEXANDER POPE'S poetry can be a specific against the prevailing intellectual and spiritual disorder of our times on two levels—the semantic and the technical. Practicing poets and critics are interested in the latter; every man is affected by the basic human dilemmas Pope's poetry presents.

In Pope's poetic universe all sins, both mortal and venial, stem from solipsism; from what Allen Tate in *The Last Days of Alice* strikingly calls "incest of spirit" and in his *Ode to the Confederate Dead* imagines as

> . . . the patient curse
> That stones the eyes, or like the jaguar leaps
> For his own image in a jungle pool, his victim.

Conrad Aiken in "Silent Snow, Secret Snow" represents solipsism as "a story that gets smaller and smaller—it comes inward instead of opening like a flower—it is a flower becoming a seed—a little cold seed."

This ingrowing process is so characteristic of the spiritual motions of the twentieth century that Aiken's clinical history of a schoolboy's gradual withdrawal from reality into himself may be taken as a symbol of the chief dilemma of the present: What shall a man do—not to be saved, but to be safe? T. S. Eliot's word for the malady was Prufrockianism, and his personal remedy everyone knows. Alexander Pope's solution, to which the whole corpus of his poetry testifies, provided him with a strong intellectual and spiritual citadel.

v

If the reader, in good neoclassic fashion, will pillage Pope's verse, as Pope for the same reason pillaged those who came before him, and take for his own whatever in it will do him good, he will find that the peace of the Augustans is indeed there and may be achieved, not merely as a historical perception and sympathy but as a mental attitude of unchanging value.

I am grateful to Barnard College, Columbia University, Yale University, and the American Association of University Women for scholarships and fellowships which enabled me to complete my general education, specialize in eighteenth-century literature, and make this study of Pope's craftsmanship; to my parents, who really believed that knowledge is more to be desired than material possessions; and to my husband, whose encouragement and active assistance with domestic and maternal duties gave me leisure to prepare my manuscript for publication.

To Professor Maynard Mack of Yale I can never be sufficiently grateful for what I learned about reading poetry, Pope's in particular, in his seminar on the Augustan Age. I am also indebted to him for his direction of this study in its early form. In admiration of his own brilliant contributions to Popian scholarship, this book is dedicated to him—with the conviction, however, that it follows his work *non passibus aequis*.

REBECCA PRICE PARKIN

Table of Contents

vii

The Poetic Workmanship of
ALEXANDER POPE

1

Introduction

T HE following chapters examine certain poetic practices of Pope as they contribute to and clarify his total meaning. His use of such devices as the implied dramatic speaker, irony, tension, parallelism, antithesis, paradox, narrative, metaphor, and tonal variation are considered as they function in the individual poem and in his work as a whole. The influence of the classical concepts of genre and imitation is discussed. It is hoped that this study will help remove some of the misapprehensions which have existed concerning both what Pope said and how he said it.

The guiding principle has been one which Pope himself repeatedly emphasized as the keystone of both metaphysical and literary criticism: The part is to be judged on the basis of its proper relation to the whole. In the *Essay on Man* Pope makes this the foundation of his pronouncements on man's place in the universe, his aims, and his possibilities for happiness. In the *Essay on Criticism* he shows how this principle may be used to evaluate a literary work of art. In the present study the reader's attention is focused on one element after another of Pope's craftsmanship in the belief that out of this will arise an enriched and deepened understanding of his poetic world.

The Pope canon has not changed notably since 1744, and the criteria of logic have presumably not changed. But it is well known that not long after Pope's death his poetic reputation began to suffer an eclipse from which it is only beginning to emerge.

The basic reason for this eclipse was the dominance during the

3

Romantic and Victorian periods of a sensibility hostile to the sort of poetry in which Pope excelled. The nineteenth century saw the full flowering of this sensibility, the beginnings of which were perceptible in Pope's own lifetime. Against this shift of values he, Gay, Swift, Arbuthnot, and the other members of the Scriblerus Club—as well as later that staunch bulwark and inheritor of their responsibility, Dr. Samuel Johnson—battled unremittingly but in the end unsuccessfully. The Fourth Book of the *Dunciad*, where the lights of civilization go out one by one, and the fundamental insight of *Gulliver's Travels* as well, were prophetic.

As a result of the direction given to English criticism by the reforms sought in the language and content of poetry in 1798, Pope came to be commended, at best, for such qualities as his dry (and by implication unpoetic) wit, his mechanical skill in manipulating the couplet, and the epigrammatic finish of his quotable commonplaces. At the worst, he was not considered a poet at all, though he was conceded to be the best substitute for one that an age of prose could produce.

Another circumstance unfavorable to Pope's reputation as a major poet was the growing tendency during the nineteenth century to read verse in the light of facts known or surmised about the author's personal life. Hence the Elwin-Croker-Courthope portrait, and many others, which depict him as an envious, conniving, spiteful, and dishonest little hunchback. Such portrayals influenced the disparagement of his brilliant achievement in satire, for example, as a mere outpouring of personal venom.

For various reasons almost all his works went under a cloud. The *Essay on Man*, with its attempt to "vindicate the ways of God to man," ran afoul of progressive thought in politics and religion. Professional philosophers, who did not distinguish between the aims of a poem and the aim of a philosophical treatise, continued to attack it as if it were a philosophic system. Professional literary critics, falling into the same error, repeated what the philosophers said and put the poem in its place as a string of epigrammatic platitudes.

4

The Rape of the Lock, though it continued to be admired as a pretty trifle, suffered misreading and a consequent diminution in stature. The *Dunciad* met with little approval, partly because it was thought to be a spiteful paying off of personal scores and partly because elucidation of its numerous topical references was assumed to be necessary for comprehension. *Eloisa to Abelard*, which happened to fall in to some extent with Romantic ideas of what a poem should be, remained popular but was sometimes arraigned as excessively rhetorical. The *Pastorals* were stigmatized as artificial and unnatural. The *Essay on Criticism* enjoyed the dubious distinction of being a mine of quotable saws, but the critical system it advocated was decried. Finally, a narrow conception of originality caused Pope's accomplishment in providing an English equivalent of Homer to be belittled.

For Pope's poetry, perhaps the most unfavorable single trait of the new sensibility was the tendency to divorce poetry from intellect. Poetry was ranged on one side of the fence under Fancy; fact and truth lay on the other side. Nineteenth-century poets, moreover, tended on the whole to produce a thin verse with only one meaning. Pope's characteristic pattern of deliberate ambiguities and layered complexities enclosed in a case of limpid surface meaning almost ceased to be recognized.

Recently the tide has begun to turn. Edith Sitwell's intuitions and George Sherburn's patient siftings of evidence have modified the unflattering biographical portrait. This has been confirmed by a clearer understanding of eighteenth-century publishing practices as well as of the attitude taken toward the literary correspondence and public decorum of a poet. Revaluation of the doctrine of imitation and of the translator's art has contributed toward a new judgment of these important areas of Pope's poetic activity. Many helpful critical insights have been supplied by Cleanth Brooks, Ian Jack, Douglas Knight, F. R. Leavis, Maynard Mack, Geoffrey Tillotson, and W. K. Wimsatt. A most significant factor has been the emergence of the so-called New Criticism, a movement which, in spite of some shortcomings, has at least not been hostile to the methods and aims of cerebral poetry.

The following pages continue the critical revaluation of Pope, showing how as a conscious and careful craftsman he used various rhetorical elements in traditional media to achieve his individual poetic communication. And this communication is by no means superficial, as has sometimes been charged. Pope's poetry deals, in a way both canny and profound, with the most urgent problems human beings have.

2

The Implied Dramatic Speaker

Use of a dramatically conceived communicator is not, of course, confined to Pope. The device is present in all poetry; it is, in fact, an indispensable condition under which every poem functions. Poets differ from each other, however, in their handling of the speaker; and an individual poet may, as Pope definitely does, vary his use from poem to poem. The reward of examining the function of the speaker—in general, in a poet's works as a whole, and in individual poems—is that, like the analysis of any part of a poem, it leads to clearer and fuller understanding of the whole.

Focusing on the dramatic role of the speaker in any poem is a valuable corrective to the biographic approach, the approach which confuses Hamlet's opinions with Shakespeare's, Lemuel Gulliver's with Jonathan Swift's, and Prufrock's with T. S. Eliot's. Both Pope's biography and his poetry have suffered from this approach. The tendency toward automatic identification of the speaker of a poem with the author is understandable, particularly when the first person is used. But it is not fair either to the author or his poems.

The concept of the implied dramatic speaker is closely related to the concept of tone. If we define the speaker as the implied fictional character—not wholly identifiable with the author—who communicates the poem, then tone may be defined as the atti-

NOTE: This chapter is an expanded version of an essay that appeared, under the title "Alexander Pope's Use of the Implied Dramatic Speaker," in *College English*, December 1949.

tude of this speaker toward the subject of the poem. A corollary of the implied speaker is the implied audience. Just as the speaker need not be, and usually is not, identical with the author, so the implied audience is an element of the poem itself. It does not necessarily coincide with a given chance reader or even with a person to whom the poem may be formally addressed. With these concepts in mind, a poem may be defined as a transaction between an implied speaker and an implied audience, the degree and kind of transaction being to a large extent determined by the subject matter and the speaker's attitude toward it.

The device and its corollaries serve five general rhetorical ends: unity, objectivity, maximum relevancy of viewpoint, dramatic tension and particularity, and identification with a specific ideological convention.

1. *Unity*, because the dramatic speaker is ordinarily not changed within a given poem. Everything said is from the viewpoint of a single person, who may develop, as any fictional character may, but who does not become another.

2. *Objectivity*, because the device enables the poet to shed the trammels of his own personality.

3. *Maximum relevancy of viewpoint*, because in an effective poem the issue is seen through the eyes of the most interesting and relevant dramatic personality that can be brought to bear on the situation.

4. *Dramatic tension and particularity*, because the speaker is a concrete individual in a particular situation which contains an element of conflict. That is, the speaker is presented as a person reacting to some aspect of the universe and trying, by the device of persuasive rhetoric, to induce his implied audience to react as he does or at least to understand his reaction.

5. *Identification with a specific ideological convention*, because, since it involves as a rule delimitation in time and place, it permits ellipsis and promotes compression, two factors which play a role in much good poetry, and especially in Alexander Pope's.

To gain some perspective on Pope's individual use of the dramatic speaker, let us first consider briefly how the device functions in poems by three other authors from three different centuries: *The Love Song of J. Alfred Prufrock*, *My Last Duchess*, and *Lycidas*.

In *Prufrock* the dramatic speaker is particularly important as a unifying force. Reverie which progresses by association of ideas rather than by overt logical structure is ordinarily more difficult for the reader to follow. A clear presentation of the character and stance of the poem's speaker can be of great help in preventing disintegration and unintelligibility. As soon as the reader has grasped the central aspect of Prufrock's character, his impulse toward heroic action and the inhibitions and indecisions which prevent him from acting, then the anesthetized evening, the pair of ragged claws, the sniggering Footman, the rolled trousers, and the reluctant mermaids begin to draw together into a comprehensible unity.

Prufrock also illustrates the way a dramatic speaker helps achieve objectivity. Since Prufrock is a persona, not automatically identifiable with Eliot, the poet can view him with greater detachment. He can make him react without the inhibitions, conscious and unconscious, that tend to operate when "I" is at all points and unequivocally equated with the poet. That Eliot was aware of this advantage is clear not only from the importance he attached to the objective correlative but also from his prefacing this particular poem with a pertinent quotation from Dante. Dante's underworld informant spoke freely only because he believed he spoke to a person who would never return to the world: *A persona che mai tornasse al mondo*.

My Last Duchess differs from *Prufrock* in possessing an overtly logical organization. But like *Prufrock* it benefits from the fact that the dramatic speaker is also the main character in the action. All minor characters and incidents are unified by being presented from the Duke's point of view. Peculiar relevancy of viewpoint is obtained by making the villain of this plot conduct himself in that role as if not he but his victim were the malefactor. This is the source of the special ironic tension of the poem.

The very man who committed the monstrous crime against his

9

wife retells it on the eve of arranging to marry another innocent young girl. He even relates it to the very person sent to represent the prospective bride's interests. Every word of self-excuse that falls from this speaker's mouth strengthens the bill of damnation against him. Additional irony arises from the identity of the implied audience, the Count's emissary, dispatched to treat of the new marriage. The Duke would seem to be assured that either man, master, or both are so corrupt that the marriage will go forward even though he admits to having murdered his first wife.

In still another way it is plain that the Duke is the best possible speaker to bring this poem to its highest point of ironic tension. His own perverted attitude toward the horrible event he recounts acts as a sort of filter for the reader's sensitivity. Furthermore, the Duke's urbanity strengthens the contrast between matter and manner. His references to art and art criticism, his use of polite locutions such as "Will't please you sit and look at her?" set a tone of cool poise which makes it possible for the story to be told. The selection of the Duke as dramatic speaker is thus at once a means of obtaining aesthetic distance from the horrible theme and of reinforcing its horror.

Lycidas, strictly speaking, has two dramatic speakers, one for the body of the poem and one for the concluding eight lines. Though these concluding lines play an interesting part in the tonal pattern of the poem, their speaker is very impersonally conceived and may for the moment be disregarded.

The main dramatic speaker embodies and focuses on the material three different ideological conventions. In the tradition of a special variant of the pastoral he is a shepherd in three senses: the idealized keeper of sheep such as Theocritus sang, the young rural poet conscious of the Greco-Roman pastoral tradition, and the Christian pastor.

Though the third sense is the most important for the emphasis of this poem, the combination of the three has a significance of its own. In his triple role the speaker has an actual counterpart in the "shepherd," Edward King, whose death was the occasion of the poem. Some of the dramatic tension derives from this fact.

King, the shepherd spoken of, is dead. The shepherd speaking—his counterpart in youth, education, poetic talent, and religious dedication—is still living. The reader's sense of the poignancy on the personal level and the misfortune on the national level of the first shepherd's untimely death is increased by the speaker's realization that what happened to Edward King could happen to him. There is a resultant decrease of hope that the unhappy national religious situation will be amended.

In this connection it may be asked why, in a poem concerned with religious issues, Milton did not deal with them directly instead of resorting to a poetic genre in which he could treat them only by means of a fortunate pun on "pastoral"? The question has a bearing on both the tone and the speaker's function here. In part the pastoral was adopted for historical reasons; there was a strong tradition of using it for elegy. But its use is also functional. In dealing with time-dulled issues like "Feed my sheep" and "Lay up treasure in heaven" the oblique approach is more likely to alert the reader than the direct. The pastoral convention operates as a screen. Instead of obscuring the problem, it stimulates the speaker into making a greater effort to see what is behind it.

There is piquancy too in the contrast the reader inevitably makes between the tranquillity reigning in the pastoral and the bitter indignation with which these matters were discussed in pre-Cromwellian England. What results is a tonal contrast based on the ideological contrast between pagan pastoralism and Puritanism. In the main body of the poem the two ideologies are united in the person of the chief dramatic speaker. They are separated again in the eight lines of postlude previously mentioned, where complete serenity is desired and obtained, partly as a result of the foregoing Christian reconciliation to death and partly from the fact that the speaker is shifted. This concluding speaker has an effect comparable to that of a Greek chorus's closing and tranquilizing comment. By oblique remarks he establishes an atmosphere above and beyond the atmosphere of the poem proper—an atmosphere which is itself a commentary on the body of the poem:

At last he rose, and twitch'd his Mantle blew:
To morrow to fresh Woods, and Pastures new.

All poets are to some extent circumscribed in their treatment of the dramatic speaker by such conventions as those of a school or a genre. In his *Pastorals* we see Pope at his most circumscribed in this matter. Since the pastoral, one of the most conventional genres, is in its very essence a tissue of traditional artifices, departures from its conventions are attended with particular peril. Few successful radical departures from its main traditions have been made by English pastoralists. Pope chose to make none at all.

The character and stance of the implied speaker of his *Pastorals* are purer—that is, closer to the traits of a hypothetical speaker for the genre—than, for instance, in *The Shepheardes Calender* or in *Lycidas*. This is especially evident in the relation of Pope's speaker to his subject matter. His stance is formal, restrained, courtly, stylized to a much greater degree than is the case with either Spenser's or Milton's speaker. Barring the brief courtly compliments to Garth and Trumbull, Pope's speaker almost never obtrudes himself directly into the action and the emotions of the poem, as Milton's speaker memorably does in *Lycidas*. He reveals nothing about himself except that he is a young poet, with classical training and aspirations, exercising himself in the pastoral landscape. Throughout all four poems he carefully maintains a decorous distance between himself and his subjects. Not once does he become passionately involved in the action and thunder forth about a non-Arcadian issue, as does Milton's speaker in such a passage as "Blind mouthes!" An important function of Pope's speaker is precisely to secure that depersonalization and objectivity which to the neoclassical mind seemed the only basis for a sane, well-rounded view of man and the universe.

Eloisa to Abelard is in direct contrast with the *Pastorals* on this matter. The ceremonial distance between speaker and subject gives way to a situation in which the speaker (technically, of course, a letter-writer) is herself the principal subject. In part a concomitant of this change, the tone of *Eloisa to Abelard* is tense, urgent, immediate in its impact, contrasting with the serenity and aesthetic exclusion which prevail in the *Pastorals*. The reason for the change is a difference in aim. Pope in this heroic epistle is not striving for restraint, but for an impression of unrestraint, of passion so strong that it can barely be contained within the bounds of communicability.

For securing this tonal effect, and for maximum relevancy of viewpoint, the advantage of being able to choose the principal sufferer in the tragedy as the communicator is obvious. The scattered details of the story are brought into sharp dramatic focus, and the reader is given the illusion of being inside Eloisa's mind. He sees the crucial issue balanced back and forth as she is torn between the pagan affirmation of physical love as a positive good and the Christian denial of the body. That the poet can count on an audience familiar with the implications of this ideological antithesis is a favoring circumstance. He need waste no time on definition and exposition but can grapple immediately with the heart of the subject.

It is an interesting fact that Eloisa has not one but several implied audiences. The four major ones are: Abelard, herself, Heaven, and literary posterity. She is always conscious of all of them; but as she directs herself primarily to one or the other, her tone varies. The audience with which she is most tense is Abelard. Least tension is involved and there is most effort at rationalization when posterity's reaction is uppermost in her mind:
To Abelard:

> Thou, Abelard! the last sad office pay,
> And smooth my passage to the realms of day:
> See my lips tremble, and my eye-balls roll,
> Suck my last breath, and catch my flying soul!
> Ah no—in sacred vestments may'st thou stand,
> The hallow'd taper trembling in thy hand,
> Present the Cross before my lifted eye,
> Teach me at once, and learn of me to die.
>   (321–328)*

* This and subsequent quotations from Pope are taken from the Twickenham edition wherever possible. Quotations from poems not yet published in that edition are from George Sherburn's *The Best of Pope* (New York, The Ronald Press Company, 1929) and in one instance (a quotation from

To posterity:

> And sure if fate some future Bard shall join
> In sad similitude of griefs to mine,
> Condemn'd whole years in absence to deplore,
> And image charms he must behold no more,
> Such if there be, who loves so long, so well;
> Let him our sad, our tender story tell;
> The well-sung woes will soothe my pensive ghost;
> He best can paint 'em, who shall feel 'em most.
>
> (359–366)

The existence of more than one implied audience and the accompanying variation of tone in speaking to each of them underlines the truly dramatic function of the implied speaker. It also shows how a poet alert, as Pope is, to the potentialities of the device, may use it to secure greater variety and flexibility. Eloisa varies her attitude with her auditor just as a person in a play varies his tone and manner when speaking to different members of the cast. Her attitude toward the Church (Heaven, God) exhibits a mixture of abject self-condemnation in conformity with the traditional stance of a postulant for salvation and a scarcely concealed contempt and hostility:

> While praying, trembling, in the dust I roll,
> And dawning grace is opening on my soul:
> Come, if thou dar'st, all charming as thou art!
> Oppose thyself to heav'n; dispute my heart;
> Come, with one glance of those deluding eyes,
> Blot out each bright Idea of the skies.
> Take back that grace, those sorrows, and those tears,
> Take back my fruitless penitence and pray'rs,
> Snatch me, just mounting, from the blest abode,
> Assist the Fiends and tear me from my God!   (279–288)

Her attitude toward herself reveals a comparable paradox. She is proud of the part she played with Abelard and of the fact that her passion for him was so strong as to blind her to every other consideration. But at the same time this memory is the cause of her abysmal despair:

Book XII of the Iliad) from the Cambridge edition of Pope's *Complete Poetical Works.*

14

I view my crime, but kindle at the view,
Repent old pleasures, and solicit new:
Now turn'd to heav'n, I weep my past offence,
Now think of thee, and curse my innocence.

(185–188)

Eloisa is most collected and unemotional when thinking of herself as a subject for future poetry; and she is aware that she is a good subject. She is most passionate, most tense, most hortatory, and her reasoning most specious, when she addresses Abelard. Her alteration of tone and argumentative method with each audience is an indication of the skill and subtlety with which the device of the dramatic speaker is exploited to achieve the purposes of this poem.

As for the ideological convention with which this speaker is identified, *Eloisa to Abelard* is one of the very few poems in which Pope has dealt sympathetically with the Romantic tenet that *grande passion* excuses everything. It would be a mistake to assume, however, that because he employs this Romantic doctrine with sympathy, he employs it with approval. Pope wished to procure the greatest possible degree of pathos and of understanding for his principal dramatic character. Eloisa is not the heroine here in the sense that Cordelia is the heroine of *King Lear*, but rather in the sense that Lady Macbeth is the heroine of *Macbeth*. Shakespeare depicts Lady Macbeth with sympathy, but he does not indicate approval of her actions or motives. The same is true of Pope's attitude toward Eloisa. The ideological framework of his poem is commonly assumed to be Christian; and according to that ideology Eloisa's character and conduct have a fatal flaw: she has preferred Aphrodite to St. Paul. But Pope's framework is really Augustan. To the Augustan, neither unbridled passion nor morbid asceticism is commendable. The norm of conduct recommended is, as always, the *via media*. Consequently, from the Augustan viewpoint, Eloisa is the victim of a double tragedy.

Before leaving *Eloisa* it is worth noting that Pope did not in this poem invent a new stance for the dramatic speaker. He drew first on the general convention that a speaker's principal subject may be himself, and, more particularly, on the speaker convention of the heroic epistle.

Eloisa has some points in common with most feminine inditers of heroic epistles. She is bereft of her love; she is not reconciled to her bereavement; and she calls posterity to witness her sufferings and fidelity. Pathetic and passionate reminiscence, together with outcry, are her basic method.

Eloisa as a speaker has some traits, however, which are individual. Because of the particular circumstances of her story, she does not, as do many of her sister speakers, have to reproach her lover with infidelity. On the contrary—and this increases the drama and pathos of her situation—she is bound to give him all her sympathy for the event which snatched him from her, an event of which she herself was, though not the instigator, the occasion. More especially, Eloisa differs from other feminine speakers of heroic epistles in being an eighteenth-century English neoclassical protagonist. To mention only one consequence of her neoclassicism, she is acutely aware of two oppositions: that of passion to reason and that of morbid asceticism to reason. She feels a compulsion to rationalize both passions, and yet is so very reason-conscious that she continually examines and exhibits the flimsiness of her own rationalizations.

Like speakers of heroic epistles, the less salient speakers of Pope's two mock epics, *The Rape of the Lock* and the *Dunciad*, have certain features in common. The most notable of these is the mock-heroic stance. The tonal unity which results from the maintenance of this throughout both poems is an important element in their success. The ironic, and hence oblique, attitude implied is marked by especial sensitivity to the discrepancy between heroic profession and human performance. Both speakers are primarily concerned with establishing a norm and then exhibiting deviation from it. In both cases, in conformity with the mock-heroic pose, the norm is established indirectly by implication rather than directly by exposition. Both speakers are sophisticates and assume worldly sophistication in their audiences. The difference in their characters is not so much absolute as occasional. And the conditioning they evince is comparable to that which would occur if the same person, holding the same basic opinions, were on one occasion addressing a learned society and on another trying to be amusing at a party.

It is clear that the implied audience of the *Dunciad*'s straightforward bawdry is composed of men only; whereas the implied audience of *The Rape of the Lock* contains both women and men. The latter poem is slanted somewhat, however, toward feminine auditors. This is not to say that *The Rape* is the less bawdy poem. But the scatology in the *Dunciad*, Book II, for example, is gross and unequivocal; while such lines as those Belinda utters in complaint against the Baron

> Oh hadst thou, Cruel! been content to seize
> Hairs less in sight, or any Hairs but these
> (IV, 175–176)

may be taken in either an innocent or a scandalous sense. This is one of the many instances, in the two poems, of modification of attitude or mode of statement in deference to the implied audience.

In thus accommodating himself to the subject matter of *The Rape* and its presumed audience, the poet has not, however, sacrificed scope. It becomes an interesting trait of the dramatic speaker that he obtains scope by indirection, implication, and, more especially, by symbolism—as when the game of ombre is made to stand for the war between the sexes. The speaker of the *Dunciad*, as is particularly evident in Book IV, deals with major issues more directly.

More than any other of Pope's poems the *Epistle to Dr. Arbuthnot* highlights the issue of the relationship between the poet and the speaker. Not only in Pope's poetry, but in poetry in general, there are admittedly situations in which the identity of the speaker and the identity of the actual poet approach each other. When this is the case, there is a particular temptation to overlook the boundary separating poetry and biography and to treat the poet's persona as if he were the actual poet.

In periods when the lyric mode is popular there tends to be a closer relationship between the situations and the opinions of poet and speaker. For example, in the case of Sidney's *Astrophel and Stella* it is known from outside biographical evidence that the circumstances of the "I" of the poems correspond in some instances to those of the author. But what of a sonnet sequence like Drayton's *Ideas Mirrour?*

The point is, not that here and there coincidental resemblances between poetic fiction and actual biography may exist, but that both these sonnet sequences are written in the same tradition of the dramatic lyric. Both Sidney and Drayton conform to the Petrarchan pose. Any similarities between aspects of that pose and the biography of either poet are as irrelevant to criticism of the poems as are points of similarity between Hamlet—or Iago—and Shakespeare.

In the *Epistle to Dr. Arbuthnot* there are unquestionable likenesses between the speaker's attitude toward a persecuting horde of incompetent and unscrupulous scribblers, and what is known to have been Alexander Pope's. The speaker makes reference by name to men who actually were Pope's friends or enemies: Dennis, Gildon, Lintot, Swift, Bentley, "Tibbald," Cibber, etc. He alludes to actual contemporary literary quarrels in which Pope was involved—for instance, the controversy about the description of the Duke of Chandos' estate in *Moral Essay* IV.

The poem contains, moreover, celebrated satiric portraits of men whom Pope actually knew and had some aversion for: Lord Hervey and Addison. Towards the close there are even references to the speaker's family life which coincide with Pope's own family circumstances. The very title of the epistle is testimony to an actual personal relationship of Pope's.

Notwithstanding, the protagonist of this poem is dramatically, not autobiographically conceived. The coincidence of certain traits and circumstances of the dramatic character with Pope's biography has nothing to do with the success of the poem as a poem. These traits are used dramatically, as an objective element in the work, to create a well-defined genre pose. The Horatian pose of the injured but superior poet is as fixed and objective as the pose of the Petrarchan sonneteer.

The speaker of the *Essay on Man* works technically in the epistolary convention. But like St. Paul in his epistles, as far as tone and substance are concerned, this speaker has taken up his stand in a pulpit. His relationship to his implied audience—mankind in general and not merely Bolingbroke—is somewhat like a preacher's to his congregation. This relationship is formal but, when man's soul is at stake, by no means unemotional. The speaker's tone is closer to the emotional urgency of a great evangelist— St. Paul again, for instance—than to the lucid didacticism of a Lucretius.

How shall a man be saved? It was the dominant question of the age preceding Pope's—the England of Bunyan and Milton. The speaker asks it in this poem with no less sense of urgency. But in conformity with the pose of enlightened reason fashionable with his presumed audience, he states and answers his question in such a way as to give the illusion of logical argument. The *Essay on Man* is not, however, primarily a logical poem. Criticism of it on the grounds of technical philosophical inconsistency does not take into consideration either its purpose or its method.

The speaker of the *Essay on Man* is a master of persuasive rhetoric. Dealing with a subject which is fundamentally incapable of logical demonstration, but convinced of the rightness of his ends, he gives the poem a logical façade the better to entice the eighteenth-century auditor into the building. As far as reason can be applied to religion, the speaker is careful to have reason on his side. But, as the poem itself emphasizes throughout Epistle II, reason is a weaker ally than passion. Since the issue is man's salvation, the implied speaker here is put on his mettle to state the situation as strongly as possible. The result is that the tone is principally one of passionate exhortation, with the speaker ready to avail himself of any rhetorical devices which will help him convince his auditors. His aim is a kind of rhetorical hypnosis, not conviction based on logic.

It is interesting to contrast the tone and attitude of the speaker of this poem with those of the speaker in *Prufrock*. Basically, both speakers are asking the same question: What shall a man do to be saved?

Prufrock in his heart divines the answer, but he is afraid of the social consequences of acting on it. The atmosphere of the society he lives in has become hostile even to asking such questions seriously, much more to answering them seriously in spiritual terms. In Pope's time this hostility was only beginning to manifest itself. It did so as a demand that questions about man's destiny be asked and answered according to the canons of enlightened reason. That the questions were urgent, that they should be put and replied to, was not yet doubted.

Pope's speaker has, as Prufrock has not, the solid ground of seventeenth–century religious feeling under him—with the addition of a Turkey carpet of enlightenment cast over that solid ground. The result is that Pope's speaker can take many things for granted. He and the implied audience have a common and positive scheme of reference.

Prufrock can take for granted in his audience only the doubts, the hesitations, and the fear to depart from conformity that he finds within himself. He can count on a literary acquaintance with—but not dogmatic convictions about—Hamlet, Lazarus, and John the Baptist. Prufrock cannot stand in a pulpit. He would not dare even to mount a soapbox. He can utter his prompting (*convictions* seems too strong a word) only if he is assured, as the question from Dante makes clear, that he will not be overheard by anyone who will return to the world.

The speaker of the *Essay on Man* is afflicted with no such diffidence. He wants the world to hear. And he takes the licence of a preacher in a pulpit to inveigh against his parishioners. In no uncertain terms he tells them the truth about their spiritual situation:

> Presumptuous Man! the reason wouldst thou find,
> Why form'd so weak, so little, and so blind!
> First, if thou canst, the harder reason guess,
> Why form'd no weaker, blinder, and no less!
>
> (I, 35–38)

The tone adopted by the speaker of the *Essay on Criticism* is altogether different. The subject of this *Essay* is the qualities of a good critic. The speaker, whose duty it is to expound them, also exemplifies them. If he did not, the poem would fail to achieve its end. As a piece of persuasive rhetoric its success largely depends on the extent to which it can convince the reader that the speaker is a reliable guide. Anyone who would prescribe how others shall write or criticize must first induce confidence in his own literary judgment and experience. Pope has therefore endowed this speaker with just those traits which an urbane and judicious eighteenth century audience approved.

Since the Augustan reader was especially wary of extreme doctrines, this speaker adopts the *via media* position on virtually every problem with which he deals. Not only the overt logical structure of the poem, but every element—diction, metaphor, syntax, and even rhyme—is used to bolster the *via media* theme and the speaker's status as an exponent of the golden mean.

It is hardly possible to mention a topic discussed in the poem upon which the speaker does not take a middle-of-the-road stand. Many of the subjects touched upon are controversial and ticklish. The speaker's sane, reasonable approach to each of them is designed to convince the reader that his judgment is sound in many realms.

The speaker's taking a sound, enlightened, reasonable religious position was of particular importance to the eighteenth-century reader. It helped build an ethos that rendered the speaker's literary opinions persuasive. It is not surprising, therefore, that this essay on literary craft contains many references to religion. In all of them the speaker deplores some extreme and, implicitly or explicitly, counsels the mean. He ridicules, for example, those eccentrics who "to Church repair,/ Not for the doctrine, but the music there" (II, 342–343). He deplores excessive subtlety in religion:

> So Schismatics the plain believers quit,
> And are but damned for having too much wit.
>
> (II, 428–429)

In this connection, Scholastic philosophy is, of course, censured:

> Once School-divines this zealous isle o'er-spread;
> Who knew most Sentences, was deepest read;
> Faith, Gospel, all, seemed made to be disputed,
> And none had sense enough to be confuted.
>
> (II, 440–443)

He disapproves of any off-center alliance between religion and vice:

> The following licence of a Foreign reign
> Did all the dregs of bold Socinus drain:
> When unbelieving priests reformed the nation,
> And taught more pleasant methods of salvation;
> Where Heaven's free subjects might their rights dispute,
> Lest God himself should seem too absolute:
> Pulpits their sacred satire learned to spare,
> And Vice admired to find a flatt'rer there!   (II, 544–551)

At the close of Part II the speaker discusses the issue of obscenity in literature. For thirty lines he advises the reader that the salacious writer should find no pardon. But then the speaker, lest he seem excessively puritanical, indicates the *via media* in this matter:

> Yet shun their fault, who, scandalously nice,
> Will needs mistake an author into vice;
> All seems infected that th'infected spy,
> As all looks yellow to the jaundiced eye.
>
> (II, 556–559)

He counsels moderation in literary aims:

> Be sure yourself and your own reach to know,
> How far your genius, taste, and learning go;
> Launch not beyond your depth, but be discreet,
> And mark that point where sense and dulness meet.
> Nature to all things fixed the limits fit,
> And wisely curbed proud man's contending wit.
>
> (I, 48–53)

A little further on he recommends restraint and control in the actual process of writing:

> 'Tis more to guide, than spur the Muse's steed;

Restrain his fury, than provoke his speed:
The wingèd courser, like a gen'rous horse,
Shows most true mettle when you check his course.

(I, 84–87)

The speaker realizes, as a matter of practical psychology, that
to obtain moderation from the average young writer, there is
more need for a warning against excessive egotism than for one
against diffidence. Therefore, on the question of following the
Ancients or striking out for one's self, the speaker, having first
equated the practice of the best Ancients with Nature, cautions
the young writer to "Learn hence for ancient rules a just esteem"
(I, 139). But instantly, lest this too should lead to an extreme, he
observes that the poet may

From vulgar bounds with brave disorder part,
And snatch a grace beyond the reach of art.

(I, 152–153)

Yet, fearful that this too might encourage extremism, he qualifies
it with the following:

But though the Ancients thus their rules invade,
(As Kings dispense with laws themselves have made)
Moderns, beware! or if you must offend
Against the precept, ne'er transgress its End;
Let it be seldom, and compelled by need;
And have, at least, their precedent to plead.

(I, 161–166)

Part II opens with a diatribe against pride, dangerous because
it is especially liable to lead one away from the *via media* of right
reason. Then, under the celebrated analogies of the Pierian spring
and the Alps, the young writer is warned against excesses due to
youthful enthusiasm. This is followed by a caveat to the critic
against missing the main highway by too fastidious a preoccupation with trivial faults in a work of art that is on the whole successful. After this comes the moralized tale of "La Mancha's
Knight," who permits his otherwise sound critical judgment to
be perverted by a "love to parts"—in his case an obsession with
the panoply of tourneys.

In more technical matters too the aspiring writer is admonished to avoid extremes: in imagery, diction, and "numbers." As for the last, as might be expected, the writer is advised to be neither too sweet nor too harsh but to pursue a middle course which provides a mixture of both, varied according to the sense.

The critic as well as the writer is warned against enthusiasm:

> Avoid Extremes; and shun the fault of such,
> Who still are pleased too little or too much.
>
> (II, 384–385)

He is told that he ought neither always to echo public opinion servilely; nor let undue *amour-propre* seduce him into eccentricities; nor yet fall into the third extreme of whirling about like a weather vane, positive in all opinions, constant in none.

Moreover, even though the good critic has safely avoided intellectual extremes, he must not go to the extreme of thinking he lives in an intellectual world only. Hence the famous admonition against intellectual pride:

> Good-nature and good-sense must ever join;
> To err is human, to forgive, divine.   (II, 524–525)

As for the quarrel of the Ancients versus the Moderns, both writer and critic are cautioned not to espouse exclusively one side or the other but to recognize that there is some good and some bad in both.

Particularly important for forming a conception of the speaker is the portrait of the ideal critic in Part III. As a critic, the speaker presumably conforms or strives to conform to the ideal presented in these lines:

> But where's the man, who counsel can bestow,
> Still pleased to teach, and yet not proud to know?
> Unbiased, or by favour, or by spite;
> Not dully prepossessed, nor blindly right;
> Though learned, well-bred; and though well-bred, sincere:
> Modestly bold, and humanly severe;
> Who to a friend his faults can freely show,
> And gladly praise the merit of a foe?
> Blest with a taste exact, yet unconfined;

A knowledge both of books and human kind:
Gen'rous converse; a soul exempt from pride;
And love to praise, with reason on his side?   (III, 631–642)

Ideologically, the passage is a series of assertions that the good critic is neither this nor that extreme but the implied or stated middle. Rhetorically, it is significant of the pervasiveness of the *via media* concept in this poem that the ideational balances are in every case reflected by syntactical balances. Line is set against line, half-line against half-line, clause against clause, parallel phrase against parallel phrase, word against word, in exact antithesis.

The reader forms his opinion of the dramatic speaker, quite properly, not only from what he says but from how he says it. The combination in the above passage of ideational with syntactical balance implies the qualities of clarity, reasonableness, and control. In spite of the obvious formal balancing, the general tone of the passage is easy and conversational. This is partly due to the infrequency of inversions and partly, as Dr. Johnson pointed out, to the fact that the ordering of the thought is juxtapositional.

But eighteenth-century French critics mistakenly accused this *Essay* of lacking method. Actually, its underlying structure is close-knit and logical; but its presentation is Horatian. The speaker is obeying his own precept that "Men must be taught as if you taught them not" (III, 574). He does not, like the speaker of the *Essay on Man*, exhort ex cathedra. His attitude resembles that which he commends in Horace, who

> . . . still charms with graceful negligence,
> And without method talks us into sense,
> Will, like a friend, familiarly convey
> The truest notions in the easiest way.
>   (III, 653–656)

The eighteenth-century French translators who attempted to introduce order into this *Essay* (the very title should have warned them) actually introduced the opposite. The poem lacks neither logic nor method; its apparent disregard of them is artfully contrived.

The effect desired is that of urbane conversation—something

like an after-dinner chat between a successful critic and man of the world and a young, eager protégé seated across the fire from him. To maintain this easy stance, the speaker must not seem to be delivering a lecture. He must eschew the grand style and choose his diction from everyday words. He must avoid scholarly jargon and technical terms, seeking out familiar phrases and colloquial turns of idiom. In short, though he must not sacrifice clarity and verbal tension, his diction too must be middle-of-the-road.

The following couplet is an example of the way the speaker favors homely words and phrases like "itching" and "the laughing side":

> All fools have still an itching to deride,
> And fain would be upon the laughing side.
>
> (I, 32–33)

He uses contractions and colloquial exaggeration:

> To tell 'em, would a hundred tongues require,
> Or one vain wit's, that might a hundred tire.
>
> (I, 44–45)

He introduces familiar saws, such as "Homer nods":

> Those oft are stratagems which error seem,
> Nor is it Homer nods, but we that dream.
>
> (I, 179–180)

In relating an anecdote he reports the direct speech, colloquial in flavor, of the characters, as in the fable of La Mancha's Knight (II, 267–284). His preference is always for short, unpretentious words:

> Be not the first by whom the new are tried,
> Nor yet the last to lay the old aside.
>
> . . . .
>
> At every trifle scorn to take offence,
> That always shows great pride, or little sense.
>
> (II, 335–336, 386–387)

He employs names of actual persons and places:

> Might he return, and bless once more our eyes,
> New Blackmores and new Milbourns must arise.
>
> (II, 462–463)

No place so sacred from such fops is barred,
Nor is Paul's church more safe than Paul's churchyard.
                                        (III, 622–623)

Occasional brief passages in a style somewhat more elevated
do occur. In such a passage the diction shows a tendency to become more general, more poetic:

Such late was Walsh—the Muse's judge and friend,
Who justly knew to blame or to commend;
To failings mild, but zealous for desert;
The clearest head, and the sincerest heart.
This humble praise, lamented shade! receive,
This praise at least a grateful Muse may give:
The Muse, whose early voice you taught to sing,
Prescribed her heights, and pruned her tender wing.
                                        (III, 729–736)

Even this is only a middling flight. The diction, though somewhat
apart from the language of ordinary conversation, is not to any
notable degree inflated. An occasional exclamatory passage can
safely be included within the normal conversational convention.
A speaker might, indeed, incur suspicion of inclining to the extreme of "correctly cold and regularly low" if he did not once
in a while try "short excursions."

If this speaker's critical dicta are to carry authority, it is important that he should appear to be a man of the world. He has
to convince the reader that he is aware, as the enlightened Augustan usually was, of the interpenetration of different realms of
value and of the undesirability of excluding any realm pertinent
to human problems. In his metaphors, therefore, the speaker
draws a conspicuous number of analogies from the life of the
Town and from unaesthetic aspects of physiology and sex; for
example—
From business life:

So modern 'Pothecaries, taught the art
By Doctor's bills to play the Doctor's part,
Bold in the practice of mistaken rules,
Prescribe, apply, and call their masters fools.
                                        (I, 108–111)

From conventions of dress:

> For diff'rent styles with diff'rent subjects sort,
> As several garbs with country, town, and court.
>
> (II, 322–323)

From sex:

> What is this Wit, which must our cares employ?
> The owner's wife, that other men enjoy.
>
> (II, 500–501)

From unaesthetic physiological phenomena:

> Those heads, as stomachs, are not sure the best,
> Which nauseate all, and nothing can digest.
>
> (II, 388–389)

From the minor ignobilia of human manners:

> What woful stuff this madrigal would be,
> In some starved hackney sonneteer, or me?
> But let a Lord once own the happy lines,
> How the wit brightens! how the style refines!
>
> (II, 418–421)

The last example reveals the speaker as a shrewd and tolerant observer of human foibles. This inspires confidence in both his perception and his judgment. It also discloses that the speaker has a sense of humor—a point by no means insignificant for the purposes of the *Essay*. The use of humor in the poem is consonant with the idea of the urbane critic who does not wish to seem too intense or boring to his audience. It is also an indication of *mens sana in corpore sano*.

The range of the humor is wide, from the scatological

> Still run on Poets, in a raging vein,
> Even to the dregs and squeezings of the brain,
> Strain out the last dull droppings of their sense,
> And rhyme with all the rage of Impotence   (III, 606–609)

to the more subtly satirical:

> Whatever nature has in worth denied,
> She gives in large recruits of needful pride.
>
> (II, 205–206)

It is important for his pose as a good-natured man that he keep his satire, barbed as it is, urbane in general effect. Though this speaker makes many bitter and cynical observations, by hedging them about with wit and ambiguity he keeps them on the drawing-room level. No matter how harsh his sense, his style remains debonair. Except in one instance (the lines on Appius) he carefully obeys his own precepts about avoiding literary contentions and unnecessarily arousing personal enmities.

Learning is another field in which the speaker displays a *via media* attitude. It is evident that he is liberally educated; but, in accordance with the conversational mode of the poem, he introduces learned allusions, when necessary, in an easy and familiar rather than a pedantic way. The most extensive display of learning occurs in the survey of the history of literary criticism in Part III. Even this review, couched in the mode of appreciative exclamation, is not an incredible part of a mellow after-dinner literary conversation.

Rhyme too plays a part in proving the speaker a conversationalist rather than an academic lecturer. In the following passage, the effect of the feminine rhymes is "unformalizing." The fact that a homely, familiar, actual place name like "Duck-lane" has been chosen for rhyme emphasis further contributes to this effect:

> Faith, Gospel, all, seemed made to be disputed,
> And none had sense enough to be confuted:
> Scotists and Thomists, now, in peace remain,
> Amidst their kindred cobwebs in Duck-lane.
>
> (II, 442–445)

Finally, though irony is dealt with mainly in the ensuing chapter, there is no need to defer mention of the fact that the speaker's frequent use of irony aids in establishing him as an experienced and sanely judging man of the world. For irony implies complexity, inclusive observation, and a sophisticated stance. Its presence in a man's speech indicates that, like the typical *eiron* in Greek drama, he is able to see through dissembling and factitious elements to the real facts of the situation. He is therefore more reliable as a guide, whether in life or in literature.

In form, irony tends toward verbal economy and often toward

litotes. Pithiness and understatement, in contrast to garrulousness and exaggeration, are speech characteristics which tend to make what a man says more readily believed. In addition, irony in its underlying structure has a particular affinity with the doctrine of the *via media*. An ironical comment, by inference, assumes a norm and condemns deviation from it.

Pope is generally conceded to excel in the art of verbal portrait painting. But in addition to such set and formal portraits as those of Addison and Lord Hervey, he produced another complete series—one for each poem—in his speakers. A study of the character traits and attitudes of these obliquely executed "sitters" often provides a valuable clue to the meaning of the poem.

It seems clear that the device of the implied speaker is used by Pope significantly. Though the use varies with the theme and approach adopted for a particular poem, it always conduces to greater dramatic tension and greater dramatic objectivity and, moreover, enlarges the possibilities for compression in ideas and phrasing, thus contributing toward that epigrammatism which is so salient a feature of Pope's style.

3

Irony

IRONY is a humanly significant disproportion between the thing itself and a limited perception of it. The intelligent observer (the Eiron) recognizes the disproportion. The unintelligent (the Dupe) takes the partial for the whole. The two intrinsic parts of irony, then, are the hidden "real real" and an apparent but misleading real. The element of human observation and perception constitutes a third aspect of the Idea (in the Platonic sense) of irony.

To borrow a metaphor from Scholastic philosophy, the above definition of irony as a humanly significant disproportion between the thing itself and a limited perception of it is the substance. The various so-called types of irony are the accidents of that substance. Much of the existing confusion in the use of the term "irony" arises from confounding various of the accidents with the substance—from failing to recognize that the alleged types have a common denominator and are not metaphysically separate.

Irony functions under a twofold aspect: psychological, as it affects the relationship between poet and reader; and metaphysical, as it affects the view of reality presented.

To consider first the psychological aspect, irony implies a sophisticated reader and a sophisticated poet, together with an awareness and acceptance, on the part of both, of their sophisticated status. In a poem it implies recognition of the poem as a deliberately made thing, an artifact, a pact in time into which two civilized men have entered. An ironic poem is, to a greater degree than some other types of poems, a ceremonial, and in the broadest sense, a social occasion.

The ironic ceremony is not, however, a rigid one, with every gesture a foregone conclusion. On the contrary, one of its established conventions is the maintenance of constant alertness, an ever present possibility of the intrusion of the unexpected. The ironical poem is not the sort of ceremony at which it is safe to doze. Indeed, one of the most valuable psychological features of irony is that it helps keep the reader alert. Since the assertions of an ironic poem cannot be accepted at face value but must be incessantly scrutinized for double meanings, the presence of irony in a poem promotes tension between reader and poet. The poem becomes a battle of wits, a game, in which the ultimate triumph is not of one against the other but of both against a hypothetical third person, the simpleton.

Another psychological value of irony, a value which impinges on the metaphysical, is its tendency to induce greater confidence in the poet as an authority on whatever issue he is dealing with. If the poet is to be guide and leader, the intelligent reader must be convinced that he has the authority resulting from wide experience. The reader must feel assured that the poet is aware of not just one aspect of his subject— this exclusiveness might betray the poet into sentimentality—but of all aspects, even incongruous ones. Irony is one way of indicating this awareness.

This function of irony is exemplified in the following passage from *Moral Essay* II: "Of the Characters of Women":

> Narcissa's nature, tolerably mild,
> To make a wash, would hardly stew a child;
> Has ev'n been prov'd to grant a Lover's pray'r,
> And paid a Tradesman once to make him stare;
> Gave alms at Easter, in a Christian trim,
> And made a Widow happy, for a whim.
> Why then declare Good-nature is her scorn,
> When 'tis by that alone she can be borne? (53–60)

It would be an easy matter to deal with this issue directly and non-ironically. Dickens, for example, might have made the ruin of a poor tradesman through a fine lady's flouting of her debts a notable tear-jerker. Daughters would be driven to lives of shame. A crippled son would die for lack of medical care. The tradesman's wife would be run down and killed by a dray as she returned home, unpaid and weeping, from an attempt to collect from the fine lady. Then the tradesman himself would take to gin and ultimately hang himself in despair.

With all respect for Dickens' ability to turn such stuff into novels not easily forgotten, so sentimental an approach may fail to allow for the intelligent reader's corrective knowledge that the tradesman's daughters might have behaved like sluts even if their father had been Lord Mayor. Given the opportunity, moreover, they might not have scrupled to act just as the fine lady did. The crippled son might easily have been envious, spiteful, and malevolent. Far from being angelic, he might even have tormented dumb animals that came within reach of his little bed, or he might have traded upon his affliction to get away with all sorts of reprehensible behavior. And so on through the family.

Pope avoids the sentimental pitfall, not in this case by actually pointing out possible turpitudes in the victims, though this is a legitimate method, but by taking up a tongue-in-cheek attitude. By affecting to accept Narcissa's own values, he reveals how vicious they are. His ostensible praise is the blackest damnation. That Pope accepts such a character as Narcissa and subjects her to dry ridicule instead of ranting about her selfishness or reaching for tears is a point the intelligent reader—wary, sceptical, and suspicious of emotional appeals—scores in his favor.

Another advantage of irony, a predominantly metaphysical one, is that it implies complexity. Hence the presumption that the ironical picture of reality is objectively truer than the non-ironical. Contrary to the credo of sentimental writers, irony does not blunt but sharpens the reader's perception of the villainy of villains and the pathos of the pathetic. It does this because, by means of inclusiveness, it establishes a universal framework for the poem. The whole universe, not just a part of it, comments on the action and the actors of the poem. Both tragedy and comedy are thus intensified. Pope's imitation of Horace's First Satire of Book II contains a striking example of this:

> [Expect]
> From furious Sappho scarce a milder Fate,
> P—x'd by her Love, or libell'd by her Hate.
>
> (83–84)

The ironical accident here is situational rather than, as in the passage previously cited, primarily verbal. Sappho injures where she hates, which is the normal and expected outcome. But by the irony of fate, even where she loves she injures. This couplet, half libel and half lament, opens a window upon the universe. It permits the reader to glimpse the working of an awesome and inalterable law: the just and exact retribution for crime. "Furious" Sappho's crime was venereal. Consequently, her punishment is, in both a physical and a spiritual sense, venereal.

Sappho is comic; for incongruity, as between expectation and event, is the basis of comedy. She is at the same time pathetic. Her ironic punishment turns on a switch that floods the couplet with the light of universal law. Against this backdrop her fury and its consequences seem pitiful. The question is whether to laugh or cry at the spectacle of a woman whose love brings, not good, but evil upon those she loves. Pope has stated Sappho's case in such a way that the emotion with which the reader views it is not simple but complex. The intelligent reader cannot skim over these verses. He must pause to allow the universal implications of the irony to sink in.

A common reaction to this couplet has been, "Even if true, what an appalling thing to say about Lady Mary." Perhaps so. But in reading Pope's verse it is important not to allow his Horatian familiarity, his use of proper names, topical references, humorous rimes, scatology, and the like, to obscure the elevation of the insights into reality which he continually, if almost always obliquely, supplies. The scope of Pope's poems is not as narrow as has often been assumed. In various ways, of which irony is one, they reach out for the ends of the universe. The down-to-earth quality of irony is valuable in gaining acceptance for statements which sometimes transcend the logic and experience of the Town.

In this way Pope's poetry—though it does not exclaim quite so explicitly as some other kinds "Ah! the wonder of it!"—manages nevertheless to produce some sense of the complex and ultimately unresolvable paradoxes of the human situation characteristic of major poetry. Eventually this leads to a view which includes recognition of reality as a mystery. Pope accomplishes, by a combination of cerebration and simulated cerebration—especially the kind of cerebration that produces ironic multiple meanings—what the Romantic poet tends to accomplish by a sort of incantation.

The types, or accidents, of irony are numerous. As a careful and conscious rhetorician, Pope is aware that employing a diversity of types is a way of achieving variety and flexibility. The *Epistle to Dr. Arbuthnot*, possibly because of the flexibility of its Horatian organization, exemplifies many of the types of irony Pope uses:

Shut, shut the door, good John! fatigu'd, I said,
Tye up the knocker, say I'm sick, I'm dead.
The Dog-star rages! nay, 'tis past a doubt,
All Bedlam, or Parnassus, is let out:
Fire in each eye, and Papers in each hand,
They rave, recite, and madden round the land.
    What Walls can guard me, or what Shades can hide?
They pierce my Thickets, thro' my Grot they glide;
By land, by water, they renew the charge,
They stop the Chariot, and they board the Barge.
No place is sacred, not the Church is free,
Ev'n Sunday shines no Sabbath-day to me;
Then from the Mint walks forth the Man of Ryme,
Happy! to catch me, just at Dinner-time.   (1–14)

The genus common to all the types exemplified here is that contained in the definition of *irony* as *a humanly significant disproportion between the thing itself and a limited perception of it* (e.g., Macbeth's interpretation of the Witches' prophecies as compared with the correct interpretation). The basic type of irony throughout the above passage might be called "irony of exaggeration." Line 4, where Parnassus equals Bedlam, provides an example of irony of false equation; so does line 6, in equating "recite" with "rave" and "madden." In line 12 occurs the "both-and" irony which arises from paradox. The irony in lines 13–14 arises from the pricking of unjustified pretence.

But mere classification, with examples of all the types of irony Pope uses, would have very little point. Merely bestowing names upon a variety of ironical accidents leads nowhere. What such a classification does reveal that is significant is a decided preference on the part of Pope for four of the types: irony that attacks violation of decorum, elegiac irony, irony of false equation, and, most of all, the both-and irony associated with paradox.

Before discussing these, it is interesting to observe two peripheral facts about Pope's use of irony. First, he knew how to take advantage of the effects to be gained by alternating ironic and non-ironic statement. In the *Epistle to Dr. Arbuthnot*, for example, the non-ironic statements are for the most part coincident with those of the autobiographical convention. Their function is one familiar to persuasive rhetoric, for they say, in effect, "Now I will abandon all the wiles of rhetoric (specifically, irony) and speak to you simply and directly." Since this depiction of the speaker and his family as good, simple people without malicious or ulterior motives helps establish the dignity and disinterestedness of the speaker's satire, the thematic part played by deliberate abstention from irony in these passages is clear.

Within such a passage, primarily non-ironic, the occasional insertion of an ironic line or epithet is, by contrast, all the more effective:

Not Fortune's Worshipper, nor Fashion's Fool,
Not Lucre's Madman, nor Ambition's Tool,
Not proud, nor servile, be one Poet's praise
That, if he pleas'd, he pleas'd by manly ways;
That Flatt'ry, ev'n to Kings, he held a shame,
And thought a Lye in Verse or Prose the same:
That not in Fancy's Maze he wander'd long,
But stoop'd to Truth, and moraliz'd his song.

(334–341)

Only line 339 and the word "stoop'd" in line 341 are ironic. They are outstanding not only because they are surrounded by non-ironical statement, but because the type of irony to which both belong reinforces their effect. The type itself is pre-eminently a shock producer. For if the basic definition of irony is kept in mind, this can be seen as a type in which the moral norm (the "real real") has been perverted by secular considerations for so long that the perversion has become the worldly norm. Adherence to the real norm seems naïve and childlike—the role of the Dupe; but in fact it is the role of the Eiron, with the worldling the actual Dupe. Basically, it is the situation of the Huron, the child of nature in Voltaire's tale, reacting with shock to the wisdom (actually, the unwisdom) of civilization.

The "perversion-of-the-norm become the norm" which is attacked is the misconception that because poetry can transcend factual truth it need not concern itself with truthfulness, but is a special realm in somewhat the way Bedlam is. The shock element in this "reversal of poses" irony is reinforced in the passage quoted above by the juxtaposition of "stoop'd" and "Truth"—the metaphor taken, of course, from the falcon's habit of circling around high in the air before suddenly swooping down and pouncing on its prey. Ordinarily we think of desirable things like truth as placed on high, to be obtained by arduous ascent. "Stoop'd to Truth" seems paradoxical at first. Pope's purpose is to stress a contrast: On the one hand, there is the *limited perception of the real* exemplified in the pretentious high-flying of his own youth and those poets whose youth in these matters is perpetual; on the other, there is the mature poet's unpretentious, realistic grappling with truth.

The second interesting general fact about Pope's irony is its multivalence—a striking constant, by the way, in Pope's dealing with every major element in his craft. His irony cuts several ways at once. The following lines, also from the *Epistle to Dr. Arbuthnot*, afford an especially happy example of this for the reason that they bear a resemblance to a passage in Donne's *The Canonization*. Defending his use of satire as a weapon, Pope says,

37

Whom have I hurt? has Poet yet, or Peer,
Lost the arch'd eye-brow, or Parnassian sneer?
And has not Colly still his Lord, and Whore?
His Butchers Henley, his Free-masons Moor?
Does not one Table Bavius still admit?
Still to one Bishop Philips seem a Wit?
Still Sappho— (95–101)

Here are the corresponding lines in Donne:

Alas, alas, who's injur'd by my love?
What merchants ships have my sighs drown'd?
Who saies my teares have overflow'd his ground?
When did my colds a forward spring remove?
When did the heats which my veines fill
Adde one more to the plaguie Bill?
Soldiers finde warres, and Lawyers finde out still
Litigious men, which quarrels move,
Though she and I do love.*

In Pope the irony of every instance given is double. In Donne
it is so only in the last two examples, soldiers and lawyers. Donne
directs no irony, for instance, against merchant shipping. In
Pope's poem the theoretical injurer, who is being vindicated, is
the weapon of satire. In Donne's poem the theoretical injurer is
love. But in all except the two cases mentioned the imputed in-
jury in Donne is to activities not themselves satirized. In Pope
each example is in itself ironic. The second irony lies in the assumption that Colley's Whore, Henley's Butchers, etc., are good
things which can be lost or hampered by satire. This is a Dupe's
assumption, and Pope is here playing the roles of Dupe and Eiron
at the same time.

Familiarity with Pope's themes and his ideological position as
a whole makes it a reasonable expectation that many of his ironic
perceptions would be directed against violation of decorum—in
the neoclassical sense of that word. For many, if not all, violations
of such decorum spring from partial and erroneous rather than
full and correct perceptions of the real.

* This and all other passages from Donne are from *The Poems*, edited
by Herbert J. C. Grierson (Oxford, The Clarendon Press, 1912).

Pope's preoccupation with irony arising from this source is evident in all his major poems. From one viewpoint, the central irony in the *Essay on Man* may be called a "violation of decorum" irony. It is indecorous, out of character, for man, situated as he is in the universe and with the powers he has, to presume to do anything except to acquiesce in whatever is, as right.

But the eighteenth century believed maintenance of decorum necessary not only in realms of primary significance, such as religion, but also in contingent and derived realms, such as speech, dress, and household management. In *Moral Essay* IV, for example, architecture and landscape gardening are the realms in which the poet is ostensibly most concerned to censure violations of decorum. As usual with Pope, however, the improprieties satirized in these fields are either springboards or metaphors for discussion of departures from propriety in other and more important fields. This is evident in the celebrated description of Timon's Villa (Timon is the Dupe and the dramatic speaker the Eiron):

> At Timon's Villa let us pass a day,
> Where all cry out, "What sums are thrown away!"
> So proud, so grand, of that stupendous air,
> Soft and Agreeable come never there.
> Greatness, with Timon, dwells in such a draught
> As brings all Brobdignag before your thought.
> To compass this, his building is a Town,
> His pond an Ocean, his parterre a Down:
> Who but must laugh, the Master when he sees,
> A puny insect, shiv'ring at a breeze!
> Lo, what huge heaps of littleness around!
> The whole, a labour'd Quarry above ground;
> Two Cupids squirt before: a Lake behind
> Improves the keenness of the Northern wind.
> His Gardens next your admiration call,
> On every side you look, behold the Wall!
> No pleasing Intricacies intervene,
> No artful wildness to perplex the scene;
> Grove nods at grove, each Alley has a brother,
> And half the platform just reflects the other.
> The suff'ring eye inverted Nature sees,

Trees cut to Statues, Statues thick as trees,
With here a Fountain, never to be play'd;
And there a Summer-house, that knows no shade;
Here Amphitrite sails thro' myrtle bowers;
There Gladiators fight, or die, in flow'rs;
Un-water'd see the drooping sea-horse mourn,
And swallows roost in Nilus' dusty Urn.

(99–126)

The "puny insect, shiv'ring at a breeze" does not perceive the unsuitability of such a huge dwelling for himself. He does not perceive that a building, a man's private home, should not try to be a town; a pond an ocean; a parterre a down. All Timon's pretensions only underline the central irony, which is that of man's situation in the universe. But the chief point that Timon does not see—and here is the irony of the human situation again—is that if man is not to be ridiculous, he must work *with* nature rather than against it. The examples Pope gives from landscape gardening could hardly be improved as instances of complete disregard of this principle: a fountain placed where there is no water supply, a summer house constructed where there is no cool shade, statues of gladiators fighting or dying in agony placed among formal flower beds.

Moral Essay IV also castigates violation of decorum on the less cosmic but still significant plane of book collecting:

His Study! with what Authors is it stor'd?
In Books, not Authors, curious is my Lord;
To all their dated Backs he turns you round,
These Aldus printed, these Du Sueil has bound.
Lo, some are Vellom, and the rest as good
For all his Lordship knows, but they are Wood.
For Locke or Milton 'tis in vain to look,
These shelves admit not any modern book.

(133–140)

It is an obvious breach of intellectual decorum to value the mechanical aspect of books, such as printing or binding, more than the contents. Stocking one's shelves with wooden dummies is flagrant. A blanket banning of modern authors, without regard

40

to their merit, violates critical decorum. The critic's decisions, as Pope so forcibly points out in his imitation of Horace's First Epistle of Book II, should be based on worth, not date:

> I lose my patience, and I own it too,
> When works are censur'd, not as bad, but new.
>
> (115–116)

Violation of decorum in religion, as elsewhere in Pope's works, is sharply rebuked in *Moral Essay* IV:

> And now the Chapel's silver bell you hear,
> That summons you to all the Pride of Pray'r:
> Light quirks of Musick, broken and uneven,
> Make the soul dance upon a Jig to Heaven.
> On painted Cielings you devoutly stare,
> Where sprawl the Saints of Verrio or Laguerre,
> On gilded clouds in fair expansion lie,
> And bring all Paradise before your eye.
> To rest, the Cushion and soft Dean invite,
> Who never mentions Hell to ears polite.　(141–150)

Just as he works against and frustrates material nature, Timon vitiates the purpose of religion. The man who imagines that jigging music, lascivious pictures, and a softening and prettifying of the law of retribution are any part of Christian religious decorum is in the role of the simpleton.

It is interesting to see how various minor factors have contributed to the underlining of the ironic intention of this passage. The even flow of the meter in the second line tends to make the reader accept as a matter of course the surprising vocable "Pride" in connection with "Prayer." The fact that these words so united are shocking is not likely to catch the reader's attention at once, but the slight delay in recognition makes the recognition more emphatic. The same is true of the juxtaposition of such artists as Verrio and Laguerre, and of a word like "sprawl" with "Saints." The choice of "Paradise"—the word usually employed in English for reference to the abode of the houris—is perhaps not without nuance. It corroborates the ironic contrast between what the poem assumes to be the true conception of religion and an imperfect and erroneous conception. Finally, there is a seeming misplacement of the adjective "soft." It is an adjective physically appropriate to the "Cushion" which precedes it, but also spiritually appropriate to the Dean. As a result of this the Dean appears to function as a kind of cushion between his parishioners and the cold, hard facts of error and punishment, which is the opposite of his proper duty.

The most profound example in the poem of irony arising from the violation of decorum, an example which leads toward what may be considered another type of irony, appears in the following passage. Here the end of Timon's pompous and sterile reorganization of his estate is prophetically envisioned:

> Another age shall see the golden Ear
> Embrown the Slope, and nod on the Parterre,
> Deep Harvests bury all his pride has plann'd,
> And laughing Ceres re-assume the land.   (173–176)

Timon has violated the decorum of human economics by turning plowed fields into pointlessly huge greenswards. But more important in this passage is what may be called "elegiac irony," an irony inherent in the human situation. This irony touches deeper issues than any of the types yet cited. Its effect here, however, is not so much tragic as humorous, since the tragic stroke is aimed at the ridiculous figure of Timon. The reader enjoys the prospect of his being taken down a peg, even though it is by a natural law to which the reader too, with all things mortal, is subject.

Incidentally, the role of the double meaning of "laughing" in reinforcing the irony should be noted. "Laughing" is meant both in the general sense applicable to all thriving vegetation and in the sense that Ceres, like the reader, is laughing at the posthumous discomfiture of Timon.

The *Elegy to the Memory of an Unfortunate Lady* provides this typical example of elegiac irony:

> So peaceful rests, without a stone, a name,
> What once had beauty, titles, wealth, and fame.
> How lov'd, how honour'd once, avails thee not,
> To whom related, or by whom begot;

A heap of dust alone remains of thee;
'Tis all thou art, and all the proud shall be!
Poets themselves must fall, like those they sung;
Deaf the prais'd ear, and mute the tuneful tongue.

                                                    (69–76)

This kind of irony is one of the most basic and universal, found
in the poetry of all nations and in all centuries. To take a random
instance, Sir Walter Scott's *Proud Maisie* is built around this
irony. The irony is stressed by the suspense involved in the ambiguity the answers have for the lady:

>   Proud Maisie is in the wood,
>   Walking so early;
>   Sweet Robin sits on the bush,
>   Singing so rarely.
>
>   "Tell me, thou bonny bird,
>   When shall I marry me?"
>   "When six braw gentlemen,
>   Kirkward shall carry ye."
>
>   "Who makes the bridal bed,
>   Birdie, say truly?"—
>   "The gray-headed sexton
>   Who delves the grave duly.
>
>   "The glow-worm o'er grave and stone
>   Shall light thee steady.
>   The owl from the steeple sing,
>   'Welcome, proud lady.' "

Pope's own use of this irony has two interesting aspects: one
which he shares with almost all poets in the Christian tradition
and another which is one of the most distinctive traits of his
verse. In Christian poets the poignant edge of elegiac irony is
sometimes dulled by consciousness that the apparent death is
really an awakening into the life beyond. Skillful Christian poets,
however, have known how to maneuver in order to avoid this
poetic loss. Even a notably pious poet like Tasso does this, making a sort of double philosophy prevail in his poem. By means of

this sleight of hand the secular world is temporarily assumed to have primary rather than secondary significance. In the sixteenth canto of his *Jerusalem Delivered*, for instance, this wholly pagan lament and wholly material advice occurs:

> With parti-colored plumes and purple bill
> A wondrous bird among the rest there flew,
> That in plain speech sung love-lays loud and shrill,
> Her leden was like human language true;
> So much she talked, and with such wit and skill,
> That strange it seemëd how much good she knew,
> Her feathered fellows all stood hush to hear,
> Dumb was the wind, the waters silent were.
>
> . . . .
>
> So, in the passing of a day, doth pass
> The bud and blossom of the life of man,
> Nor e'er doth flourish more, but like the grass
> Cut down, becometh withered, pale and wan.
> Oh, gather then the rose while time thou hast,
> Short is the day, done when it scant began,
> Gather the rose of love, while yet thou mayest,
> Loving, be loved; embracing, be embraced.*

Pope, like Tasso and most Christian poets, is adept at permitting this double outlook to function. Sometimes the Christian viewpoint is simply avoided. A poem or passage is conceived within a framework other than Christian and specific references to Christian doctrine, particularly *de contemptu mundi*, are omitted. This is true to a large extent of the *Elegy to the Memory of an Unfortunate Lady*. Sometimes a degree of distance sufficient to prevent direct contrast is put between pagan elegiac irony and the Christian idea that death is the beginning of a new phase of life. This can be done either by separating the two by many lines or by such a rhetorical device as Tasso's bird-song, which represents not necessarily Tasso's sentiments but the bird's. In this connection, incidentally, *Eloisa to Abelard* is somewhat unusual in rec-

---

* Translation of Edward Fairfax, under the title *Godfrey of Bulloigne, or the Recovery of Jerusalem*, 1600; spelling modernized by J. W. Hebel and H. H. Hudson in *Poetry of the English Renaissance* (New York, Appleton-Century-Crofts, Inc., 1938).

ognizing the conflict overtly and, in fact, making it the crux of the poem.

Especially distinctive of Pope is the use of this elegiac irony in an ambivalent way. Ambivalent or both-and irony, by far Pope's favorite type, is discussed in greater detail later in this chapter. It is sufficient here to give one example of the way it is used to state an elegiac irony obliquely. In the *Dunciad* the virtuoso whose flower has been spoiled by another virtuoso's butterfly complains to the goddess of dulness:

> . . . "Hear thy suppliant's call,
> Great Queen, and common Mother of us all!
> Fair from its humble bed I rear'd this Flow'r,
> Suckled, and chear'd, with air, and sun, and show'r,
> Soft on the paper ruff its leaves I spread,
> Bright with the gilded button tipt its head,
> Then thron'd in glass, and nam'd it CAROLINE:
> Each Maid cry'd, charming! and each Youth, divine!
> Did Nature's pencil ever blend such rays,
> Such vary'd light in one promiscuous blaze?
> Now prostrate! dead! behold that Caroline:
> No Maid cries, charming! and no Youth, divine!
> And lo the wretch! whose vile, whose insect lust
> Lay'd this gay daughter of the Spring in dust.
> Oh punish him, or to th' Elysian shades
> Dismiss my soul, where no Carnation fades."
> He ceas'd, and wept. (IV, 403–419)

The elegiac motive is as unmistakably present here as in a straight elegy such as Shakespeare's song in *Cymbeline*:

> Golden lads and girls all must
> As chimney-sweepers, come to dust.

In the passage quoted above from the *Dunciad* two ironic disproportions are hit with one stone. The poignancy of Pope's elegiac irony is unquestionable; but it is embedded in such a context that, for all its proper seriousness, it becomes a weapon of ridicule against the simpleton virtuoso who carries on about a carnation as if it were a tragically violated young girl.

Pope delighted in irony of false equation. The classical instance

45

of this is perhaps the following passage from *The Rape of the Lock*:

> Whether the Nymph shall break Diana's Law,
> Or some frail China Jar receive a Flaw;
> Or stain her Honour, or her new Brocade;
> Forget her Pray'rs, or miss a Masquerade;
> Or lose her Heart, or Necklace, at a Ball;
> Or whether Heav'n has doom'd that Shock must fall.
>
> (II, 105–110)

The irony lies in the reader's perception of the distortion of viewpoint in the feminine mind that regards the cracking of a China vase or the staining of a new brocade as equivalent in seriousness to a violation of the double standard. Another signal example of this is the following passage:

> Not louder Shrieks to pitying Heav'n are cast,
> When Husbands or when Lap-dogs breathe their last,
> Or when rich China Vessels, fal'n from high,
> In glitt'ring Dust and painted Fragments lie!
>
> (III, 157–160)

This type of irony animates the following couplet from the *Essay on Criticism*, in which "unconquered" is ironically equated to "uncivilized":

> But we, brave Britons, foreign laws despised,
> And kept unconquered, and uncivilised.   (III, 715–716)

And likewise these lines from the *Essay on Man*:

> . . . happy frailties to all ranks apply'd,
> Shame to the virgin, to the matron pride,
> Fear to the statesman, rashness to the chief,
> To kings presumption, and to crowds belief.
>
> (II, 241–244)

The presumption of kings and the belief of crowds, though rhetorically equated, are not happy frailties like the others. The casualness with which these disparates are slipped in with the others would seem, from the frequency with which Pope does it and from its contribution to the effectiveness of this type of irony, to be deliberate—and a deliberate utilization of the alerting value of irony.

The celebrated passage beginning "Lo, the poor Indian" from the *Essay on Man* is an instance of the way Pope uses both-and irony to achieve the greater metaphysical inclusiveness (and hence an exacter and truer statement of reality) mentioned earlier:

> Lo, the poor Indian! whose untutor'd mind
> Sees God in clouds, or hears him in the wind;
> His soul, proud Science never taught to stray
> Far as the solar walk, or milky way;
> Yet simple Nature to his hope has giv'n,
> Behind the cloud-topt hill, an humbler heav'n;
> Some safer world in depth of wood embrac'd,
> Some happier island in the watry waste,
> Where slaves once more their native land behold,
> No fiends torment, no Christians thirst for gold!
> To Be, contents his natural desire,
> He asks no Angel's wing, no Seraph's fire;
> But thinks, admitted to that equal sky,
> His faithful dog shall bear him company.   (I, 99–112)

It might almost be said that here irony floats on the ambiguity. Half of the irony is directed against the poor Indian; half against the Christian who thinks himself, but who in some respects at least is not, superior to the Indian. It is not easy to say whether in these lines we are being told that it is good or bad to ask for an angel's wing or a seraph's fire. The fact is, we are being told both. On the one hand, it seems that the Indian is being praised for his common sense in resting content with natural being and not desiring such chimeras as angelic wings and seraphic fires. The Christian who insists on these is condemned as arrogant and a fool. On the other hand, it would seem that it is the savage, poor and untutored, with his idea of paradise as physical comfort and security, who is being satirized; whereas the Christian is being commended for his less material aspirations.

Actually, both of these things are being done at once. The result of this paradoxical procedure is a closer approach to completeness of statement. The insight here seems more complex, more conscious of the inadequacy resulting from the expounding of one viewpoint *or* the other, than would have been true if the

47

poet had confined himself to an unambiguous, non-ironic statement.

When this particular instance of ambivalent irony is related to the central meaning of the *Essay on Man*, it is seen to be especially significant. In one sense, the untutored Indian's attitude is superior to the Christian's; and in another sense, the latter's to the former's.

The important point is that both are satirized, both are fallible, both have need to submit to a reality greater than they. This is also emphasized by the lines immediately following the "Lo, the poor Indian" passage. Here the European Christian who imagines himself superior is shown to be as effectively limited by his human nature as the Indian in any attempt to comprehend and pass judgment on the workings of Providence:

> Go, wiser thou! and, in thy scale of sense
> Weigh thy Opinion against Providence;
> Call Imperfection what thou fancy'st such,
> Say, here he gives too little, there too much;
> Destroy all creatures for thy sport or gust,
> Yet cry, If Man's unhappy, God's unjust.
> (I, 113–118)

Moral error and limited perception of reality, Pope implies, come to the same thing. The nominal Christian in the above lines carries human presumption to an extreme that is patently absurd. It is recognition of the absurdity which convinces the reader, and thus assists in conveying the central communication of the poem.

This *Essay* as a whole has often been misunderstood and disparaged because of the reader's failure to perceive the both-and nature of its main statement. "Whatever is, is right" has frequently been misinterpreted as a fatalistic acceptance of the *status quo*, however bad. Ignored was the fact that the whole tenor of the *Essay* emphasizes the necessity for individual ethical struggle. The paradox involved was not invented by Pope; it is a cornerstone of the Christian religion, as of other religions and philosophical systems. Nowhere in the *Essay* does Pope condone an individual's complacency in vice. His assertion is that God, in spite of evil-doing on the part of individuals, will make all come right in the end.

There is an underlying irony, of course, as this poem stresses, in the very situation of man in the universe:

> Plac'd on this isthmus of a middle state,
> A being darkly wise, and rudely great:
> With too much knowledge for the Sceptic side,
> With too much weakness for the Stoic's pride,
> He hangs between; in doubt to act, or rest,
> In doubt to deem himself a God, or Beast;
> In doubt his Mind or Body to prefer,
> Born but to die, and reas'ning but to err.
>
> (II, 3–10)

This irony is the mainspring of all such passages where Pope castigates man for attempting to ignore the realities of his circumstances:

> What would this Man? Now upward will he soar,
> And little less than Angel, would be more;
> Now looking downwards, just as griev'd appears
> To want the strength of bulls, the fur of bears.
>
> (I, 173–176)

The ironic disproportion noted here is inherent in man's nature: man dupes himself about himself when he tries to be either a god or a beast. Whether he aspires to angelhood or to animal qualities, he fails equally. But if man does realize his isthmian position in this regard and act in accordance with it, "soaring humbly," then, as far as his individual conduct is concerned, he is no longer a target for irony.

Pope points out in the same poem another source of irony in man's relation to human society, to God, and to the universe:

> Each individual seeks a sev'ral goal;
> But HEAV'N's great view is One, and that the Whole.
> That counter-works each folly and caprice;
> That disappoints th' effect of every vice.   (II, 237–240)

Bluntly put, Pope implies that man is always the Dupe and God is the Eiron, though, of course, man becomes less of a Dupe in so far as he puts himself on God's side. Man can never see the whole situation. Even though he can to some degree control his own acts, he can never be sure of controlling the results of his acts. He may intend evil, and good may come of it; and conversely. Yet the fact remains that if whatever is, is to be right, man cannot be released from his moral responsibility. He must will good and do good in so far as he can see it.

Recognition and acceptance of this paradox is actually recognition and acceptance of God as all-wise and all-powerful. "The fear of the Lord is the beginning of wisdom." Man must go ahead and act as if he were an Eiron and yet never for a moment forget that he is always in the position of the Dupe. Man is neither god nor beast. He is both somewhat godlike and somewhat beast-like. The truth lies not in exclusion but in inclusion.

Even in so slight a genre as pastoral, this both-and irony can be detected at work. Pope is not, of course, individually responsible for its presence in the genre. Pastoral both-and irony worked for Theocritus and Virgil very much as it worked for Pope. The effect is subtle and perhaps more unconscious than conscious. Still, the "action" in *Spring* affords a clear example of it: Two impossible entities designated Daphnis and Strephon have a contest, which is not a contest, to decide whose girl is the more desirable. The question is left undecided and the prizes, properly speaking, unawarded. The shepherd who put up the lamb gets the bowl and vice versa. All that happens is this lamb-bowl transfer, and the superficial effect of the poem as a whole is static prettiness.

But things here are not what they seem. The tranquil and really conflictless people and situation constitute a utopia, a mental place fenced off from human urgency—"at the still centre of the turning world"—and this fact is undoubtedly one source of the appeal of pastoral to harassed humanity. It is at the same time the source of its primary weakness.

The extreme preciousness resulting from the exclusion of the seamy side of everything carries its own negation. The difficulty is like that of the average human attitude toward the traditional picturing of heaven. The good man does not want to sit around resting on his laurels and twanging a harp; he wants to do something. He cannot exclude the devil, the element of resistance, from his thinking.

Conflict may in itself seem undesirable, but a human situation without that factor is unthinkable. There must be a sense of struggle, with the possibility of either triumph or defeat. Pastoralism is, therefore, from the human standpoint, both desirable and undesirable. The pastoral world is both Utopia and not Utopia.

The effect of this is to stress once more the irony of the human situation. Whether man chooses conflict or absence of conflict, he is at a disadvantage. For he is still in the inferior position, the position of the unknower and partial-viewer. It is impossible that man should not aspire toward the stasis of Utopia. It is equally impossible that, once in Utopia, he should not desire, as did Buddha and Rasselas, to scale the fence and experience pain and struggle.

There is a similarity between the pastoral and the mock epic in this respect. In both *The Rape of the Lock* and the *Dunciad* special realms (Duncedom and the Boudoir) inhabited by people seemingly satisfied with them (Dupes) are contrasted with the sane world. This is the world of the knowing reader who perceives the limitations and errors of Duncedom and Boudoirism.

In *The Rape of the Lock*, however, it is not so much in the genre as in the choice and treatment of subject within the genre that the principal both-and irony inheres. Here it is not mankind in general but woman who is faced with a both-and paradox: the desire not to be violated and yet explicit preparation for it.

After Cleanth Brooks' perceptive analysis of the theme of this poem in *The Well Wrought Urn*, it is not necessary to insist that the story of the belle, the lap dog, and the snipped ringlet are only the tinkling symbols for another and more significant story. Just as generic man loses if he tries to be either god or beast, so does generic woman, represented by Belinda. If Belinda remains inviolate, she will lose in one sense; if she does not, she will lose in another.

A woman wins the war between the sexes by losing it under the proper conditions—by honorable surrender. For Belinda, either spinsterhood or dishonorable surrender is disadvantageous, just as either angelhood or animality would be for mankind in general. And just as mankind can escape these disadvantageous extremes by recognizing his middle nature and soaring humbly, so Belinda can to some extent combine the advantages of her two extremes by the middle course of lawful marriage.

This is the *via media* again, which is Pope's, and in general the eighteenth century's, solution to the otherwise unalleviated role of dupeship humanity must play. This sane and reasonable solution of the basic problem of generic woman or generic man, a livable solution on the level of practical everyday conduct, should not blind the reader to the way the solution was reached. It was not by ignoring what the Romantic might call the wonder and mystery of reality. It was by presenting the human paradox in a way characteristic of cerebral poetry—by the use of ambivalent irony to reveal the insufficiency of human reason for dealing with reality, which by implication transcends reason. Once again Pope is forcing his reader away from his narrow self out into a realization of his dependency upon a transcending and all-including Reality.

Humor

Irony has a humorous facet, but Pope's use of humor has aspects which go beyond concern with the operation of any one humorous mode. Humor in general plays a part in establishing three important qualities of his poetry—qualities, incidentally, in which contemporary poetry is sometimes considered deficient. These are clearness, balance of viewpoint, and universal appeal.

Humor is, moreover, like metaphor, a cognitive device: it is a way of getting at knowledge as well as a manner of communicating it. Set against the background of the gods' inextinguishable laughter, a subject gains in perspective and hence in precision, and these are qualities Pope was certainly not indifferent to. In this connection it is important to remember, in view of the frequent undervaluing of Pope's poems, that the presence of humor in a poem may, paradoxically, make it more, not less, serious.

So consistent a moralist did not, of course, overlook the didactic value of humor. By jarring the reader's sense of fitness, humor focuses attention on the discrepancy between the ideal and the actual. It implies a positive scale of values and recommends positive standards of human conduct.

As an Augustan poet, Pope must also have been influenced by the fact that humor involves a public attitude; humor is urbane. But far from being high-flown, it demands the humble and the concrete. It counters the eccentric with the concentric; and it

NOTE: This chapter is an expanded version of an essay that appeared, under the title "The Quality of Alexander Pope's Humor," in *College English*, January 1953.

53

does this indirectly, sometimes ambiguously. Most important, humor is a foe to boredom; it entertains. Hence it is a prime instrument for those who believe with Horace that the purpose of poetry is to instruct delightfully.

Except for *Eloisa to Abelard* and the *Messiah*, not one of Pope's longer poems fails to rely considerably upon humor of some kind. Many of his poems are conceived entirely within a humorous context.

To see how humor works for Pope and to isolate some of its distinctive characteristics, the *Essay on Criticism* is particularly well adapted for a beginning. In this poem the most important single function of the humor is to sweeten the instruction. The quality of the humor itself is rarely sweet, but it does make the precepts more palatable. Humor is not as inextricably fused with precept here as humor is with narrative in the *Dunciad*. On the contrary, in the *Essay on Criticism* humor and precept can often be detached:

> Some praise at morning what they blame at night;
> But always think the last opinion right.
> A Muse by these is like a mistress used,
> This hour she's idolised, the next abused.
>
> (II, 430–433)

The first couplet makes a statement in a relatively nonhumorous manner. The second couplet repeats the idea in terms of a humorous comparison. The picture drawn is so sordid that the humor is considerably submerged. This submerging is desirable because the unsavory picture points up the inappropriateness of treating a divinity, the Muse, in a fashion so changeable and outrageous.

Approach to the Muse, as Pope envisages her, has its decorums, which would be more like those of a church than like Gin Lane's. Barbarians who first supplicate a god and then, when the request is not granted, vilify it, are at the same time pitiable and comic. Similarly, in the lines above, Pope's treatment of fickle poetic judgment in brothel terms brings together two incongruous emotions. The serious and the comic interplay and by their incongruity make the principal point of the passage.

It is typical of Pope's economy to utilize this same incongruity to make other points. The second couplet, touched as it is with the sorry wisdom of the Town, helps establish the worldly experience of the poem's speaker and flatters the reader's vanity by making the assumption that he too is versed in the ways of the world. Its representation of unconventional sex mores, moreover, has an undeniable and immediate appeal to certain of the reader's emotions. But these secondary enriching meanings are compelled by the surface logic to serve what is syntactically prominent—the humorous comparison.

This passage, incidentally, exemplifies the fact that humor does not subsist on abstractions. It draws its vitality from the concrete particular charged by usage with connotations both relevant and irrelevant to the syntax. Humor helps to provide the essential "thingness" of poetry, and this is particularly important where an Augustan poetics prevails.

The Janus aspect of Pope's humor is one of its most constant qualities:

> If Maevius scribble in Apollo's spite,
> There are who judge still worse than he can write.
>
> (I, 34–35)

By Apollo Pope signifies that aspect of divine attention which concerns itself with the poet's craft. And the decorum of the poet's relation with Apollo demands not defiance but reverent supplication. When Apollo refuses countenance to a would-be writer, that writer's only sane course is to desist. If he scribbles on in spite of the god, he is impious and as absurd as a man trying to row a boat in the middle of a desert.

The grimmer implications of this couplet are subdued by the comic element in the picture of the puny man defying reality. The contemptuous connotation of "scribble" and the use of a pagan divinity's name to an audience that is nominally Christian divert attention from the couplet's seriousness. Syntax too plays a part. The Maevius clause is only a preamble to the main statement: that there are critics worse than the worst uninspired poets. The main clause itself is humorous, administering a kind of mock consolation to Maevius: Though damned, he is not the most damned.

Pope also uses humor as an aid to brevity:

> 'Tis with our judgments as our watches, none
> Go just alike, yet each believes his own.   (I, 9–10)

This couplet, easy, colloquial, and perspicuous as it is, is a triumph of much in little. From its planned indirection certain positive statements emerge: Regardless of what individual watches may register, there is an objectively arrived at and correct time. And regardless of how individual minds may differ, there is an objective truth. The couplet temporarily equates the homely, everyday object, "watch," with that comparatively noble faculty, human reason. The logical coupling ground is the human failing of preferring one's own, whether judgment or watch and whether right or wrong. An unreasonable self-love, trivial in the one case, serious in the other, will pervert the purpose of either.

Pope, however, is not concerned primarily with judgments about the time, but with judgments about poetry and, by implication, with all the more important human concerns. He might have stated the graver part of the proposition alone, without reference to watches, without humor. But had he done so, the couplet would have been less immediately perspicuous and would have lost some of the appeal resulting from an amusing and easily grasped comparison. And some of the precision of Pope's insight into the absurdity of priding oneself on human reason would have been sacrificed.

The ready comprehensibility and universal appeal of humor are factors in the success of the following passage, in which the speaker berates bad poets:

> What crowds of these, impenitently bold,
> In sounds and jingling syllables grown old,
> Still run on Poets, in a raging vein,
> Even to the dregs and squeezings of the brain,
> Strain out the last dull droppings of their sense,
> And rhyme with all the rage of Impotence.
>   (III, 604–609)

The most prominent humorous device is the ambiguous metaphor developed in the last four lines. The process involving "raging," "dregs," "squeezings," "strain," and "dull droppings" is not identified. Is it a process of the privy, the bedroom, or even perhaps the kitchen? The ambiguity makes it possible to suggest all three. It is the width of the gap between poetry and the privy, poetry and the kitchen, poetry and sexual impotence that makes the point: Good poetry is the reverse of this straining and futile rage.

There is little tenderness in the humor of the *Essay on Criticism*. It is masculine in tone, forceful, and predominantly low in its associations. These are the qualities required for the function it has to perform. Bad poets and critics deserve neither execution nor coddling, but rather the "purgings, pumpings, blankettings, and blows" mentioned in the *Dunciad*.

In *The Rape of the Lock* the prevailing quality of the humor is very different. The poem condemns certain feminine frailties, most of which are as diminutive in the scale of moral values as the Sylphs and Gnomes who personify them. They are foibles, not crimes; and their perpetrators are not grave critics but belles. The sources drawn upon for humor in the *Essay on Criticism* would be inappropriate. There is innuendo but little overt grossness. The humor comes, in Pope's own words, "thro' some certain strainers well refin'd." Satire is mixed with sympathy:

> While Peers and Dukes, and all their sweeping Train,
> And Garters, Stars, and Coronets appear,
> And in soft sounds, Your Grace salutes their Ear,
> 'Tis these that early taint the Female Soul,
> Instruct the Eyes of young Coquettes to roll,
> Teach Infant-Cheeks a bidden Blush to know,
> And little Hearts to flutter at a Beau. (I, 84–90)

Pope is aware that both courtly pageantry and feminine coquetry have a grace which may be harmless. But when beauty sells itself corruptly for rank, Pope's humor can be sharp, as in this couplet from *Moral Essay* III:

> His daughter flaunts a Viscount's tawdry wife;
> She bears a Coronet and P—x for life. (391–392)

Aside from the element of beauty so prominent in *The Rape of the Lock*, a further conditioning factor of the humor is the consciousness, never lost sight of, that all this beauty, whether of the woman herself or of the objects and culture patterns surrounding her, is transient and easily destroyed:

> For, after all the Murders of your Eye,
> When, after Millions slain, yourself shall die;
> When those fair Suns shall sett, as sett they must,
> And all those Tresses shall be laid in Dust . . .
> (V, 145–148)

By means of a pun on "die" Pope makes a humorous, down-to-earth sexual allusion in these lines; but it is softened by the reference to Belinda's mortality and the short date of all things sweet and rare.

The most important conditioning factor of the humor in *The Rape of the Lock*, however, is the ambivalence central to the poem—the attempt at the same time to build up and tear down the importance of the feminine concerns with which the poem deals. In such passages as the description of Belinda's toilet table in terms of an altar, the treatment of the game of ombre as an epic combat, and the ultimate stellification of the lock, the prime purpose is magnification. Yet all these passages are undercut by the mock-heroic mode. Once Belinda is presented as a goddess, even in mock-heroic, humor can be used to undermine her precarious divinity:

> What tender Maid but must a Victim fall
> To one Man's Treat, but for another's Ball?
> (I, 95–96)

These verses reveal the goddess's all too human susceptibility.

Though the prevailing tone of the humor is playful, tolerant, and compassionate, there are exceptions. One of the most notable is the description of the Cave of Spleen, the "hell" of the poem where "sinners" are punished. The humor here is not qualified by either beauty or compassion. It is grotesque and coarse. But the altered tone is functional; the structure of the poem demands that the consequences of prudery be shown realistically.

In the *Essay on Man* humor is couched frequently in the invective mode. Within this mode Pope achieves a kind of humor which can only be called sublime. Human pride personified, as blind to reality as Jenny was to the louse on her bonnet, swells into blasphemy:

> Ask for what end the heav'nly bodies shine,
> Earth for whose use? Pride answers, "'Tis for mine:
> For me kind Nature wakes her genial pow'r,
> Suckles each herb, and spreads out ev'ry flow'r;
> Annual for me, the grape, the rose renew
> The juice nectareous, and the balmy dew;
> For me, the mine a thousand treasures brings;
> For me, health gushes from a thousand springs;
> Seas roll to waft me, suns to light me rise;
> My foot-stool earth, my canopy the skies.   (I, 131–140)

The puffed-up little mortal who speaks these lines, by applying to himself praise reminiscent of that reserved in the Christian tradition to celebrate the glory and power of God Almighty, achieves a sort of inverse sublimity. If spoken by a being worthy of having seas roll to waft him and suns rise to give him light, the speech would be straightforwardly sublime. But with the speaker what he is, the mounting self-magnification undermines itself as it goes. Counterpointed against the rising line of sublimity there is a falling line of satire, and the humor is the product of the counterpointing.

The religious decorum of this poem makes impossible the use of privy jokes and brothel ribaldry found in the *Essay on Criticism*, and it discourages the type of innuendo pervading *The Rape of the Lock*. But it does not prevent plain speaking:

> Why has not Man a microscopic eye?
> For this plain reason, Man is not a Fly.
>   (I, 193–194)

The fly is a homely object, so homely that in translating from the Greek Pope resorted to periphrasis to avoid naming it in an epic context. But if a religious poem of the ceremonial kind represented by the *Essay on Man* must be decent, it need not, like a heroic poem, avert its eyes from the humble. Thus Pope can still maintain the distance between realms of reference required for humor.

The metaphysics of his *Essay* makes it possible for him to depend substantially for this upon the disparity between different beings on the Great Scale. This is the source of the humor in the couplet ending "Man is not a Fly." And the source may be exploited in both directions, up and down:

> What would this Man? Now upward will he soar,
> And little less than Angel, would be more;
> Now looking downwards, just as griev'd appears
> To want the strength of bulls, the fur of bears.
>
> (I, 173–176)

The Great Scale is also the origin of the humor in the analysis of man's middle nature which opens Epistle II. The passage ends:

> Sole judge of Truth, in endless Error hurl'd:
> The glory, jest, and riddle of the world!   (II, 17–18)

The tone of the humor here is no longer dry and downright; it is impassioned. In verse after verse man has been granted a positive quality only to have it immediately snatched away. The picture which emerges is of man as a very ecstasy of antitheses. This tonal excitement and the humor condition each other. Both interact with the steel control of the rhetoric to keep the passage from losing perspective and urbanity under the pressure of religious urgency.

The humor is also based on the Great Scale in these lines from Epistle III, yet the tone again differs. Man is described as follows:

> Of half that live the butcher and the tomb;
> Who, foe to Nature, hears the gen'ral groan,
> Murders their species, and betrays his own.
> But just disease to luxury succeeds,
> And ev'ry death its own avenger breeds;
> The Fury-passions from that blood began,
> And turn'd on Man a fiercer savage, Man.
>
> (III, 162–168)

The tone is not as mobile and ecstatic as in the passage cited previously. Yet it is so heavily charged with the horrible that it too skirts the danger of emotional overflow. Pope keeps this dreadful humor within the bounds of pulpit decorum, partly by the inexorable balancing inherent in the patterns of divine retribution and partly by making his rhetorical patterns imitate that balancing.

An important special adjunct to the grim humor of the above passage is the "container" image pervading it. Man has turned foe to the animal creation, and animals are antagonistic to him; but man's collective stomach encloses them. That collective stomach is also spoken of as a tomb; hence the animals are doubly enclosed, in space and in death. But every death, whether of beast or fellowman, breeds and hence contains its own avenger. The last line, "And turned on Man a fiercer savage, Man," encloses man's savagery within mankind. The humor itself is savage, but it cannot break through the rhetorical containment. Unable to disperse itself, it must remain concentrated within the doubly controlling walls of meaning and rhetoric.

In Dialogue I of the *Epilogue to the Satires* the prevalent humor is in some sort a composite of that in the *Essay on Criticism* and the *Essay on Man*. The intimacy of the dialogue form removes some of the restraints of pulpit oratory; but the moral import of the subject, graver than the writing or judging of verse, acts in some degree as a check on ribaldry.

To a considerable extent the humor is bound up with the dialogue form. The axis of the poem is the tension between the apparent meaning as the Friend sees it and the real movement as the poet is managing it. The Friend is a Dupe throughout, completely blind to moral values, completely enslaved by appearances, completely a thing of the Court. As the poem proceeds it becomes clear that he thinks of himself not as immoral but as amoral, and so conceives of satire as a morally neutral tool in the service of morally neutral issues. He accepts satire as a device for ridiculing whatever does not happen to meet current courtly convenience. The poet, on the contrary, respects satire as a moral and religious force. Between these polar conceptions the poem moves.

The dialogue form places the poet-as-persona in an advantageous strategic position. He can profit from the fact that the Friend has apparent dramatic autonomy. But actually the Friend does not speak a word not put into his mouth by the poet-as-writer. The all but technical identity between the poet-as-persona and the poet-as-writer makes the latter a very comforting ally. It permits the double-edged humor in the Friend's recommendation that the poet imitate Horace:

> But Horace, Sir, was delicate, was nice;
> Bubo observes, he lash'd no sort of *Vice*:
> Horace would say, Sir Billy *serv'd the Crown,*
> Blunt *could do Bus'ness,* H-ggins *knew the Town,*
> In Sappho touch the *Failing of the Sex,*
> In rev'rend Bishops note some *small Neglects,*
> And own, the Spaniard did a *waggish thing,*
> Who cropt our Ears, and sent them to the King.
> His sly, polite, insinuating stile
> Could please at Court, and make AUGUSTUS smile:
> An artful Manager, that crept between
> His Friend and Shame, and was a kind of Screen.

(11–22)

The poet-as-writer puts into the mouth of this spiritual Babe-in-the-Woods the most sly and insinuating Horatian satire of his own Court friends. The litotes derives especial point from its revelation of the courtier's moral density. The climax of his inversion of satire's true function is reached in the concluding metaphor—that of the satiric poet as "a kind of Screen" between his friends and shame. The metaphor is particularly appropriate in the mouth of this speaker, whose corrupt concern for nothing but appearances has effectually screened him off from the perception of moral truth.

As the Dialogue progresses, the Friend is more and more revealed as a creature of the abyss. And the breach between the humor of the revelation and the moral seriousness of the subject widens. The contrast between subject and manner underlines the depravity of the Friend's viewpoint. The climax is reached when Vice is pictured as the Scarlet Woman of the Apocalypse making her triumphal procession through England:

Hear her black Trumpet thro' the Land proclaim,
That "Not to be corrupted is the Shame." (159–160)

This is not humor in the comic sense, but in the cosmic. The inversion of moral values expressed in the proclamation toward
which the whole movement of the poem tends is so complete in
its enormity that it suggests the "humor" of Milton's Devil defying and aping God.

In contrast, the humor of the *Dunciad* rolls the reader back
away from the divine as actuality to the divine as metaphor, from
cosmic humor to humor based, at a remove, on cosmic implications. The fundamental humorous device in the *Dunciad* is also
inversion, a favorite rhetorical technique which Pope uses so
persistently that every apparently trivial turning upside down
of natural order and fitness—as in the notorious mixture of holy
and profane objects on Belinda's dressing table—is apt to be symbolic of a graver moral disorder. But in the *Dunciad* it is not
merely one foolish belle or a single interlocutor who is blind to
truth. It is all the sons and daughters of Dulness, a shoal of fools,
who threaten to "make one mighty Dunciad of the land." Though
Dialogue I of the *Epilogue* vividly conveys the menace of moral
corruption, the menace of the *Dunciad* is more inclusive, since
fools are always more numerous than villains.

In Dialogue I the blindness of the Friend is presented realistically. Every remark of his bears the sign of everyday credibility.
But the blindness of the Dunces is presented ideally, as in the
following prayer of the future King of Dulness to the goddess:

O! ever gracious to perplex'd mankind,
Still spread a healing mist before the mind;
And lest we err by Wit's wild dancing light,
Secure us kindly in our native night.
Or, if to Wit a coxcomb make pretence,
Guard the sure barrier between that and Sense;
Or quite unravel all the reas'ning thread,
And hang some curious cobweb in its stead!
(I, 173–180)

The actual dullard does not pray to be dull but to be clever—as he sees it. In constructing this prayer, and in general throughout the poem, Pope sacrifices the illusion of realism in actions and speech in order to achieve a greater ideal truth. The effect of this is to heighten the deeds and utterances of the dull to a bedlam strain of inspiration. The whole poem moves within the current of this crackling, farcical, madhouse magnetism.

Dialogue I gives the illusion of actual conversation; its inverted humor is the humor of the actual. But as real as the inversions of the *Dunciad* may be, the atmosphere in which they are presented is that of a fairy tale. If the humor of Dialogue I moves close to the ground, that of the *Dunciad*, like a magic carpet, flies always parallel to but far above the ground.

Yet the consistent farcical exaggeration, or high-flying, makes the humor neither tedious nor unsympathetic. The heir apparent of Duncedom is, for example, thus described:

> Swearing and supperless the Hero sate,
> Blasphem'd his Gods, the Dice, and damn'd his Fate;
> Then gnaw'd his pen, then dash'd it on the ground,
> Sinking from thought to thought, a vast profound!
>
> (I, 115–118)

The hero is by no means completely unsympathetic. While the reader laughs, he pities. Pope's lethal shafts are reserved for serious criminals, a Peter Walter or a peeress who starves her sister to death. He merely ridicules uninspired poets, occasionally tempering his ridicule with a touch of pathos.

A deeper compassion pervades this poem in connection with the theme of the triumph of Dulness as the destruction of civilized morals and arts. Every ludicrous mock-elevation of the broad-faced goddess and her train is accompanied by the premonition that this advances the day of doom for civilization:

> Thus at her felt approach, and secret might,
> Art after Art goes out, and all is Night.
>
> (IV, 639–640)

Though the *Dunciad* is highly comic, it is not lacking in the cosmic humor which consists in being, in the etymological sense, anti-cosmic—destructive of fit order and arrangement.

Not only in this poem but in Pope's verse as a whole the range of humorous tones is wide. The quality of his humor is not one but multiple, differently conditioned from genre to genre and poem to poem. The humor adds depth and another dimension to what is already being presented in Pope's characteristically multi-dimensional way. Humor's particular facility, which no other component of poetry possesses so eminently, of making the complex statement plain and ingratiating is especially serviceable in a poetry so rich in texture as Pope's.

5

Parallelism, Antithesis, and Paradox

Parallelism, antithesis, and paradox are closely related to one another. Antithesis is a special kind of parallelism, and paradox may be defined as a special kind of antithesis in which both halves of the antithesis are asserted to be true.

The predominance, of the first two especially, in neoclassical English poetry and particularly in the poetry of Pope, has long been acknowledged and commented on. There is no major poem of Pope's in which all three are not in some degree exemplified.

Pope's main purpose in using them is to achieve an effect which is itself paradoxical: motion in stance. It is a question of setting up the strongest possible tensions and then balancing and confining them in the strongest possible way—somewhat as if a life and death struggle were carried on in an enclosed formal garden. Examining Pope's use of these three devices throws light on one principal way he went about solving the old poetic problem of diversity in unity.

Parallelism is the element which makes for stability and repose. Its basic function is the establishment of a fixed and harmonious framework against which complicating factors like antithesis and paradox can be played off. The three elements, therefore, usually act in close conjunction with one another and are structurally complementary.

They are not, however, found in the same proportion in each poem. Neither are they used in the same way, though they are always used for the same basic purpose. Parallelism is undeniably the most indispensable of the three. No poem—and, in fact, no work of art—can exist without it. Likewise antithesis, whether expressed or implied, is hardly dispensable.

But good poems may and do exist in which paradox is lacking or negligible. The *Epistle to Dr. Arbuthnot*, for example, unlike the rest of Pope's major poems, is not dominated by significant paradoxes inextricably bound up with the central meanings. Yet it has always been acknowledged one of Pope's best poems. The absence of significant paradox is unusual and is to be accounted for on specific grounds of subject and approach.

The subject, a defence of satire, is one which, unlike the relationship of man to the universe, can be examined carefully without encountering significant paradoxes. The place of paradox as a structural factor making for tension and complication is supplied in this poem by antithesis, irony, and the convention of autobiographical truth.

Not all paradoxes, of course, are profound. Romeo's to Benvolio provide a good instance:

> Why then, O brawling love! O loving hate!
> O any thing! of nothing first create!
> O heavy lightness! serious vanity!
> Mis-shapen chaos of well-seeming forms!
> Feather of lead, bright smoke, cold fire, sick health!
> Still-waking sleep, that is not what it is!
> This love feel I, that feel no love in this.
> Dost thou not laugh?
>
> *(Romeo and Juliet*, I, i, 181–188)

Nor are paradoxes which touch on profound issues always profoundly used. Witness the conventionalization of the "sweet foe" type of epithet applied by the cavalier to his lady in the Petrarchan mode. Paradox is, notwithstanding, one of the most important devices available to a poet for making mature, complex, subtle, and accurate statements.

Whenever men have thought deeply about the nature of man, God, and the universe, and the relations of these to one another, they have tended to resort to paradox. Why this is true is a matter for philosophers to settle. If one takes a religious view of reality, it would seem that paradox is a condition of human thinking comparable in function to the withholding of peace in George Herbert's *The Pulley*. A man who has thought to a point at which he concludes that life is death, death is life, evil is good, etc., has reached the limits of human reasoning. He has reached the limits of the use of reason as a tool for comprehending the universe. He has advanced to a point at which reason no longer functions, where it begins to give him mutually contradictory *yet true* statements about reality.

From the religious standpoint, then, this is where the individual must recognize the insufficiency of human reason for comprehending reality. For any further insight, man must wait upon what in Christian tradition is called divine grace.

Regardless of why so much of the profoundest thinking of philosophers, theologians, and poets has been expressed in paradox, the fact of its having been so expressed is undeniable. It is enshrined, in our present civilization, in print for all who read to verify. A few examples will suffice:

Verily, verily, I say unto you, Except a corn of wheat fall into the ground and die, it abideth alone: but if it die, it bringeth forth much fruit.

He that loveth his life shall lose it; and he that hateth his life in this world shall keep it unto life eternal. (John 12:24-25)

> Fountain of Light, thyself invisible
> Amidst the glorious brightness where thou sit'st
> Thron'd inaccessible, but when thou shad'st
> The full blaze of thy beams, and through a cloud
> Drawn round about thee like a radiant Shrine,
> Dark with excessive bright thy skirts appear,
> Yet dazle Heav'n, that brightest Seraphim
> Approach not, but with both wings veil their eyes.
> (*Paradise Lost*, III, 375-382)

At the still point of the turning world. Neither flesh nor fleshless;
Neither from nor towards; at the still point, there the dance is.
But neither arrest nor movement. And do not call it fixity,

Where past and future are gathered. Neither movement
from nor towards,
Neither ascent nor decline. Except for the point, the still
point,
There would be no dance, and there is only the dance.
I can only say, *there* we have been: but I cannot say
where.
And I cannot say, how long, for that is to place it in
time.   (*Burnt Norton*, II, 16–23)

Paradox in Pope is not always explicitly stated; it is often implied. Even when the degree of rhetorical salience is low, as in
the case of the *Pastorals*, it can possess much significance. As
might be expected in a genre which strives for ideal tranquillity,
both antithesis and paradox are subordinated to parallelism, and
the parallelisms stressed are in content primarily conducive to
reassurance and serenity.

The major parallelism which runs through all four *Pastorals*—
that between the life of man and the life of external nature—is
stabilizing, as any congruence is stabilizing. It is especially reas-
suring to little and insecure man, since it stresses resemblances
between his little world within and the great outside world. He
feels himself part of a universal harmony and rhythm of event.

Pope's use of parallelism in the *Pastorals* is generally formal and
overt. In *Spring* every speech of Daphnis corresponds exactly in
length and sense to every speech of Strephon. When Strephon
invokes in four lines the aid of the gods and promises a sacrifice
if successful—

Inspire me, Phoebus, in my Delia's praise
With Waller's strains, or Granville's moving lays:
A milk-white bull shall at your altars stand,
That threats a fight, and spurns the rising sand—

then Daphnis immediately does the same in the same number of
lines—

O Love! for Sylvia let me gain the prize,
And make my tongue victorious as her eyes;
No lambs or sheep for victims I'll impart,
Thy victim, Love, shall be the shepherd's heart.
                                                  (45–52)

If one propounds a riddle, so does the other. If one lady feigns to hide only to be found, the other feigns to run in such a way that she is soon caught. If Strephon in the end wins the bowl, Daphnis wins the lamb. If the swains are said to be blessed in Nymphs who "in every grace excel," the Nymphs are immediately asserted to be blessed in swains who "those graces sing so well."

Such antitheses as are necessary to prevent the poem from being all stance and no motion are mild. The principal one is the artistic contest between Daphnis and Strephon, who vie in seeing which can praise his ladylove the more adroitly. The weapons of their harmonious war are songs and riddles. Temporary antitheses occur, like those between man and linnet and man and star:

> Why sit we mute when early linnets sing?
>
> . . . .
>
> Why sit we sad when Phosphor shines so clear?
>
> (25–27)

But these are at once harmonized by Strephon's resolution in the lines beginning "Sing then," etc.

None of the stated paradoxes touches on any very serious matter. The behavior of the shepherdesses, for instance, hiding and running but wanting to be discovered and caught, is paradoxical. But these *Pastorals* do contain both an important implied antithesis and a serious and significant paradox. The antithesis is that which underlies all pastoral and gives it its peculiar charm: the contrast between the specially secluded and select world of pastoral and the everyday world. In the latter, struggles are for life and death. Contests are waged, not with songs and riddles, but with bullets and bombs. By comparison, the pastoral world seems at first very desirable. But as was pointed out in Chapter III in connection with both-and irony, no human being would be content to live forever in such a static world, however prettified. Pastoral antithesis, then, involves a restatement of a well-known paradox in human nature. There is at the same time a desire for and a shrinking from conflict and a desire for and rejection of complete tranquillity.

It is especially interesting to see how in the *Pastorals* Pope resolves antitheses into certain paradoxes with a tranquilizing effect. (Transcendental theology, incidentally, is full of such resolutions.) The most important antithesis in *Winter*, that between life and death, is resolved into the Christian paradox, Death is Life. The resolution is made formally, in the course of several parallel refrains. The first six are despairing, of the type, "Daphne, our grief! our glory now no more!" (68). Then, just as in *Lycidas*, comes recognition of the fact that the person lamented as dead has really entered into eternal life. This is at once reflected in the refrain, "Daphne, our Goddess, and our grief no more!" (76).

Pope, recognizing the dangers of overfacility and sentimentality which lurk in the cliché use of this pious paradox, has given it a characteristically oblique twist. By adding another statement he creates a double paradox. The second assertion is superimposed upon the Christian formula "Life is death, and conversely." It is "Nevertheless, death is death." This idea, which in some sort contradicts the first, is not made in the poem until Thyrsis' last speech:

> But see, Orion sheds unwholesome dews,
> Arise, the pines a noxious shade diffuse;
> Sharp Boreas blows, and Nature feels decay,
> Time conquers all, and we must Time obey.
>
> (85–88)

But its terminal position and the strong contrast in which it stands to the gentle side of nature hitherto presented give it force. Thus Pope seeks to counteract the overcomplacency and oversimplification which may arise from the use of the first paradox.

In contrast to the *Pastorals*, *Eloisa to Abelard* is primarily a poem of conflict. Its fundamental action is the struggle which goes on in Eloisa's mind between pagan and Christian ideologies. The aim of the poem is to present, not tranquillity and a world far removed from human passions and perplexities, but the strongest possible picture of a woman in the throes of emotional anguish and intellectual despair. No mild or immediately resolved antitheses and no tranquilizing paradoxes are needed or used.

Of the three structural features under consideration, antithesis is the one dominant in this poem. There is, however, one very important parallelism: *In Eloisa's mind* God and Abelard are parallel. But it is of consequence to remember that this parallelism exists only subjectively. Objectively viewed, as by the reader, it is clearly seen to be an erroneous parallelism. Its effect is to suggest more strongly the antithesis between error and truth.

It is this parallelism, as a matter of fact, and not sexual passion in itself that Eloisa conceives to be her chief sin. Paralleling Abelard with God involves, according to the religion she professes, a culpable equating of physical with spiritual values. Yet she admits,

> I waste the Matin lamps in sighs for thee,
> Thy image steals between my God and me,
> Thy voice I seem in ev'ry hymn to hear,
> With ev'ry bead I drop too soft a tear.
> When from the Censer clouds of fragrance roll,
> And swelling organs lift the rising soul;
> One thought of thee puts all the pomp to flight,
> Priests, Tapers, Temples, swim before my sight;
> In seas of flame my plunging soul is drown'd,
> While Altars blaze, and Angels tremble round.
>
> (267–276)

Her ultimate expression of what is for her blasphemy comes when, in speaking of Abelard's name, she confesses that in her heart it is confused with God's (lines 11–12).

The chief paradox of the poem is a fact of being rather than an idea. Eloisa herself is in a sense a walking paradox. A Christian nun by her vows, her outward habit, and her conscious intellectual persuasion, within she remains, in her own eyes, a sensualist and a sinner. Actually, from the Augustan viewpoint, she is the confused victim of an unsound theology which is in conflict with reality. It is in her flesh, however, that the two poles of the poem's basic antithesis meet.

Aside from this metaphorical paradox of being, the whole

reliance of the poem is antithesis; and the whole method of conducting the poem is antithetical. Strong walls have been set up, but the reader is not allowed to rest within the enclosure. He is tossed by the antithetical movement, first against one wall and then against another. There is no arrest of movement in ideological paradox, for no such stance is desired.

To appreciate the fact that the entire ordering of the poem, as well as the content, is antithetical, it is necessary to read the poem as a whole, observing how it proceeds solely by one contrast after another. And there is no solution which resolves these antitheses or includes two opposites reconciled in a new positive. There is nothing but the pattern of constant tossing to and fro and the recognition that only exhaustion (death) can bring it to an end—an end, not a solution.

As far as content is concerned, all the minor antitheses are closely related to the major one. These derived antitheses are such as the contrast between Abelard's castrated calm and Eloisa's ill-subdued passion, between the happy past and the unhappy present, between Eloisa's turmoil and her imaginative depiction of "the blameless vestal's lot," between the sensuous beauty of life and the cold horror of death.

The antithetical ordering of the poem can at least be glimpsed in the following passage. Eloisa advances rapidly from a grovelling state of grace to a passionate appeal to Abelard; then to a passionate renunciation of Abelard; and finally to a rapturous (but temporary) reconciliation to asceticism with a religious veneer:

> While prostrate here in humble grief I lie,
> Kind, virtuous drops just gath'ring in my eye,
> While praying, trembling, in the dust I roll,
> And dawning grace is opening on my soul:
> Come, if thou dar'st, all charming as thou art!
> Oppose thyself to heav'n; dispute my heart;
> Come, with one glance of those deluding eyes,
> Blot out each bright Idea of the skies.
> Take back that grace, those sorrows, and those tears;
> Take back my fruitless penitence and pray'rs;

Snatch me, just mounting, from the blest abode,
Assist the Fiends and tear me from my God!
  No, fly me, fly me, far as Pole from Pole;
Rise Alps between us! and whole oceans roll!
Ah come not, write not, think not once of me,
Nor share one pang of all I felt for thee.
Thy oaths I quit, thy memory resign:
Forget, renounce me, hate whate'er was mine.
Fair eyes, and tempting looks (which yet I view!)
Long lov'd, ador'd ideas! all adieu!
O grace serene! oh virtue heav'nly fair!
Divine oblivion of low-thoughted care!
Fresh blooming hope, gay daughter of the sky!
And faith, our early immortality!
Enter each mild, each amicable guest;
Receive, and wrap me in eternal rest!   (277–302)

The Rape of the Lock affords an excellent vindication of the assertion made at the beginning of this chapter: that parallelism, antithesis, and paradox are intimately related, and to some extent only aspects or degrees of the same thing. Throughout this poem three realms of existence run parallel to one another: the epic world, the world of social trivia, and the world of serious human issues. The action of parallelism, antithesis, and paradox in this connection is such as, not to negate, but to affirm each of these three realms.

As noted earlier, Cleanth Brooks has shown throughout the poem a parallelism between details connected with the symbolic rape and the actual facts of human relationship. To this it may be added that the third parallel realm, the mock-heroic, has the effect of concentrating disproportionate interest and attention on the trivial realm—as when the Baron builds an altar of gilt French romances, garters, gloves, and billets-doux. The result is that the seeming trivia, already disproportionately emphasized as far as sane human values are concerned, are more readily accepted as not trivial at all but symbols of something more serious.

Parallelism and paradox are more important than antithesis in *The Rape of the Lock*. The antitheses, as a matter of fact, arise from the parallelisms. The major antitheses are, on the one hand,

74

between the apparently frivolous subject matter and the heroic manner in which it is set forth; and, on the other, between the actually serious human issues and the frivolous guise under which they are presented. The relationship here between parallelism and antithesis is comparable to the working of metaphor, in which resemblances derive their point from differences.

The central paradox of the poem has already been touched on in connection with both-and irony—Belinda's desire to retain her chastity and yet her definite expectation of and preparation for losing it. This is only the statement, in feminine terms, of a broader human paradox: Use, even legitimate use, of any human faculty is destruction. It is the idea that, even in consenting to live, a human being is in a sense consenting to a sixty-year-long suicide. Belinda is like a flower, which cannot be picked and at the same time left on the stem. Though the flower will die if picked, it will wither and die just as surely if left on the stalk.

The choice which she must make is, therefore, not an absolute but a relative choice. Since living is dying, all Belinda or anyone can choose is the manner of dying. In the eighteenth century usage of the term, Belinda wants to "die" on the best possible terms for her—not actual rape but marriage.

The full truth of this human situation could not be stated without paradox. It would be pure conjecture to maintain that it could not be stated forcefully in direct terms. But it is undeniable that presented as it is, it is especially effective. The meaning is conveyed in terms of a double, metaphorical parallelism. Both the mock-heroic and the boudoir elements are extended metaphors for the real subject. Both these metaphors are drawn from realms which contrast provocatively with the realm in which the paradox is serious.

Because of the graduated, hierarchical nature of existence as portrayed in the *Essay on Man*, there can be no question of absolute antitheses, only relative ones. Even the antithesis between moral evil and moral good is resolved by "Th' eternal art educing good from ill." Every entity in the hierarchy, though it may seem antithetic to some other, is always parallel to every other. For the

75

position of each entity is relative both to what is above and what below it, and it is subject to the laws governing the whole system.

Most of the significant parallels in the poem arise from the concepts of the Great Chain and the Great Scale. Out of the union of these concepts a paradoxical situation results: All things are interconnected on a scale of graduated importance, and yet they are completely and democratically equal in God.

Everything in the Scale is at once greater than the thing below it, less than the thing above it, and equal to each of them! Though Pope throughout emphasizes man's littleness in comparison with angelic intelligences and God, he also places much stress on the parallel aspect of the components of the Great Scale. He paints a very vivid picture of what would happen if the least unit should abandon its necessary place:

> . . . On superior pow'rs
> Were we to press, inferior might on ours:
> Or in the full creation leave a void,
> Where, one step broken, the great scale's destroy'd:
> From Nature's chain whatever link you strike,
> Tenth or ten thousandth, breaks the chain alike.
>   And if each system in gradation roll
> Alike essential to th' amazing whole;
> The least confusion but in one, not all
> That system only, but the whole must fall.
> Let Earth unbalanc'd from her orbit fly,
> Planets and Suns run lawless thro' the sky;
> Let ruling Angels from their spheres be hurl'd,
> Being on Being wreck'd, and world on world,
> Heav'n's whole foundations to their centre nod,
> And Nature tremble to the throne of God.
>
> (I, 241–256)

Much of the tension of the poem depends upon this paradox of "parallel and yet not parallel" or "equal and yet not equal" in the components of the universe. But this doctrine receives a more directly Christian expression in the lines following:

> Who sees with equal eye, as God of all,
> A hero perish, or a sparrow fall,

Atoms or systems into ruin hurl'd,
And now a bubble burst, and now a world.

(I, 87–90)

Because these lines alter the emphasis of the Biblical reference to the sparrow, they have sometimes been adversely criticized. But the alteration is for the purpose of emphasizing another and equally important aspect of God's relation to the sparrow. The fall of a hero and the fall of a sparrow are represented as, paradoxically, both of equal and unequal value in the eyes of God. It is the way in which hero and sparrow are parallel, however, and not the way in which they suggest physical and spiritual antitheses, that is here stressed.

This concept of "parallelism in God" is even more strikingly expressed in the following celebrated passage:

As full, as perfect, in a hair as heart;
As full, as perfect, in vile Man that mourns,
As the rapt Seraph that adores and burns;
To him no high, no low, no great, no small;
He fills, he bounds, connects, and equals all.

(I, 276–280)

It is a relative antithesis that exists between "hair" and "heart," between "Man" and "Seraph." This involves the central paradox of the poem: Man is little, considering his place in the Scale; but he is big, considering God's concern for him. It is a theological paradox; and, carefully considered, the *Essay on Man*, far from being a mere collection of platitudes, expresses intuitions shared with the avowed mystic poets of the English language. It does so, of course, under the camouflage of reason and common sense.

From this basic theological parallelism many subsidiary parallelisms follow. For example, the familiar parallel, central to pastoral poetry, between man and external nature is in this *Essay* seen as logically valid because both are parts of the Great Scale:

If the great end be human Happiness,
Then Nature deviates; and can Man do less?
As much that end a constant course requires
Of show'rs and sun-shine, as of Man's desires;

77

> As much eternal springs and cloudless skies,
> As Men forever temp'rate, calm, and wise.
> If plagues or earthquakes break not Heav'n's design,
> Why then a Borgia, or a Cataline?
> Who knows but he, whose hand the light'ning forms,
> Who heaves old Ocean, and who wings the storms,
> Pours fierce Ambition in a Caesar's mind,
> Or turns young Ammon loose to scourge mankind?
>
> (I, 149–160)

Pope achieves an additional interesting group of parallelisms by comparing relatively antithetical exemplifications of the organs of sense to be found within the Great Scale.

> What modes of sight betwixt each wide extreme,
> The mole's dim curtain, and the lynx's beam:
> Of smell, the headlong lioness between,
> And hound sagacious on the tainted green:
> Of hearing, from the life that fills the flood,
> To that which warbles thro' the vernal wood:
> The spider's touch, how exquisitely fine!
> Feels at each thread, and lives along the line.
>
> (I, 211–218)

Not only here but throughout the *Essay* parallelism acts in close conjunction with both antithesis and paradox, a fact which makes both for a high degree of tension in repose and for very close semantic integration.

In the second Epistle antithesis predominates, however. Man is presented as a battleground, or perhaps a compromise, between two opposed principles, roughly Good and Evil. If there is any absolute antithesis in the poem, it is between good and evil. To admit that there is no clear-cut distinction between good and bad in moral conduct, even though the distinction may not always be easily visible to man, would have made this poem, to say the least, unacceptable to an English audience.

Nevertheless, the poem maintains that, though absolute good and evil exist for the individual, they do not exist on the divine plane. Quite orthodoxly, Pope asserts that God is able to make even the Devil serve his purpose and turn evil into good. Just as in the *Pastorals*, though here in a more intense and momentous context, the resolution of opposed forces in paradox serves the fundamental hortatory aim of the poem: the individual's reconciliation with and acquiescence in *what is*.

In Epistle II the antithesis between Reason and Passion is emphasized, and the opposition between the two principles made quite clear:

> Self-love, the spring of motion, acts the soul;
> Reason's comparing balance rules the whole.
> Man, but for that, no action could attend,
> And, but for this, were active to no end;
> Fix'd like a plant on his peculiar spot,
> To draw nutrition, propagate, and rot;
> Or, meteor-like, flame lawless thro' the void,
> Destroying others, by himself destroy'd.   (II, 59–66)

Their opposition, however, is seen to be not hostile but complementary: "Self-love and Reason to one end aspire" (II, 87). Though opposed in nature, they supplement each other and work to the same end.

This is true likewise of the antithesis repeatedly stated between little man and the big universe. There is no doubt that man is little and weak in comparison with presumptive beings higher in the Scale and with the system as a whole. Pope presents this with great insistence, stressing that the big-little relationship is not unjust, but harmonious and right. Order depends upon proper subordination:

> ORDER is Heav'n's first law; and this confest,
> Some are, and must be, greater than the rest,
> More rich, more wise.   (IV, 49–51)

The relationship, moreover, has a benevolent aspect:

> Ask of thy mother earth, why oaks are made
> Taller or stronger than the weeds they shade?
> > (I, 39–40)

> Safe in the hand of one disposing Pow'r,
> Or in the natal, or the mortal hour.
> > (I, 287–288)

79

See! and confess, one comfort still must rise,
'Tis this, Tho' Man's a fool, yet GOD IS WISE.
                                    (II, 293–294)

The result of this metaphysical antithesis is not to suggest a
David-Goliath situation but one in which God's superior strength
and goodness put upon him the burden of *noblesse oblige*—to
man's inestimable advantage. Again the antithesis is directed, in
accordance with the constant aim of the poem, toward harmony
and reconciliation of man to the ways of God.

Closely related to this concept of order accomplished by subordination is the antithesis, ever present in this poem, between
order and possible chaos. The latter is usually presented as a sort
of fire-and-brimstone threat to presumptuous man who, in his
blindness, often wishes to violate the order. It is important to
remember, however, that even the concept of possible chaos is
limited. Nature may tremble, Pope says, *up to* the throne of God.
The reader is confronted again with the paradox of free will and
the possibility of making a wrong moral choice in a universe
where nevertheless all things work together for good. This antithesis between order and possible chaos, then, is also limited
and qualified.

Connected with the antithesis between man's worse and better
natures is Pope's consistent depiction of man as "sufficient to
have stood, though free to fall." Man should neither overvalue
nor undervalue himself; yet, since the more common human tendency is toward the former, Pope devotes more space and emphasis to reminding man of his shortcomings than of his kinship with
the angels.

The most celebrated passage in which the middle nature of
man is set forth, that which opens the second Epistle, has already
been quoted. There man resolves the antithesis of "God or Beast"
by realizing that his nature partakes of both and that if he is sat-
isfactorily to perform his human duty in the great plan, he must
achieve a balance between them. Again, an antithesis is resolved
in the direction of tranquillity and acceptance of whatever is, as
right. "This hour a slave, the next a deity" (I, 68)—this line in-

volves still another antithesis ultimately resolved. Man can be either high or low on Fortune's wheel, his position apparently depending on chance. But "All chance," says Pope "[is but] Direction which thou canst not see." In Epistle IV Pope refers to a number of instances in which diversity and sudden reversals of material well-being exist, but he immediately indicates several reasons for which man should be reconciled to them:

> Honour and shame from no Condition rise;
> Act well your part, there all the honour lies.
> Fortune in Men has some small diff'rence made,
> One flaunts in rags, one flutters in brocade;
> The cobbler apron'd, and the parson gown'd,
> The friar hooded, and the monarch crown'd.
> "What differ more (you cry) than crown and cowl?"
> I'll tell you, friend! a Wise man and a Fool.
> You'll find, if once the monarch acts the monk,
> Or, cobbler-like, the parson will be drunk,
> Worth makes the man, and want of it, the fellow;
> The rest is all but leather or prunella.   (IV, 193–204)

This is the Great Scale again. Antitheses in economic fortune as well as in metaphysical rank are, in the first place, only relative, and in the second, necessary to the welfare of the whole. Man is further dissuaded from repining by the envisioning of a hypothetical state of equality in fortune, with the following unfavorable probable result suggested:

> But Fortune's gifts if each alike possest,
> And each were equal, must not all contest?
> If then to all Men Happiness was meant,
> God in Externals could not place Content.
> (IV, 63–66)

Having drawn upon the traditional Christian argument with which Boethius consoled himself, Pope then suggests that fear on the part of the "haves" and hope on the part of the "have nots" in some sort equalize matters. It is an attempt to nullify by an appeal to the interior and spiritual the undeniable exterior and material antithesis between rich and poor, fortunate and unfortunate on this earth.

A very significant antithesis, constantly stressed in this poem, and one which has its complement in the opposition between man and seraph, is that between man and animals. But the antithesis is two-edged. Man's general superiority is acknowledged:

> The lamb thy riot dooms to bleed to-day,
> Had he thy Reason, would he skip and play?
>
> (I, 81–82)

> To each unthinking being Heav'n, a friend,
> Gives not the useless knowledge of its end:
> To Man imparts it; but with such a view
> As, while he dreads it, makes him hope it too.
>
> (III, 71–74)

But this relative degree of antithesis between man and animal, inherent in the Great Scale, is blurred by the fact that carnivorous man, making himself morally culpable toward the animal creation, has himself somewhat tarnished the glory of his situation. God, says Pope, "Made Beast in aid of Man, and Man of Beast" (III, 24). And in the Golden Age,

> Man walk'd with beast, joint tenant of the shade;
> The same his table, and the same his bed;
> No murder cloath'd him, and no murder fed.
>
> (III, 152–154)

But this ideal state of affairs changed; man slew animals for food and clothing. In turning *against* animals, man turned *toward* them. Eventually, identifying himself, by his behavior, with the brutes, he also turned against his own species:

> The Fury-passions from that blood began,
> And turn'd on Man a fiercer savage, Man.
>
> (III, 167–168)

The existence of a sharp, though relative, antithesis between man and beasts on the Great Scale is assumed, since "Whatever is, is right," to be just and fair. Any blurring or reduction of this antithesis, it is implied, is a sin against the divine ordering of the universe, and hence morally wrong.

Moving up on the Scale, it has often been supposed that the poem presents an antithesis between civilized man and primitive man as exemplified in the noble savage. The antithesis is rather between man depraved by civilization and that philosophical construct which the eighteenth century sometimes persuaded itself real savages resembled. In other words, in his passages on the noble red man, Pope is not attacking civilization but abuses of it.

His method is to use antithesis ironically. The juxtaposition of "fiends" and "Christians" in line 108 of the famous passage beginning "Lo, the poor Indian" is by no means without significance.

The antithesis between "fiends" and "Christians" is apparent only, not real (irony of false equation). In straight, non-ironic language Pope says that, in the matter of treatment of Indians, Christians, civilized men, and fiends are one and the same thing.

The savage, unlike froward and discontented civilized man, does not aspire to the perquisites of ranks above him in the Great Scale. But, as noted previously in another connection, it would be a mistake to infer that the Indian's assumption and desire that his faithful dog will accompany him to Heaven is presented as commendable. The above lines must be read in the light of the others on the noble savage in Epistle IV:

> Weak, foolish man! will Heav'n reward us there
> With the same trash mad mortals wish for here?
> The Boy and Man an individual makes,
> Yet sigh'st thou now for apples and for cakes?
> Go, like the Indian, in another life
> Expect thy dog, thy bottle, and thy wife;
> As well as dream such trifles are assign'd,
> As toys and empires, for a god-like mind.
>
> (IV, 173–180)

What has happened to the antithesis between urbanized man and the noble savage? Though the roles are not reversed, the Indian has ceased to be the positive pole of the antithesis. He and depraved, urbanized man are now on the same reprehensible level. Both are contrasted with an ideal man, not with each other.

Set over against these modified antitheses is an especially meaningful group in which the antithesis arises from depiction of extremes in conduct morally viewed. Pope was not, as he has sometimes been misinterpreted as being, a chirping Pippa. He did not pass over the very real existence of evil and discomfort for the individual. From the individual's viewpoint, evil is evil and good is good. Moreover, from the standpoint of practical morals, it is necessary to point out that evil conduct brings down on the malefactor here and now and on this earth unpleasant punishment. Since the poem as a whole is directed against overweening pride in human beings, Pope is particularly concerned to show that what appears to be happiness gotten by pre-eminent wealth or power is not happiness but more often misery:

> There, in the rich, the honour'd, fam'd, and great,
> See the false scale of Happiness complete!
> In hearts of Kings, or arms of Queens who lay,
> How happy! those to ruin, these betray.
> Mark by what wretched steps their glory grows,
> From dirt and sea-weed as proud Venice rose;
> In each how guilt and greatness equal ran,
> And all that rais'd the Hero, sunk the Man.
> Now Europe's laurels on their brows behold,
> But stain'd with blood, or ill exchang'd for gold,
> Then see them broke with toils, or sunk in ease,
> Or infamous for plunder'd provinces.
> . . . .
> Alas! not dazzled with their noon-tide ray,
> Compute the morn and ev'ning to the day.
> (IV, 287–306)

The two types of antithesis used in the *Essay on Man*—the modified and the straight, or relative and absolute—in themselves constitute an antithesis, and a very significant one. Balance asserts itself again in the refusal of the judicious and reasonable man to be content with a one-sided view. He seeks inclusiveness, even to the point of paradox, rather than risk the falsification of reality which may result from exclusiveness.

As with all the other elements of his craft, Pope's use of parallelism, antithesis, and paradox reveals the careful attention he paid to propriety—to the decorum demanded by a sane view of reality, by a genre, and by a subject. In accordance with the demands of accuracy in matter and decorum in means, he adjusted and modified these three interrelated structural elements in each poem.

6

Metaphor

METAPHOR, like irony and paradox, is one of the means available to the poet of making his communications about reality fuller and more accurate than is possible within the confines of accepted, current speech. Metaphor is therefore basically a pioneering technique. A poet with a new insight cannot always convey it in existing idiom, accepted, like paper money, at declared value. He must have recourse again to whatever, standing behind the currency, gives it value—to things themselves. He must furthermore, if meaning is to be conveyed, make clear to his readers one or more connections or similarities between things in different categories. And, if his metaphors are to perform their essential cognitive function, the connection must be freshly perceived and applied so that there is an increment to existing insights.

This is the primary function of metaphor. The term "metaphor," incidentally, is used throughout this work to indicate a comparison made between things in unlike categories whether the analogy is stated, as in the traditional simile, or implied, as in the traditional metaphor, and whether the comparison involves animation of an inanimate object, as in the traditional personification, or de-animation of an animate one.

Certain subsidiary functions of metaphor are also important to poetic communication. One of these is the obtaining of a shock effect from the meaningful linking of two things the reader has

NOTE: Part of this chapter was published, under the title "Mythopoeic Activity in the *Rape of the Lock*," in the *Journal of English Literary History*, March 1954, and is reprinted by permission of the author and the director of The Johns Hopkins Press, publishers of the *Journal*.

not before thought of as having any connection. It is here that the differences existing between the things compared contribute to the effect achieved—an increase of tension and wonder.

An example of this is the comparison of Belinda in *The Rape of the Lock* to creative deity:

> The skilful Nymph reviews her Force with Care;
> Let Spades be Trumps! she said, and Trumps they were.
>
> (III, 45–46)

The parodied Biblical passage is "And God said, Let there be light. And there was light." All mock-epic metaphor—the genre itself is in some sort an extended metaphor—derives some of its force from the shock element in such a comparison as this between God Almighty creating light and a coquette playing cards. The comparison could not function, however, unless there were an element of valid similarity; and there is, in the fact that Belinda is throughout the poem presented as a sort of goddess to the worshipers of love and beauty.

This shock aspect of metaphor was carried to an extreme by the seventeenth-century English metaphysical poets; but it is in some degree active in all metaphor. Kennings of the "whale's road" and "swan's bath" type were doubtless mere ritual language to the contemporaries of the *Beowulf* poet. Their shock effect was dulled by repetition and familiarity. But it must have been present originally, as it is for modern readers. That celebrated evening in Eliot which is "like a patient etherized upon a table" is a striking instance of this shock effect.

Compression is another subsidiary function of metaphor. It helps a poet achieve more concentrated utterance largely because it juxtaposes two objects or concepts which merely by the fact of their juxtaposition in a given context may speak volumes. For example, in *The Rape of the Lock* Pope insistently juxtaposes frail nymphs and frail China vessels. An ornate, precious, but fragile China jar and feminine chastity—no more need be said. The reader's mind will busily, and almost instantaneously, perceive the multiple congruences between the two components of this metaphor.

Metaphor is also valuable for promoting concreteness. Metaphors in which both terms are abstractions are rare. Usually, one or both of the components is a concrete object. Concrete objects can, of course, be introduced into a poem non-metaphorically, as "candles" in the following lines from Yeats' "Among School Children":

> Both nuns and mothers worship images,
> But those the candles light are not as those
> That animate a mother's reveries . . .

Donne's use of candles ("Tapers") in "The Canonization" is quite different:

> Call us what you will, wee are made such by love;
> Call her one, mee another flye,
> We' are Tapers too, and at our owne cost die.

In the first passage, since candles are mentioned primarily as a utilitarian source of light, very little attention is centered on them. In the second, intense interest is concentrated on them; for they are at once and paradoxically representative of the idea that death is life and life is death, and recall the Phoenix riddle which is the central concept of the poem.

Extension of cognition, with its corollary of greater precision of statement; shock; compression; and concreteness—all these general functions of metaphor are exemplified in Pope's works, as in the works of any poet who has relied considerably on metaphor. In the analysis of Pope's individual use of metaphor, the interest lies in perceiving the skill with which he adapted this element of poetry to his broad poetic ends; or, in the language of neoclassical criticism, it lies in perceiving the *decorum* of his use of metaphor in a particular poem.

Pope's pastoral metaphors have long been adversely criticized as being eighteenth-century stock metaphors. That they have an important relationship to a common poetic stock or treasure-house of metaphors is true. That they are stock metaphors in the sense of inviting a stock response on a low level of complication is far from true. Even in 1709 Pope was not a simple or uncomplicated poet. Much of the unfavorable criticism of his pastoral metaphors springs from a misunderstanding of the genre and, consequently, of the part metaphor should and does play in it. But some of the unfavorable criticism arises from overfacile and unhistorical reading—that is, from failure to distinguish between the abuse of this type of metaphor by Pope's imitators and the subtlety and propriety of Pope's use of them.

Moreover, in mid-twentieth century our *Zeitgeist* simply is not favorable to pastoral. The average citizen is persuaded that he *ought* to read newspapers and news magazines, listen to news broadcasts and telecasts, do his share of worrying over national and international events; he is convinced, in short, that it is his duty to expose himself to what Richard Weaver in his *Ideas Have Consequences* calls "The Great Stereopticon." To a citizen so persuaded the tenants of the pastoral landscape are of much less concern than the possibility of inhabitants on Mars.

But *is* pastoral what it is now commonly thought to be? Is it mere escape poetry, tranquil and agreeable but without significant relationship to the realities of life? Pastoral does create a world apart; but when the acknowledged masterpieces in the genre (not the spate of shallow imitations) are examined, it becomes plain that that world is not so much escapist and unreal as a selection from the real for a particular purpose.

It might be said that pastoral verse, like the Christian soul, dies that it may live. Pastoral surrenders the limited, partial, and semi-true world of immediate utility in order to see and present the world as a contemplative whole. The pastoral convention is one of the ways a poet has of gaining philosophic and aesthetic distance. In pastoral this necessary detachment, it must always be borne in mind, is achieved in a highly traditional, highly formalized, and restricted way.

Pope's, like all pastorals, take the reader out of doors, away from towns and into the country, close to rivers, mountains, woods, fields, caves, flowers, birds, and sheep—close to external nature. But nature in a pastoral does not behave as it is ordinarily conceived to do in a common-sense, everyday, utilitarian world. Nature in pastoral personally and intimately concerns itself with mankind. It serves not only as a mirror and replica of the world of man; it sympathetically and sometimes passionately participates, for or against, in human affairs. In pastoral the utilitarian partition between microcosm and macrocosm is knocked down, and the actual symbiotic relationship between human and non-human nature is revealed.

Statements of various kinds and degrees of sympathy between man and nature are not, of course, confined to pastoral poets. But while they may be incidental in a drama like *King Lear*, they are the constant and central element in pastoral. And while they may be directly, overtly, and spontaneously made in a poem like *Tintern Abbey*, or obliquely and with conscious artifice in such a poem as Gerard Manley Hopkins' *Spring and Fall: To a Young Child*, in a pastoral they are habitually made in a still different way.

This is not the way of individual discovery at all. It is the way of a very rigid and impersonal convention. In unsuccessful pastorals, trees withering from grief, floods swelling from passion, echoes mourning, and breezes caressing seem both incredible and boring; and this is true of the majority of pastorals by bulk. It is not true of the good ones. It is not true of Pope's.

Viewed for a moment from the narrower technical angle rather than from the broader aspect of meaning, the poet's problem in pastoral is to get life and interest into something ordinarily regarded as static—landscape. The principal means by which this is accomplished in Pope's four seasonal pastorals, and to some extent in *Windsor Forest* as well, is by the use of animating metaphor, that is, personification.

Quantitatively, there are fewer metaphors in *Spring* than in the other three "seasons." Presumably this is because in *Spring*, non-metaphorical statements of the type "Now hawthorns blossom" can be substituted for the animating function of personification. There is motion—indeed, an astonishing amount of twinkling, dancing life has been introduced into this little tableau—but it is motion in stance.

Mention is made of the "various seasons of the rolling year," of night changing to day, of flowers opening and closing, of the nightingale beginning and the thrush ceasing his song, etc. But all such motion takes place within a fixed framework of natural order. The general principle governing the poem is that there shall be no motion of *débordement* either in the human or the natural world, and that all agitating discords shall be eliminated. To this end, as has been previously noted, irony, though present, is not of the bitter and upsetting kind. And the paradoxes are of the tranquilizing sort inherent in the orderly working of the pleasant side of nature. Only mild and decorous antitheses are permitted; and it is parallelisms which are stressed.

The non-metaphorical motion is enclosed within a fixed and tranquil framework of natural event. The metaphorical motion is to a large extent determined by parallelism, the most important metaphorical parallelism being that between human action and nature. In *Spring* Delia and Sylvia, for example, are said by their smiles or frowns to control the metaphorical equivalent of these in external nature:

STREPHON

All nature mourns, the Skies relent in showers,
Hushed are the birds, and closed the drooping flowers;
If Delia smile, the flowers begin to spring,
The skies to brighten, and the birds to sing.

DAPHNIS

All nature laughs, the groves are fresh and fair,
The Sun's mild lustre warms the vital air;
If Sylvia smiles, new glories gild the shore,
And vanquished nature seems to charm no more.

(69–76)

Most of the personifications in the poem are made unobtrusively, sometimes so ambiguously it is possible to debate their existence. The Thames, for example, is mildly personified by being addressed in this manner: "Fair Thames, flow gently from thy sacred spring." And in the line, "Let vernal airs through trembling osiers play," the word "play" can be so understood as to make the airs volitional and capable of enjoying play. "Trembling" functions similarly for "osiers." These gentle semipersonifications are exactly suited to the soft, subdued tone maintained throughout the poem.

Another functional characteristic of this pastoral metaphor is the absence of complication in the relations between the two terms of the metaphor. Instead of the rich, multiple congruences found, for example, in the satires, these pastoral metaphors typically have only one or two points of contact.

This is true of the comparison, in *Spring*, of Sir William Trumbull to a nightingale and of the poet himself to a thrush:

> So when the Nightingale to rest removes,
> The Thrush may chant to the forsaken groves.
>
> (13–14)

The only connections between Trumbull and the nightingale are that the nightingale is a better singer than the thrush and, in poetic tradition, is esteemed a nobler bird. Compared with what Keats does with the nightingale as a symbol in his "Ode" or with the intense and complex use Bridges makes of these birds in his *Nightingales*, Pope's metaphoric treatment of the nightingale here is undeniably thin.

Sheep are described metaphorically in line 20 as "Fresh as the morn, and as the season fair." Again, the sheep are compared to the morning and to the season of spring in one point only: "fresh" in the case of the morning and "fair" in the case of the season. The sheep are neither stated nor implied to resemble morn and spring in any other respect. Nor is the thin relationship between the terms of this metaphor fattened by the fact that the sole point of congruence inheres in such vague, general adjectives as "fresh" and "fair."

But a thin metaphor is just what is wanted here. In such pastorals as Pope's, emotional intensity and metaphysical complexity would counter the effect desired. Abstention from excessive complication is a requirement for the decorum of metaphor in pastoral of the pure or classical Virgilian type.

It may be objected that in *Summer* and *Autumn* there is much passionate metaphor. And all the pastorals contain hyperbolical metaphor.

As far as passionate metaphors are concerned, the pastoral tradition has always included the element of contrast. Despairing shepherds and shepherdesses plunge over cliffs or into rivers. Hideous, warring satyrs irrupt into a peaceful scene, frighten the fluting and garland-weaving tenants away, and proceed to spoil the landscape. They dislodge rocks and uproot trees to hurl at each other. They muddy the fountains and foul the streams with bloody, dismembered corpses.

Occasional exceptions from the rule are needed for the sake of contrast on the rhetorical level and for the sake of truth on the metaphysical level. It would be a falsification to depict all shepherdesses as kittenishly playful and tender like Delia and Sylvia. Aegon in *Autumn* has become enamored of one who makes him cry out

> I know thee, Love! on foreign Mountains bred,
> Wolves gave thee suck, and savage Tigers fed.
> Thou wert from Aetna's burning entrails torn,
> Got by fierce whirlwinds, and in thunder born!
>
> (89–92)

This outburst is the more emphatic for being contrasted with the gentle plaints of Hylas which precede. Though the terms of Aegon's metaphor suggest savagery and violence, the relationship between the terms (Love on the one hand; "Wolves," "Tigers," "Aetna," "whirlwinds," and "thunder" on the other) remains simple and uncomplicated. Nothing like the many and subtle congruences between Donne's two lovers and the tapers is involved.

The hyperbolical metaphors which have received most attention are in the main those depicting the participation of external nature in human sorrows and joys. The following passage from *Autumn*, where all nature is said to mourn Delia's delay in coming to Hylas, is typical:

> For her, the feathered quires neglect their song;
> For her, the limes their pleasing shade deny;
> For her, the lilies hang their heads and die.

Ye flowers that droop, forsaken by the spring,
Ye birds that, left by summer, cease to sing,
Ye trees that fade when autumn-heats remove,
Say, is not absence death to those who love?

(24-30)

Here the hyperbole involves direct personification. Sometimes classical mythology intervenes, as in this couplet from *Winter*:

Ye weeping Loves, the stream with myrtles hide,
And break your bows, as when Adonis died.

(23-24)

And sometimes it seems to be extremely unnatural nature, as in this passage, also from *Winter*:

For her the flocks refuse their verdant food.

. . . .

In hollow Caves sweet Echo silent lies,
Silent, or only to her name replies;

. . . .

The silver flood, so lately calm, appears
Swelled with new passion, and o'erflows with tears;
The winds and trees and floods her death deplore.

(37, 41-42, 65-67)

Pastoral hyperbole is not essentially an inflated and hollow convention. From the common-sense standpoint, these hyperboles are indeed absurd. Sheep do not refuse to eat grass, nor the laws of sound with respect to echo suspend themselves because any woman dies. Yet these seeming extravagances, ridiculous as they appear on one plane, are deadly serious, and exactly and precisely true on another—as true as the fact that in Hopkins' *Spring and Fall* Margaret, mourning over the unleaving of Goldengrove, is mourning her own mortal transience.

Serious poets of all ages and nations have perceived this analogy between human processes and the processes of external nature. Though a particular flower may not wither *because* a particular young girl pines away and dies, still, one is a symbol or prognosis of another. Both are subject to the same general law.

Shakespeare uses this analogy for Perdita's pretty speech in *The Winter's Tale*:

> . . . pale prime-roses,
> That die unmarried, ere they can behold
> Bright Phoebus in his strength, a malady
> Most incident to maids . . . (IV, iv, 122–125)

In this connection, a group of personifications in *Winter* is interesting. The objects personified act, not in consonance with their own natures, as when a breeze sighs or a flood weeps, but against nature. In the line, "Her fate is whispered by the gentle breeze," the whispering which personifies the breeze is an action running parallel to the natural facts about breezes. But when Pope, speaking of the effect of Daphne's death on the natural landscape, says, "Inscribe a verse on this relenting stone"; or "The balmy Zephyrs, silent since her death"; or "In hollow caves sweet Echo silent lies," stone, zephyrs, and echo are personified only that they may be shown behaving contrary to their natures. The result of this is a heightening of the impression that external nature is sympathizing with human sorrow over Daphne's death. A "relenting stone" is a paradox among stones, a stone behaving like the antithesis of stone. Such an antithesis, however, does not disturb the carefully wrought harmonious tone of this poem. The antithesis in stony conduct only places the stone in a reversed but still parallel relationship with a central concept of pastoral poetry: the analogy and symbiosis between the Great World and the little world within man's self.

Metaphor has a different task to perform in Pope's argumentative and satiric poems. (The term "argumentative and satiric" is more inclusive than distinctive, since Pope's prime argumentative weapon is satire.) Metaphor in these poems must *give the effect of* logical proof. Logicians may debate whether argument by analogy should convince; poets simply accept the fact that it does. The reader of poetry is much less apt to be convinced when an abstraction is used to prove an abstraction than when an abstraction is shown to have parallels in one (or preferably many) concrete realms.

This type of metaphorical proof is, after all, allied to a fundamental poetic method: that of the epiphany or "sudden revelation of the wonder of it." When a poet shows that an abstractly stated relationship is paralleled by an always existing but hitherto unnoticed or unemphasized relationship between two things in a concrete realm, the reader is disposed to accept the validity of the abstraction. He accepts it as an additional confirmation of what poets, as well as most theologians, have always asserted: Everything in the universe is articulated in a cunning plan, and everything in the universe subsumes everything else. Tennyson's "Flower in the crannied wall," for example, is a simple and obvious statement of this.

Pope's adaptation of this logical function of metaphor—an aspect of its general cognitive function— shows that he was able to enhance its effect by various devices likely to make it especially telling with an eighteenth-century audience and, indeed, with readers of any century.

The first of these was terseness. In the argumentative and satiric poems lengthy, involved, and elaborate metaphors are exceptional. Pope is utilizing the psychological principle that people who "protest, protest, protest" are more liable to be questioned than those who state what they have to say concisely and with assurance. This terseness contributes also to the everyday, down-to-earth conversational tone desired in the satiric and didactic poems. And this tone in itself helps carry conviction. It was particularly convincing to the Augustan reader, since it was the opposite of the nebulous, rhapsodic approach he distrusted.

In this connection it is essential to distinguish between the presence in a poem of many metaphors referring to the same realm and the elaboration of various aspects of a single metaphor. For example, both the *Essay on Criticism* and the *Dunciad* contain important light-darkness metaphors. But the *Essay* is not pervaded by the light-darkness metaphor, as the *Dunciad* is.

A typical use of the equation Pope wishes to establish in the *Essay on Criticism* between light and critical acuteness or literary skill is found in these lines:

> But true expression, like th' unchanging Sun,
> Clears and improves whate'er it shines upon,
> It gilds all objects, but it alters none.
>
> (II, 315-317)

The reference is brief and to the point. After it, Pope shifts to another totally different concrete realm (clothing) for his metaphors. He does not, after the lines just quoted, expand and ramify the sun metaphor, though some eighty lines onward he uses *another* sun metaphor.

This clearly contrasts with the pervasive identification of Belinda with the sun in *The Rape of the Lock*. There, once the analogy has been drawn, it does not cease to operate. It cannot be picked up and then put down again. Belinda's sunlike qualities are an essential part of the concept of Belinda: Wherever she moves, they accompany her like a halo—to the very end of the poem.

The sun metaphor in the *Essay on Criticism* may also be contrasted with the paradoxical use of the light-darkness metaphor (discussed in detail below) which informs all four books of the *Dunciad*. There the basic motif of the poem—the reversal of natural order, with Dulness exalted and Intelligence put down—is emphasized by the double equation of Dulness to light (ironically) and to darkness, and of Intelligence to darkness (ironically) and to light.

This type of distinction also exists between Pope's use of clothing metaphors in the *Essay on Criticism* and Shakespeare's use of them in *Macbeth*. The purpose of the metaphor in *Macbeth*, as Cleanth Brooks has pointed out, is to emphasize that Macbeth's usurped dignities fit him ill, like a suit of clothes too big for him. The metaphor thus not only ties in with the usurpation theme, but does so in a pervasive way. Once that train of thought has been started by the metaphor, its influence is continuous. Like the sun metaphor in *The Rape of the Lock*, it has a silent effect on whatever else is being said, even when it is not itself specifically referred to.

It is true that Pope's clothing metaphors in the *Essay on Criti-

96

cism have a connection with the central theme. Literary decorum is an aspect of fundamental decorum-at-all-levels, of which clothes-decorum is a facet. And it is true that the clothing metaphors are tied in with the metaphors conveying "Light equals critical insight." Light, like proper dress, is conceived as a heightener or improver, but not as a distorter. In some cases light is thought of almost as a kind of clothing which clarifies the nature and quality of the critical object as clothes tend to do in a hierarchical society.

Nevertheless, Pope's dress metaphors do not pervade the argument of the *Essay on Criticism* to the same degree that his sun metaphor pervades the action of *The Rape of the Lock*. In conformity with the more discursive method of the *Essay*, Pope turns the dress metaphor on and off as one might an electric light. He uses a dress metaphor to prove a particular point. Then he drops it, using another metaphor from a different area—and most often, not as in the case of the light metaphor, an area without strong thematic relation—to reinforce the next argument. Though a little further on he may resort to another dress metaphor, the reader has no feeling of inescapable continuity from one to the other. Moreover, these metaphors relating to dress usually stress different aspects of it each time rather than one *idée fixe*, as does *Macbeth*.

In addition to this tendency away from pervasiveness, metaphors in the satiric and argumentative poems are often given the appearance of reasoned, judicious statements. Frequently they take the form, "As this to this, so that to that." This employment of the locutions of formal logic puts a sort of legitimate cheat upon the reader's practical daylight attitude. Considering himself safe in the academic grove, he can forget the bristling side arms he has held in readiness against any invasion of his common-sense world by transcendental concepts. The metaphors, thus camouflaged, are then free to work in their own powerful way—a way sanctioned by Plato if not by Aristotle.

This is the effect, for example, of the metaphors in the following passage from the *Essay on Man*:

Ask of thy mother earth, why oaks are made

97

Taller or stronger than the weeds they shade?
Or ask of yonder argent fields above,
Why JOVE's Satellites are less than JOVE?   (I, 39–42)

As oaks are in size, strength, and beneficent relationship to weeds,
so is the universe to man. And as satellites are in derivation from
and dependency on their planet, so is man to the universe (i.e.,
the planet Jupiter, Jove, or God). The persuasive validity of these
metaphors does not derive from any actual, immediate, and logically demonstrable connection of satellites and oak trees with
human religious attitudes. It arises from acceptance of the fact
that oaks are larger than weeds, and planets than their satellites,
plus an illogical assumption that hence man cannot be otherwise
than little and weak in comparison with the universe.

Underlying this acceptance may be a latent disposition to regard as true the precept of "thrice-great Hermes": "Everything
above is like everything below, and everything below is like
everything above." Poets generally claim that every relationship
in the universe subsumes every other relationship.

The same quasi-logical device is found in the following passages.
From the *Essay on Criticism*:

But as the slightest sketch, if justly traced,
Is by ill-colouring but the more disgraced,
So by false learning is good sense defaced.
                              (I, 23–25)

From Moral Essay II:

Or Sappho at her toilet's greasy task,
With Sappho fragrant at an evening Mask:
So morning Insects that in muck begun,
Shine, buzz, and fly-blow in the setting-sun.
                              (25–28)

And from the *Epistle to Dr. Arbuthnot*:

Yet let me slap this Bug with gilded wings,
This painted Child of Dirt that stinks and stings;
Whose Buzz the Witty and the Fair annoys,
Yet Wit ne'er tastes, and Beauty ne'er enjoys,
So well-bred Spaniels civilly delight

In mumbling of the Game they dare not bite.
Eternal Smiles his Emptiness betray,
As shallow streams run dimpling all the way.   (309–316)

As compared with the *Pastorals*, *Windsor Forest*, the *Messiah*, *Eloisa to Abelard*, *Elegy to the Memory of an Unfortunate Lady*, *The Rape of the Lock*, and the Greek translations, the argumentative and satiric poems employ metaphors from a much greater diversity of realms. Almost nothing is barred. Things in themselves ugly and ignoble are, in fact, rather more apt to be used for comparisons than things in themselves beautiful and admirable.

In the metaphors quoted above Sappho is compared to a muckborn, fly-blowing insect (her career summarized for the worse in the "shining" of her youth, the literary "buzzing" of her maturity, and the promiscuity Pope attributed to Lady Mary in her riper days). Sporus is likened to a gilded but noisome bug and to a spaniel slobbering over game. The reasons for these comparisons are not far to seek. On the one hand, there is the destructive immediate effect, felt instinctively before being analyzed. On the other, after analysis, the delayed intellectual recognition of the fact that moral and mental triviality—or dirtiness, or clumsiness, or depravity—has been presented in physical terms increases the force of the presentation. The Augustan was inclined, moreover, like the catholic reader in any age, to distrust exclusion, except briefly and for a special purpose.

Weeping floods and trees protectively crowding into a shade would have been as much out of place in the satires as allusions to defecation and green vomit in the *Pastorals*. By recruiting his satiric metaphors from many different realms Pope demonstrated that he was not attempting to hide anything—especially not the seamy side of things. Moreover, he showed that what he asserted to be true was true not once but many times and on many varying levels.

In *Eloisa to Abelard* a chief concern of Pope's is to submerge the mechanics of metaphor so as not to interfere with the flow of passion. The primary aim of the poem is to present Eloisa's internal conflict in the strongest possible terms. Metaphor must conduce to that end, not interfere with it. Consequently, the reader will look in vain for the "As this to this, so that to that" type of metaphor found predominantly in the *Essay on Man*, the *Essay on Criticism*, and the satiric poems. A metaphor introduced by this locution suggests a measured reasoning process, totally foreign to the purpose of the metaphorical texture of *Eloisa to Abelard*.

Neither will the reader find in *Eloisa to Abelard* any of the lengthy, involved, and highly elaborated metaphors appropriate to calmer states, such as the comparison of Belinda's toilet to a religious rite. Even similes, since they involve an *as* or a *like* that draws attention from the emotion to the fact that a comparison is being made, are rare.

The metaphors in *Eloisa to Abelard* have, in fact, been made as syntactically inconspicuous as possible. They are characterized by ellipsis, achieved in various ways. Personification, obtained with a single adjective or, more often, with a verb, is frequently used to attain verbal economy in metaphor. For example, "relentless" in "Relentless walls! whose darksom round contains . . ." and the combination of an imperative verb and the nominative of address in

> Hide it, my heart, within that close disguise,
> Where, mix'd with God's, his lov'd Idea lies.
> (11–12)

Or with the single verb "usher'd" in

> Oh name for ever sad! for ever dear!
> Still breath'd in sighs, still usher'd with a tear.
> (31–32)

The basic purpose of personification here is not greatly different from its purpose in the *Pastorals*. Eloisa delivers herself of a monologue three hundred and sixty-six lines long. Her landscape is partly exterior (the convent and its environs) and partly interior (her own thoughts and feelings). In the *Pastorals* the dramatic tension and significance of the central human action was increased by showing the landscape (and by implication, the universe) participating. So the participation, at least in Eloisa's eyes, of everything surrounding her in her impassioned struggle magnifies and intensifies the central action of the poem. Eloisa is not alone upon her stage. Hundreds of forces, some for and some against, some concrete and some impalpable, are—through personification—there with her.

Love and chastity, for example, are personified and shown acting in opposition to each other in these lines:

> Ev'n here, where frozen chastity retires,
> Love finds an altar for forbidden fires.
>
> (182–183)

Abelard is, of course, the god worshiped on this altar and with these forbidden sacrificial fires. A great deal of significant metaphorical comparison is packed into these two lines and in such a way that Eloisa's central conflict, the struggle between warm pagan love and chill Christian asceticism, is again presented, in miniature.

Antithesis has already been mentioned as a dominating force in this poem. The content of the metaphor reflects this. The antithesis between Christianity and paganism, between passion and asceticism, is so familiar to an English audience that it does not require farfetched and involute metaphorical insistence. It is moreover cosmologically and conventionally associated with a heat-light-life metaphorical group on the one hand and a cold-darkness-death group on the other. This is an important factor, permitting and favoring the ellipsis demanded by the urgency of the dramatic circumstances. It is well illustrated in the following passage:

> Come Abelard! for what hast thou to dread?
> The torch of Venus burns not for the dead;
> Nature stands check'd; Religion disapproves;
> Ev'n thou art cold—yet Eloisa loves.
> Ah hopeless, lasting flames! like those that burn
> To light the dead, and warm th' unfruitful urn.
>
> (257–262)

Symbolic metaphor in Pope is by no means confined to *The*

Rape of the Lock and the *Dunciad*, though it is especially characteristic of them. In *Eloisa to Abelard* the freezing chastity and burning love metaphors just discussed are symbolic metaphors. The two terms of these metaphors exhibit the approach toward fusion with each other, combined with an approach toward fusion with the central concept of the poem, which is the distinctive mark of symbolic metaphor.

The symbolic value of a metaphor is a question of degree. In the *Essay on Criticism*, for instance, there is a large group of metaphors in which unskillful writing and criticism are equated with various sorts of unsatisfactory sex relationships:

> Each burns alike, who can or cannot write,
> Or with a Rival's or an Eunuch's spite.   (I, 30–31)

> But Dulness with Obscenity must prove
> As shameful sure as Impotence in love.
>   (II, 532–533)

Though these metaphors tend toward symbolic value, they never achieve the degree of continuous rapport which exists between Belinda and the sun or between Belinda's chastity and the frail China vessel.

The whole system of the Sylphs is a symbolic metaphor. The analogy drawn between their airy, shifting qualities and feminine honor is never lost sight of. It is consistently maintained and developed from the beginning of the poem to the end. The metaphoric texture of *The Rape* as a whole is, in fact, a palimpsest of symbolic metaphors, large and small, interlocking and superimposed.

Within the "sylph-feminine honor" metaphor, for instance, there is the concept of the sylphs as a military organization. This military figure is developed in detail. Military commands are given; rank is insisted on; the general exhorts his troops before sending them into action. A special patrol, moreover, is detailed to guard that special enemy objective, Belinda's petticoat. Sylphian articles of war, with the military punishments for violating them, are promulgated.

This military concept does not stand by itself, however, as a mere ingenious piece of elaboration. It is tied in with, and reinforced by, the military metaphor in the card game (itself a completely worked-out system of metaphorical harmony) and with the battle of the belles and the beaux which follows the successful perpetration of the central military stratagem, the clipping of the lock.

By no means to be disregarded is the religious metaphor: the rites of Belinda's toilet, the Baron's altar of twelve gilt French romances, his prayer to Love, the bowing of the side-box from its inmost rows to women adored like angels, the worshiping and sending up of vows to the stellified lock, etc. This metaphor is linked to the "war between the sexes" metaphor. Both sides appeal to deity for aid. Belinda, while arming herself for the fray, addresses the deity revealed in her mirror; the Baron, Love.

The mock-epic convention, which continually draws an analogy between big and heroic and little and ordinary, provides another metaphor, inherent in the genre, a sort of ocean on which all the other metaphors float. This metaphor, never abandoned throughout the course of the poem, conduces to the very high degree of metaphoric integration which prevails in *The Rape of the Lock*. It invades all the major metaphors, and with ironic effect—since in the mock-heroic convention the pointing out of similarities only serves to emphasize differences. For example, in the celebrated lines

> And now, unveil'd, the Toilet stands display'd,
> Each Silver Vase in mystic Order laid.
> First, rob'd in White, the Nymph intent adores
> With Head uncover'd, the Cosmetic Pow'rs.
> A heav'nly Image in the Glass appears,
> To that she bends, to that her Eyes she rears;
> Th' inferior Priestess, at her Altar's side,
> Trembling, begins the sacred Rites of Pride
>
> (I, 121–128)

the whole point of the metaphor derives from the actual disparity between the realms of make-up and religion.

The Rape of the Lock also exemplifies, though not in so salient a degree as the *Dunciad*, Pope's oblique approach to pure beauty in metaphor. Pope's conception of beauty was more catholic than that which prevailed in the nineteenth century. The Augustan habitually saw beauty in urban realms as well as in the greenwood. Pope distrusted any sort of exclusiveness in outlook, any stress upon one aspect of reality to the exclusion of others, any viewing of the part as if it were the whole.

Though beauty is to some extent a matter of context (compare Pope's description of Belinda's toilet with Jonathan Swift's excursion into a lady's boudoir), there is, nevertheless, a set of factors inherent in human life which may be described as a "universal context." In this context certain objects are almost always conceded to be in themselves beautiful; e.g., flowers, stars, moonlight, music, and positive, constructive human emotions.

Pope's verse contains important metaphors which draw upon this stock of aesthetic objects and concepts; but he characteristically introduces such metaphors with qualification. This is illustrated in the passage below in which the Sylphs are threatened with condign punishments if they betray their various charges:

> Whatever Spirit, careless of his Charge,
> His Post neglects, or leaves the Fair at large,
> Shall feel sharp Vengeance soon o'ertake his Sins,
> Be stopt in Vials, or transfixt with Pins;
> Or plung'd in Lakes of bitter Washes lie,
> Or weg'd whole Ages in a Bodkin's Eye:
> Gums and Pomatums shall his Flight restrain,
> While clog'd he beats his silken Wings in vain;
> Or Alom-Stypticks with contracting Power
> Shrink his thin Essence like a rivell'd Flower:
> Or as Ixion fix'd, the Wretch shall feel
> The giddy Motion of the whirling Mill,
> In Fumes of burning Chocolate shall glow,
> And tremble at the Sea that froaths below!
>
> (II, 123–136)

The divine punishments in Greek and Christian mythology to which this passage has reference are terrible and sublime. Nor do they altogether lose that quality here. But the Luciferian lake has become a puddle of spilled face lotion. The chaotic media through which Lucifer with difficulty made his way to Eden have become hairdressing pomades. Ixion's wheel has dwindled into that of a mechanical gadget to grind chocolate beans. The minuscule size of the beings concerned and the frivolity of the boudoir environment alter the Miltonic sublimity into another kind of sublimity, another kind of beauty, a beauty which incites to wonder as surely as the Miltonic kind.

Again, no one would expect to find the Chaucerian "fresh, young, clear" type of beauty in a card table and a pack of cards. But Pope's description of the figures painted on the cards, through the metaphor by which he presents them as military combatants, has qualities reminiscent of the clarity and freshness of detail with which Chaucer describes his Canterbury pilgrims. The scene on the velvet-covered card table might almost be a landscape from the *Book of the Duchesse*:

> Behold, four Kings in Majesty rever'd,
> With hoary Whiskers and a forky Beard;
> And four fair Queens whose hands sustain a Flow'r,
> Th' expressive Emblem of their softer Pow'r;
> Four Knaves in Garbs succinct, a trusty Band,
> Caps on their heads, and Halberds in their hand;
> And particolour'd Troops, a shining Train,
> Draw forth to Combat on the Velvet Plain.   (III, 37–44)

Considered directly, without reference to the card game, the above description might, with some changes of orthography, be fitted into, say, *The Knight's Tale*. Pope's reader, however, cannot for a minute forget that these embattled heroes are a pack of cards. In responding to the aesthetic element in this metaphor, the reader must respond complexly, with an awareness of the double realms being manipulated.

Silver lamps, japanned trays, and ocean waves dashing against the shore line until the white foam looks like smoke are in themselves beautiful. The culinary process of preparing a hot drink has homely rather than aesthetic associations. But in the follow-

ing passage Pope has mixed the two, with no loss of beauty and
an increase in piquancy:

> For lo! the Board with Cups and Spoons is crown'd,
> The Berries crackle, and the Mill turns round.
> On shining Altars of Japan they raise
> The silver Lamp; the fiery Spirits blaze.
> From silver Spouts the grateful Liquors glide,
> While China's Earth receives the smoking Tyde.
>
> (III, 105–110)

The importance in this poem of qualifying the "stock beauty"
element in metaphor is that such qualification symbolically reinforces the concept of values central to *The Rape of the Lock*:
These things are simultaneously trivial and beautiful in the way
that cutting the lock is simultaneously frivolous and portentous.

In fact, in this poem actual divinity is in varying degree postu-
lated of almost everything: of Belinda, the Baron, the Scissors,
the sparkling Cross, the Lap-Dog, the Petticoat, and the Lock,
as well as of Love, Fate, Jove, and the Sylphs and Gnomes with
all pertaining to them. The finite realm of beaux and belles and
the most trifling objects in their surroundings are presented as
larger than mortal, shot through, so to speak, with the Infinite.
This divinity metaphor touches them all. Even Belinda's patch box,
which falls thrice from her hand as a warning, is a thing possessed.
Like the tottering china that shakes without a wind, it functions
on a superhuman as well as a human level. And the Sylphs and
Gnomes, creatures of fantasy though they are, are as real as feminine beauty, frailty, and honor, or as frustration, malice, and mis-
chief in the human heart.

The ground of the reader's assent to this two-edged presentation is in part Pope's use of the classical epic framework. In the
Homeric world everything that exists, whether stationary or kinetic in its mode of being, is sacredly alive. Everything is imbued
with divinity—"they in Zeus and He in them." All the phenomena
of nature, even bread, grass, and the dawn, are holy.

To this Pope adds, especially by his frequent Miltonic echoes,
the world of Christian miracle: the world in which angels may

appear bodily to instruct man and the devil converse in the form
of a toad; a world in which the eating of an apple can entail consequences enormously disproportionate if considered without reference to the special qualities of that apple.

Together, the Homeric and Christian myths help suggest a
spiritual approach to reality and to human affairs, preparing the
way for the divinity metaphor. The solemn theological postulate
that the divine is concerned with man and the things of man because in some way the divine is *in* man is, of course, treated in
terms of puffs, powders, patches, and billets-doux. In an age skit-
tish about a direct approach to the world of usual life as a divine
mystery, this is a telling way to deal with such matters. Main-
taining the predominance of Greco-Roman and Rosicrucian rather
than Christian mythology further aids Pope in achieving an indirect approach.

Divinity is most prominently embodied in the person of Belinda. Intimations of her divinity range from such conventional-
ized, sleeping etymological expressions as the hope that she, like
the goddess Muse, will inspire Pope's lays, to the passage quoted
above describing the sacred rites of her toilet.

Establishment of her divinity falls into three major classifica-
tions: the general deification of the sex to which she belongs; the
special treatment accorded Belinda, such as Sylphic attendance,
together with the superhuman value placed on everything connected with her, such as her "sacred Lock"; and finally, the insistence throughout the poem that she is a kind of sun goddess.

In Canto I we are told that

> Oft when the World imagine Women stray,
> The Sylphs thro' mystick Mazes guide their Way.
>
> (91–92)

In addition to this divine guidance, it is said that when their role
on earth is over women will return to their "first Elements."
Termagants will become Salamanders, "soft yielding Minds"
Nymphs; prudes will turn into Gnomes, and coquettes become
airy Sylphs. During life the sex as a whole has Sylphic assistance "to curl their waving Hairs, Assist their Blushes, and inspire

their Airs" (II, 97–98). The gift of a lady to her knight, specifically Clarissa's offering of the scissors, is received "with rev'rence."
When the Fair pay visits on "solemn" days, "numerous Wax-
lights in bright Order blaze." They are "Angels call'd, and Angel-
like ador'd," and at the theater the side-box bows to them "from
its inmost Rows." When the belles fight the beaux they exhibit
more than mortal powers. Enraged Thalestris "scatters Deaths
around from both her Eyes." Chloe kills Sir Plume with a frown
and then revives him with a smile.

But Belinda outshines all her sex in divine attributes and Olympic importance. She is told that she is the "distinguish'd Care/ Of
thousand bright Inhabitants of Air!" The head Sylph, Ariel himself, comes to warn her of the impending disaster. Her own
"heav'nly Image in the Glass" is the goddess she worships during
the sacred ceremony of her toilet. When the Baron desires a
favor from her, he builds an altar to Love—which is, in a sense,
Belinda herself.

Sylphs who are careless in attending Belinda are, as we have
seen, threatened with hellish punishments, all of them within Belinda's Rhadamanthine power: being "stopt in Vials," "transfixt
with Pins," "plung'd in Lakes of bitter Washes," and shrunk with
alum styptics. When she is angry lightning flashes from her eyes,
and by the use of "Cosmetic Powers" she can make these light-
nings keener.

Not only is her lock sacred, but as the symbol of her chastity
it is called an "inestimable Prize." When it is lost she "burns with
more than mortal Ire." Canto IV opens with a long list of grievances, mostly greater than the snipping of a curl; yet Belinda's
rage at the loss of the lock is said to exceed that of the victims of
all these other grievances. This heightens the significance of her
loss and exhibits her emotions about it as above the average mortal run. Finally, the surest proof the poem gives that the lock is
too exalted a trophy for a mere mortal is its ascension into heaven
and its perpetual glorification there. Future lovers will send up
vows to it and human fates are to be foretold by its celestial motions.

Furthermore, Belinda and the objects associated with her can work miracles. Sailing forth on the Thames,

> On her white Breast a sparkling Cross she wore,
> Which Jews might kiss, and Infidels adore.   (II, 7–8)

The kissing and adoration are in a sense miracles of the Cross, though of the sparkling not the bloody one. And this conversion of Jews and infidels is owing not to the power of Christ but to the power of female beauty. Yet, somewhat like a deity willing to undergo tortures and to sacrifice herself for the good of mankind, Belinda points out that she bound her locks in "Paper-Durance," wreathed her tender head with "tort'ring Irons" and fillets, "And bravely bore the double Loads of Lead." The Baron himself petitions her for a miracle. Rather than die, he begs ". . . ah let me still survive, And burn in Cupid's Flames,—but burn alive" (V, 101–102).

This brings us to the question of Belinda's Olympian pedigree, about which it is possible to conjecture with some accuracy. Repeatedly the poem suggests her kinship with the sun. In Canto I her eyes are said to eclipse the sun. At the opening of Canto II this sun comparison is extended:

> Not with more Glories, in th' Etherial Plain,
> The Sun first rises o'er the purpled Main,
> Than issuing forth, the Rival of his Beams
> Lanch'd on the Bosom of the Silver Thames.
> Fair Nymphs, and well-drest Youths around her shone,
> But ev'ry Eye was fix'd on her alone.
>
> . . . .
>
> Favours to none, to all she Smiles extends,
> Oft she rejects, but never once offends.
> Bright as the Sun, her Eyes the Gazers strike,
> And, like the Sun, they shine on all alike.   (II, 1–14)

Not only is she the center of this youthful solar system boating on the Thames, but she has an effect like sunshine on the world as a whole: "Belinda smil'd, and all the World was gay" (II, 52). Not all her sun functions, however, are benevolent. In Greek myth the daughters of the sun—such as Circe, Medea, and the nymphs who guard the cattle of Helios—are endowed with special terror. Like the sun itself, they possess a strong destructive power.

In Belinda's case, the spellbinding and enchantment activities of a Circe and the thirst for cruel vengeance of a Medea are exerted, properly, only in the hyperbole of courtship. Her "cruelty" is directed, as a belle's must be, toward her beaux. She nourishes her shining locks for the "Destruction of Mankind"; and as the sun destroys with its rays, so Belinda can make fops "die" by glances from her eyes.

However, Pope reminds us, the "fair Suns" of Belinda's eyes are destined to set (V, 145–148). He thus undercuts the myth of Belinda's divinity—specifically her sunship—by references to her actual mortality. The time of the poem is conceived as a single day, its progress marked by frequent references to the progress of the sun in the sky. The implication is that Belinda's course, like the sun's, will ultimately end in darkness.

Pope frequently undercuts the beautiful or heroic structures he builds up, either in the interest of realism or to achieve shock or risibility. Here by the juxtaposition of two seemingly contradictory aspects of Belinda's nature, her divinity and her mortality, he makes this sun myth come to grips with actuality in a reverberating way.

For there is an actual level on which Belinda the woman, with all her frivolities, is divine. As a woman, she is a volitional, morally responsible part of God's universe. The good sense or lack of it which she brings to bear upon the great business of the Hampton Court scene, her selection of a husband, will have its effect upon her own future, that of her children, and ultimately of the human race. She is also the physical vehicle of that future. As such she is sacred in the same way as, but in an intenser degree than, Homer's "holy" grass, bread, and dawn.

It is necessary for Pope to begin by stressing Belinda's divinity. The affront offered her, though slight in appearance, must be felt as a serious and real affront—as, in fact, sacrilege. The snipping of the lock must signify simultaneously not only a trivial youthful folly but also, symbolically, the rape of a woman and the outrage of a goddess.

But if Belinda's mortality were not also stressed, the myth of her sunship would lose much of its acceptability. Western civilization has tended to turn away from the conviction that everything that lives is God-related—we in Christ and He in us. The more enlightened of the Chinese and Indian traditions have never lost sight of this, and our own major poets have had to turn their eyes toward a unifying spiritual center. But the poet of an age of common sense may find it good strategy, as Pope did with Belinda, to qualify goddess-ship by emphasizing finite, human qualities. The scene at Belinda's dressing table where she is both the mortal high priestess and the goddess worshiped in the mirror is an especially felicitous example of this strategy.

The miraculous power exerted by Belinda's eyes and the cross on her bosom has already been indicated. So potent is her beauty —for it is through the actual force of female beauty that her divinity operates—that a single hair from the belle's head can do wonders:

> Love in these Labyrinths his Slaves detains,
> And mighty Hearts are held in slender Chains.
> With hairy Sprindges we the Birds betray,
> Slight Lines of Hair surprize the Finny Prey,
> Fair Tresses Man's Imperial Race ensnare,
> And Beauty draws us with a single Hair.   (II, 23–28)

This is at once miraculous and literally true. Sporting with the tangles of Neaera's hair is well recognized as synecdoche for the actual sexual attraction of the female for the male.

Within the field of this God-given attraction all the trivia connected with Belinda achieve accessory deity. Her powder, her washes, her furbelows, and her blushes are sanctified, receiving the care of heavenly spirits. Her chastity too, under the metaphoric disguises of "some frail China Jar" and the portentous Petticoat, achieves a sacred character. Yet the very frailty and transience of blushes and chastity bring forcibly to mind this goddess's humanity.

The status of Shock as an object belonging to Belinda has particular interest in this connection. Ariel ends his review of dangers threatening the heroine with the climactic suggestion that perhaps Heaven has doomed Shock to fall. In the context of this speech Shock's fall has been made to seem more important than Belinda's forgetting her prayers, losing her heart, or staining her honor. This impression is reinforced by Ariel's decision to assign lesser points of danger to lesser Sylphs. Early in the poem the foppish lovers are compared to lap-dogs—a minor theriomorphic myth which gains in importance when it becomes clear that to belles lap-dogs are in a sense lover-substitutes. Thus the concern of Belinda and her guardian Sylph for Shock is not eccentric but a recognition of the belle's major interest in life, her relations with eligible men.

This is typical of the way values are deliberately confused in the poem. What appears trivial—the exaggerated anxiety over Shock—is actually significant; and conversely. When Belinda says "Let Spades be Trumps! . . . and Trumps they were," she only seems to be going through the routine procedure of a card game. In a sense she is a goddess creating and lighting a world. These two meanings are linked by the fact that Belinda, representing generic woman, is the physical means by which the "little worlds" of mankind are brought into being. Her beauty and the feminine graces, of which this poem makes so much, actually are a light of daily living and one of the ordering forces of the world.

Though the poem focuses primary attention on the· deity of Belinda, her male compeers also come under the cognizance of Olympus. Belinda's status is multiple. She is a belle, an epic champion, and a sun goddess. But the fops' elevation seems at first to go no further than the heroic, and even that is precarious. In the context of Hampton Court it is easier to believe in the ladies' divinity than in the fops' heroism. For the women, in spite of their frivolity, are functioning in an environment proper to them; whereas the men are out of a specific manly context. Their attributed heroism is nowhere exhibited unless in the Baron's surreptitious severing of Belinda's lock, an act which on the goddess level is sacrilege, on the epic level a war trick, and in the polite world a piece of rudeness.

Both in the game of cards and in the crowning battle fought with fans, snuff, and killing frowns these "heroes" are overcome by the ladies. Even Jove decides for the latter:

> Now Jove suspends his golden Scales in Air,
> Weighs the Men's Wits against the Lady's Hair;
> The doubtful Beam long nods from side to side;
> At length the Wits mount up, the Hairs subside.
>
> (V, 70–74)

The myth of the beaux' heroism seems to be a mock myth—one not substantiated in the action of the poem. But it would be mistaken to suppose that this pseudo myth is not functional. On the contrary, the irony of its relation to actuality, compared to that of the Belinda myth, reinforces the theme of false and confused values. In the eyes of belles, these fops *are* godlike heroes. The belles, like certain other deities, are purblind.

Based also on imperfect vision are two twin myths which pervade the poem: that seeming is being, and conversely; and that the little is big, and conversely. Set against these myths of confused vision is the reader's correct view of actuality, the view in which appearances are seen through, where big things are always and everywhere big, and little ones always and everywhere little.

But the relation of these two myths to actuality is not simple. Within the actuality of the fashionable sphere in which Belinda moves, seeming *is* to some extent being and has real effects. If Belinda is to marry reputably she must seem—but not necessarily be—"first in Virtue as in Face." Her virtue may be put on for public consumption as are her clothes and complexion. On the other hand, though the belle may in reality be virtuous, if she is made to seem questionable—as by a fop's displaying a curl of hair snipped from her person—then her actual virtue, as Thalestris points out to her, counts for nothing:

> Methinks already I your Tears survey,
> Already hear the horrid things they say,

Already see you a degraded Toast
And all your Honour in a Whisper lost!
How shall I, then, your helpless Fame defend?
'Twill then be Infamy to seem your Friend!

(IV, 107–112)

As far as the fashionable world is concerned, big things, such as the loss of virtue, may have no important consequences; whereas little things, the snipping of a curl, may be disastrous. These twin ideological myths have a two-way connection with actuality: the actuality of the moral absolute and the actuality of the world of Sir Plume and Thalestris.

This conflict of actualities is reflected in the Rosicrucian machinery. Among other things, the Sylphs represent the fashionable actuality, and the Gnomes with the Cave of Spleen the vengeance absolute actuality always takes when flouted. It is this contrast of actualities which gives the poem its deepest significance.

The effectiveness with which the contrast functions derives not so much from the abstract truth underlying it as from the extent to which Sylphs and Gnomes are liberated from fairyland and made denizens simultaneously of London and the New Jerusalem. Similarly, their human charges are inhabitants of fashionable London, relatives of Zeus, and pilgrims to eternity. It is this coming together of fictional and real, their interaction, and their partial fusion that helps give *The Rape of the Lock* its exceptional degree of integrated ambivalence.

A prime factor in achieving this richness without sacrificing unity is the care Pope takes to anchor each of the poem's nonce myths in a variety of established mythologies. He borrows impartially from Greeks, Romans, Christians, Hebrews, and Rosicrucians, not to mention public or natural myth and such special areas as Shakespeare's world of diminutive fairies. Nor is it merely a question of mythological systems. The Cave of Spleen, for instance, has a rich overlay both of general underworld concepts and of visits to underworlds in specific poems. Yet all these diverse borrowings are subjugated to the particular purpose of

Umbriel's visit to this particular Hades. It is the *curiosa felicitas* of Pope's design that the whirlwind of metaphoric activity going on in the poem is so tempered by its presentation that on the surface it makes little more noise than a beau's whisper in the ear of a belle. Pope's own metaphoric method here is, in effect, this:

> When Florio speaks, what Virgin could withstand,
> If gentle Damon did not squeeze her Hand?   (I, 97–98)

The *Dunciad* does not exhibit in the same degree that continual close integration of individual metaphors with the central theme characteristic of *The Rape of the Lock*. This is partly because the *Dunciad* is a longer poem and partly because it has a much looser construction. The *Dunciad* does, however, show symbolic fusion of metaphor with theme to an eminent degree. In addition, it has a wealth of richly implicated elliptical metaphors of the type, already mentioned, in *Macbeth*. Throughout the poem there is a tendency for metaphors, their content drawn from many diverse realms, to come thick and fast, so that the effect is one of great richness and complexity. The metaphor of *The Rape of the Lock* is more immediately perspicuous as a system. That of the *Dunciad* is more many-faceted and moves in a less exclusive world.

Book II opens with an extended metaphor:

> High on a gorgeous seat, that far out-shone
> Henley's gilt tub, or Fleckno's Irish throne,
> Or that where on her Curls the Public pours,
> All-bounteous, fragrant Grains and Golden show'rs,
> Great Cibber sate: The proud Parnassian sneer,
> The conscious simper, and the jealous leer,
> Mix on his look: All eyes direct their rays
> On him, and crowds turn Coxcombs as they gaze.
> His Peers shine round him with reflected grace,
> New edge their dulness, and new bronze their face.
> So from the Sun's broad beam, in shallow urns
> Heav'ns twinkling Sparks draw light, and point their horns.
> Not with more glee, by hands Pontific crown'd,
> With scarlet hats wide-waving circled round,
> Rome in her Capitol saw Querno sit,
> Thron'd on sev'n hills, the Antichrist of wit.   (II, 1–16)

Mock-heroic ambiguity is used here, as throughout the *Dunciad*, for packing a thesaurus of meanings into a small, metrically defined space. The metaphoric system of this passage is, in fact—and this is the chief characteristic of symbolic metaphor—a "Dunciad" in little.

One of the main comparisons is sidereal; the monarch is a sun and his assistants planets. Though this metaphor is not explicit and unmistakable until the ninth line, it has been prepared for, both directly and indirectly, from the first line. The sun metaphor, though this is not its most important function, serves to increase magnificence and gorgeousness in the passage. Hence it is linked in purpose to, and prepared for by, all the words suggesting glitter and refulgence: "out-shone," "gilt," "Golden," "rays," "shine," "bronze," "Sun's broad beam," "twinkling Sparks," and "light." In an indirect way, all this emphasis on light and shining serves to unify the passage. More directly, these references to the Cibberian sun on his throne, surpassing Henley and Fleckno on theirs, increase the satirical point of the sun metaphor when it is stated explicitly.

The relationship between Cibber and the sun is rich and complex. Shining (ironically understood of Cibber) is not their only point of congruence. The physical sun is an elevated and conspicuous object in the heavens. Cibber too, alas, is an exalted and conspicuous object sitting "High on a gorgeous seat." The physical sun has a transforming or modifying effect on materials on which it shines—for example, on butter or seeds in the earth. So it is with those mortals who direct their attention to Sun Cibber, for "crowds turn Coxcombs as they gaze." Moreover, just as the sun imparts light to the planets in its system and changes the color of men's skins, so too Cibber's

> . . . Peers shine round him with reflected grace,
> New edge their dulness, and new bronze their face.
>
> (II, 9–10)

The paradox implicit in the sun-dulness metaphor is here reinforced by statement in a new metaphor—that of sharpening some swordlike instrument to "new edge" its dulness.

The planetary relationship of the less dull to Cibber is elaborated by the following lines:

So from the Sun's broad beam, in shallow urns
Heav'ns twinkling Sparks draw light, and point their horns.

(II, 11–12)

"Broad" is ambiguously used. The existence of such phrases as "broad nonsense" and the association of broadness with stupidity at other points in this poem increase the force of the identification between Cibber and the sun. They make possible that ironic functioning of the antithesis between "broad" and "shallow" which not only underlines the planetary relationship but permits an additional meaningful ambiguity in "shallow." Cibber's planets are indeed dull, but even their capacity for dulness is shallow, compared with his.

In the second line quoted above "Sparks" is also ambiguous, permitting the additional metaphor of the dull as fops—Heaven's *sparks*. In the second half of the line additional ironic ambiguities are built up in the sun-planet relationship. "Point their horns" has, of course, a plain astronomical meaning. But since Milton is being parodied in this passage, with Cibber as Lucifer and the inferior dull as lesser devils, the fact that they point their horns also means that by gazing on Cibber they wax more skillful in crimes perpetrated against good sense.

The identification of Cibber with the Christian Devil is significant in another way. One of the cardinal points of congruence between Dulness and Lucifer is that Dulness makes itself more conspicuous and obnoxious through pride, the Satanic sin. Querno would not have become the butt of cardinals and the ecclesiastical Pope if he had remained in his native village. Henley's pulpit would not have attracted so much scorn if he had left it, like the other dissenting "tubs," plain, instead of garnishing it with velvet and with gold. Satan might have remained in heaven if pride had not seduced him to his fall. So Dulness, if it had not aspired to shine, would not have been betrayed to its enemies, discerning critics.

The richness and complexity of this passage; the use of ambiguity and paradox to convey ironical meanings in metaphor; the constant interlocking and interplay of the metaphors; and the tendency of them all to converge toward the central theme or to stand for it in little—these are the characteristics of *Dunciad* metaphor as a whole.

The concern of this passage with light symbolism is typical of the poem throughout. Inversion of the natural light symbolism has already been mentioned. This inversion for ironic purposes (Dulness as light and Good Sense as darkness) holds throughout the first three books.

In the fourth Book the natural symbolic equation is restored. Pope's eighteenth-century readers would have been aware that Longinus had cited God's command and its immediate performance in Genesis—"Let there be light, and there was light"—as an instance of the sublime. In a straight epic Pope could not have reversed this quotation. But to reverse it in mock epic was one of the most powerful things a writer in the West European Christian tradition could have done. Thus Dulness, of whom it is said, "Light dies before thy uncreating word" (IV, 654), becomes the reverse of God.

The concern of this passage depicting sunlike Cibber on his throne, and of the poem as a whole, with religion is by no means casual. As different as the approach here must be, in conformity with the mock-epic tradition, the stress the *Dunciad* places upon "correctness" in religious thinking is fully as serious as in the *Essay on Man*.

The reversal of the usual symbolism based on natural light has been used powerfully in this connection. And, parodying Milton, Pope has made enthroned Dulness represent Lucifer and his court. Nor is the reference to Henley's gilt tub without special significance. The enlightened Augustan disapproved of dissenters who, departing from century-long, tried traditions approved by the intelligence of generation after generation, presumptuously followed the will-o'-the-wisp of their own upstart convictions. Dissenters were, from the standpoint of the established church, somewhat in the relationship of Satan to Heaven. The Dissenters' rebellious motives, like Satan's, were felt to stem from pride in their own faculties.

In Henley's case, what was perhaps the Dissenters' strongest point—a stripping away of ritualistic trappings in order to come to grips more nakedly and essentially with spiritual truth—was, through Henley's dulness, nullified. Henley longed for Dissent; but he longed equally for the flesh-pots. Hence his bare "tub" was swathed in velvet and adorned with gold. Henley could not even be "intelligently dull."

The castigation of Henley as the representative of dulness in religion is carried on, in conjunction with the poem's general inversion metaphor, in Book III. Henley, having placed his "tub"

> . . . where each Science lifts its modern type,
> Hist'ry her Pot, Divinity his Pipe,
> While proud Philosophy repines to show,
> Dishonest sight! his breeches rent below,
>
> (III, 195–198)

is arraigned:

> Oh worthy thou of Aegypt's wise abodes,
> A decent priest, where monkeys were the gods!
> But fate with butchers plac'd thy priestly stall,
> Meek modern faith to murder, hack, and mawl;
> And bade thee live, to crown Britannia's praise,
> In Toland's, Tindal's, and in Woolston's days.
>
> (III, 207–212)

Each ostensible compliment is a calumny. The symbolism of the mock meaning is fighting against the symbolism of the real meaning throughout this passage as throughout the poem. It is no praise for a preacher to have his pulpit bolstered by debased history, smoke-dream divinity, and tatterdemalion philosophy. Nor should he conduct himself in the pulpit as if he were a performing monkey. Nor should he strive to propagate by violent and butcherly means a religion in which the meek are called blessed. Certainly it is not to Henley's credit to be linked with Toland, Tindal, and Woolston, who were, from the orthodox standpoint, the reverse of stars in Britannia's crown.

In Book IV even the amusingly portentous hat of Bentley becomes a symbol of the inverting of religious thinking and observances by the dull:

> His Hat, which never vail'd to human pride,
> Walker with rev'rence took, and lay'd aside.
> Low bow'd the rest: He, kingly, did but nod;
> So upright Quakers please both Man and God.
>
> (IV, 205–208)

Characteristically, the same ironical statements that ridicule Bentley's individual pride castigate the Quakers, as well—a sect pre-eminent even among Dissenters (a "bad eminence," like Satan's and Cibber's) as followers of the "inner light." The tenor of the passage is that refusing to remove one's hat or to bow is not a sign of humility but of exceptional pride. In Bentley's case, as long as the hat must, in deference to Dulness, be doffed, it would certainly be more unassuming to do it himself than to have it removed by the Vice-Master of Trinity.

Pope implies that the Quaker hat, "never vail'd to human pride," is actually a pharisaical badge of proud difference, the Quaker's self-bestowed sign marking his spiritual superiority to duller mortals. Who but the dull would elevate the observance or nonobservance of minor social courtesies to a plane of religious significance?

The same sort of doubleness appears in the choice of adjective in the phrase "upright Quakers." The adjective can indicate both physical and spiritual uprightness. But what sort of spiritual uprightness is this which pleases both mundane and spiritual judges? It sounds suspiciously like an inversion of the time-honored Christian admonition that the World, the Flesh, and the Devil are on one side and God on the opposite side.

The doubleness which is reprehensible in spiritual matters may be commendable in poetic communication. Pope's poetic method here and elsewhere resembles his conception of God's own method of setting to work in the universe. Pope describes it thus in the *Essay on Man*:

In human works, tho' labour'd on with pain,
A thousand movements scarce one purpose gain;
In God's, one single can its end produce,
Yet serves to second too some other use.   (I, 53–56)

As one exemplification of this, Pope in *The Rape of the Lock* qualified "beautiful" metaphors with some admixture of the homely, ugly, or unaesthetic. "Ugly-beautiful" metaphors are especially frequent in the *Dunciad*. In addition to the general function they perform, which has been previously discussed, in the *Dunciad* they also make their contribution to the underlying inversion metaphor: The ugly becomes the beautiful.

This was illustrated in the passage cited and analyzed from the opening of Book II. To what is the gorgeous seat on which Cibber is enthroned compared? A pillory. What are those "fragrant Grains and Golden show'rs" which the all-bounteous Public pours "on her Curls" (by which is meant both such miscreant publishers as Edmund Curll and the Public's hair, which she is here dressing)? Refuse malt and rotten eggs. These things are beautiful in the same way that Cibber is a source of intellectual light and Lucifer of spiritual light.

The ugly-beautiful inversion prevails also in these lines from the "heroic games":

First Osborne lean'd against his letter'd post;
It rose, and labour'd to a curve at most.
So Jove's bright bow displays its wat'ry round,
(Sure sign, that no spectator shall be drown'd)
A second effort brought but new disgrace,
The wild Meander wash'd the Artist's face.   (II, 171–176)

"Jove's bright bow" and the "wild Meander" are aesthetic and classical in their associations, and the allusion to the rainbow's promise is Biblical. The contrast emphasizes the homely quality of the physiological function, described as if it were a noble essay in a Homeric contest.

A similar effect is obtained in the well-known description of Jove on the privy-seat and in the passage toward the close of the Second Book where a crowd of the "vulgar," "hush'd with mugs of Mum," is compared to a grove of sensuously nodding pine trees. The comparison, a mild degree of depersonification, is ludicrous; but out of these most unlikely elements Pope has created sensuous beauty:

> Soft creeping, words on words, the sense compose,
> At ev'ry line they stretch, they yawn, they doze.
> As to soft gales top-heavy pines bow low
> Their heads, and lift them as they cease to blow:
> Thus oft they rear, and oft the head decline,
> As breathe, or pause, by fits, the airs divine.
> And now to this side, now to that they nod,
> As verse, or prose, infuse the drowzy God.   (II, 389–396)

The powerful and tragic apotheosis of these inversion metaphors is accomplished in Book IV. All, in reality, combine to form one damning metaphor which symbolizes the theme of the entire poem: In the eternal war of What-ought-to-be with What-is, the latter (the Ass) wears the lion's skin and kings it on the throne. The dramatic reversal of What-ought-to-be, in this Book, is, in sober literalness, terribly sublime.

Everything good and desirable (Fancy, Wit, Art, Religion, etc.) is now conceived in terms of light; all opposites in terms of darkness. Item by item the components of civilization are extinguished until the climax is reached—utter darkness. Though the effect of the whole is elegiac, the doubleness of the mock-heroic convention is not abandoned. The ostensible syntactic meaning and the tone preserved imply the achievement of something desirable, the complete triumph of a great power. Thus, till the very end, the true and inverted symbolisms fight with each other. Much of the effectiveness of the passage and the poem derives from the tension thus created:

> She comes! she comes! the sable Throne behold
> Of Night Primaeval, and of Chaos old!
> Before her, Fancy's gilded clouds decay,
> And all its varying Rain-bows die away.
> Wit shoots in vain its momentary fires,
> The meteor drops, and in a flash expires.
>
> .   .   .   .

See skulking Truth to her old Cavern fled,
Mountains of Casuistry heap'd o'er her head!
Philosophy, that lean'd on Heav'n before,
Shrinks to her second cause, and is no more.
Physic of Metaphysic begs defence,
And Metaphysic calls for aid on Sense!
See Mystery to Mathematics fly!
In vain! they gaze, turn giddy, rave, and die.
Religion blushing veils her sacred fires,
And unawares Morality expires.
Nor public Flame, nor private, dares to shine;
Nor human Spark is left, nor Glimpse divine!
Lo! thy dread Empire, CHAOS! is restor'd;
Light dies before thy uncreating word:
Thy hand, great Anarch! lets the curtain fall;
And Universal Darkness buries All.   (IV, 629–656)

Considering Pope's use of metaphor in his poems as a whole, the most prominent feature is his versatility and ingenuity in developing and controlling his metaphor to meet the demands of a poem as an individual creation within a genre. Pope clearly took immense pains to impart to both his individual metaphors and his metaphoric systems the special felicity an Augustan poet seeks in a poem; namely, the precise and careful integration of the minutest parts into a whole governed by the requirements of an established, mature, and sophisticated decorum.

Pope achieves this integration while working with a great variety of metaphoric modes, ranging from the deliberately thin, pretty metaphors of the *Pastorals* to the dry, shrewd, down-to-earth metaphors of the didactic and moral poems, and from the daring mock-epic sublimity of the metaphoric systems in *The Rape of the Lock* and the *Dunciad* to the consciously elevated yet moving metaphor of his English equivalent of Homer.

Yet the scrupulous nicety with which Pope tailored his metaphor to fit the individual poem did not betray him into sacrificing metaphoric vitality. Surely Pope's handling of metaphor is a sign (as Aristotle long ago maintained metaphor to be) of a powerful, major poet, in full and sensitive control of his material and technique.

Tension

Poetry is expected to communicate with an urgency higher than that of prose. The most obvious attribute differentiating most poetry from prose, regularity of rhythm, helps achieve tension. So does rhyme and, when used as a line-marker especially, alliteration. Once expectations of repetition—not to mention phonic processes subtler than repetition—in meter and sound have been set up, the reader's ear remains alert to have them satisfied.

This physical satisfaction is not, however, the only aspect of the poetic exploitation of sound which helps produce tension. As soon as a reader with even a little experience in poetry hears the first few measured lines of a new poem, he forms certain intellectual expectations also. He knows that the realm of everyday prose, whether written or spoken, is on the whole less taut intellectually than the realm of poetry. The tension existing objectively in the art form and arising in part from poetic attitude toward subject matter, creates a corresponding subjective tension in the reader.

To both the physical and intellectual expectations there are exceptions. Good free verse, for example, compensates for lack of traditional metrical tension by special emphasis on tension secured in other ways, metaphor in particular. And bad poetry can be slacker than good prose.

NOTE: This chapter is an expanded version of an article, "Tension in Alexander Pope's Poetry," which appeared in *The University of Kansas City Review*, Spring 1953.

Too frequent, inept imitation of the heroic couplet, for instance, combined with a *Zeitgeist* unfavorable to the form and to the outlook it habitually expressed, did especial damage to Pope's reputation in regard to tension. Less gifted imitators, unable to equal his handling of closure, balance, antithesis, compression, precision, epigrammatic finish, and other qualities, lowered the couplet's tension. As a writer of couplets, Pope was anything but slack. Examination of his larger structures likewise reveals that he was alive to the necessity of creating the greatest possible tension in whatever unit he was working with.

Vitiation of a poet's style by followers lacking ability is not, of course, a phenomenon confined to Pope. The Spenserian, Miltonic, and Shakespearean patterns have been similarly mishandled. With almost every issue our little magazines sprout would-be Eliots, Audens, and Dylan Thomases. And the Romantic lyric would be abashed to recognize its descendants in our housewives' magazines and middle-brow general magazines.

The twentieth-century reader must make some effort to regain the expectation of the brilliance and nervous energy Pope infused into the heroic couplet. He must scrutinize whole poems closely, with a mind freed as far as possible from the common misconception that Pope's poems tend to be constructed loosely and even haphazardly.

By far the most crucial element in creating tension is meaning. Since genre is broadly a categorizing of what and how a poem may mean, individual genres exhibit certain distinctive tensions. To a neoclassic poet this is of prime importance. The tension proper to epic, for instance, arises chiefly from the conflict of heroes with heroic adversaries and in some degree of both with fate. Achilles opposes Hector in the knowledge that hard upon the heels of victory will come the termination of his own brief life. Beowulf fights Grendel and the firedrake, but is himself overcome by man's mortality. Adam and Eve are set within a garden to combat the Devil himself, but within the framework of omnipotent God's—and the reader's—foreknowledge that they will not combat successfully.

As for the fundamental tension of mock-heroic, it resides in the constant comparison it promotes between this epic tension and low, frivolous, contemporary matters. The distinctive tension of satire lies in the pull between the norm of right conduct and the castigated deviations from it.

Within the limits of each genre the individual poet may achieve certain characteristic modifications of the prevailing tension. Epics though they all are, *Beowulf*, *The Faerie Queene*, and *Paradise Lost* are highly individual in degree and quality of tension. Likewise, *Sir Thopas*, *Hudibras*, *The Dispensary*, and *The Rape of the Lock*, though all mock-epics, operate at different levels of tension.

Of this group *The Rape of the Lock*, in spite of its surface frivolity, offers the most serious and inclusive comment on human life. The *Dunciad* in this respect surpasses *The Rape*; since public, general, "masculine" interests carry more weight than private, domestic, "feminine" interests. One poem is concerned with the relations of men to women; the other with the possibility of a whole civilization's slipping into a new dark age. Either of these subjects is more significant in its human import than criticism of pseudo knighthood or even the question of free pharmaceuticals for Londoners. And tension is in large part a concomitant of seriousness of subject matter.

Pope utilizes this fact in such a way that he very nearly turns mock-epic tension back into epic tension. He does not maintain the genre tension between low subject and high style in a simple one-to-one fashion; he brings in a third dimension. For in neither of his mock epics is Pope's real subject matter low. Belinda's boudoir, as we have seen, and even Duncedom's games have a serious aspect. The two-way tension inherent in mock-heroic is transformed by Pope into a three-way tension pointing back toward epic seriousness. Clarissa's speech in Canto V, for instance, underlines several of the serious emphases of *The Rape of the Lock*:

Oh! if to dance all Night, and dress all Day,
Charm'd the Small-pox, or chas'd old Age away;

Who would not scorn what Huswife's Cares produce,
Or who would learn one earthly Thing of Use?
To patch, nay, ogle, might become a Saint,
Nor could it sure be such a Sin to paint.
But since, alas! frail Beauty must decay,
Curl'd or uncurl'd, since Locks will turn to grey,
Since painted, or not painted, all shall fade,
And she who scorns a Man, must die a Maid;
What then remains, but well our Pow'r to use,
And keep good Humour still whate'er we lose?
And trust me, Dear, good Humour can prevail,
When Airs, and Flights, and Screams, and Scolding fail.
Beauties in vain their pretty Eyes may roll;
Charms strike the Sight, but Merit wins the Soul.

(V, 19–34)

Belinda, no less than Achilles, is cursed wtih a glorious but—
because curled or uncurled, locks *will* turn to gray—brief domin-
ion over the hearts of beaux. The sun she personifies and "the
Suns of her Eyes" will set. Old age for Belinda is the firedragon
which will put an end to her proper career. The lack of applause
with which Clarissa's speech is greeted makes it clear that virtue
and useful skills are not an acceptable alternative for conquests
of hearts.

Nor does Clarissa herself recommend virtue from the right
motive. Her radically contorted female philosophy makes it appear that the typical belle, somewhat like Adam and Eve in the
garden, is so enmeshed in fate that she has no reasonable probability of rising above Clarissa's narrow, hypocritical opportun-
ism. The more serious issues underlying the depiction of Belinda's
dressing table as an altar at which she worships the deity revealed
in the mirror have already been discussed. This does not make
The Rape of the Lock an epic; but not very far beneath its amusing, lacquered surface lurk graver issues, not ordinarily treated
in mock epic. The interaction of these with the more conventional mock-epic qualities, produces a special type of tension very
characteristic of Pope.

A source of tension notably exploited in the *Dunciad* and the
Satires is reference to particular people and particular events. The

following passage from Dialogue I, *Epilogue to the Satires*, is typical. The Friend remonstrates with Pope:

> Ye Gods! shall Cibber's Son, without rebuke,
> Swear like a Lord? or Rich out-whore a Duke?
> A Fav'rite's porter with his Master vie,
> Be brib'd as often, and as often lie?
> Shall Ward draw Contracts with a Statesman's skill?
> Or Japhet pocket, like His Grace, a Will?
> Is it for Bond or Peter (paltry Things!)
> To pay their Debts or keep their Faith like Kings?
>
> (115–122)

The reading of this passage is undoubtedly enriched by knowledge of the details of Bond's or Peter's perfidy, but such information is not necessary for understanding the satiric point. Sappho, Cibber, and Ward lived and were poetically pilloried in Horace's day; they live too in our own.

That this naming of names increased the tension of such passages for Pope's contemporaries is borne out by the protests they occasioned. Even in our time, merely the realization that Pope is referring not to fictional ghosts but to actual people and happenings augments tension. The reader does not have to know personally the characters stigmatized or even to be acquainted with their biographies to recognize the heightening of satiric level Pope achieves by making "those not afraid of God afraid of him."

Wherever he can, Pope uses the rhetorical devices at his disposal to avoid a one-sided, narrow presentation of reality. Through irony, metaphor, paradox, layering of meaning, and tonal variation he gains an inclusiveness which makes his work comprehend something approaching the whole and not just a part of human experience. This inclusiveness, this attraction into the poem of many different facets of human experience, of itself powerfully increases tension. If the given subject of the poem is thought of as an animal body centered in a spider-web arrangement of ropes, it can be said that to tug on many ropes simultaneously will cause more agony than to tug on just one rope—and, incidentally, this will keep the body in the center of the web instead of pulling it out eccentrically to any one side.

In individual couplets and passages one of Pope's most interesting ways of securing tension is to make syntax or meaning fight against form. A notable instance of a poem in which this device provides the complete motivation is the *Temple of Fame*.

Chaucer in Book III of the *House of Fame* secures tension chiefly in other ways. Both poets employ a combination of devices for securing tension, but even where the same factor is used the emphasis differs.

The unpredictable actions reflecting the capricious nature of Fame are utilized by both. Pope places his main reliance on them, but a broader narrative element dominates Chaucer's poem. Pope's narrator is just having a dream. The interest is focused on the metaphysical and moral implications of the dream itself. Chaucer's narrator is experiencing a very strange adventure which holds the reader in suspense. What further marvelous happenings are in store for the man snatched up through the air by the eagle? What will be the long expected love tidings?

Pope's poem is a vision, but its emphasis is upon the normal, not the extraordinary. Pope's narrator dreams of a paneled room, so to speak; but in the dream of Chaucer's narrator the panel slides to reveal a vast dark place ruled by a goddess with

> . . . also fele upstondyng eres
> And tonges, as on bestes heres;
> And on hir fet woxen saugh y
> Partriches wynges redely.
> (III, 1389–1392)*

When anything can happen to anybody, when the order of the day is miracle, a considerable source of tension is being tapped.

The danger in this source is that it may be nullified by complete detachment from actuality. Where anything can and does happen, soon nothing that happens possesses much excitement or significance. Chaucer guards against this by casually mixing in

---

* All quotations from Chaucer are from *The Complete Works*, edited by F. N. Robinson (Boston, Mass.: Houghton Mifflin Company, 1933).

homely proverbs, folksy allusions, altercations, and other situations suggestive of everyday life. The very mixture produces additional tension, as exemplified in this passage where the goddess who has as many eyes as "fetheres upon foules," whose feet touch earth and whose head reaches heaven, scolds her suppliants like a fishwife:

> "Fy on yow," quod she, "everychon!
> Ye masty swyn, ye ydel wreches,
> Ful of roten, slowe techches!
> What? false theves! wher ye wolde
> Be famous good, and nothing nolde
> Deserve why, ne never ye roughte?
> Men rather yow to hangen oughte!
> For ye be lyke the sweynte cat
> That wolde have fissh; but wostow what?
> He wolde nothing wete his clowes."
>
> (III, 1776–1785)

But the extremely unusual and the miraculous are not necessary for tension. Everyday life—as those who live it can testify—produces tension enough. Pope depends very little upon the marvelous. He uses a dream in which Fame appears personified as a goddess to make normalized comments about the impact of fame on everyday life. "Normalized" is important. Pope is following the neoclassical idea that the more universal the experience, the more significant it is, and hence the more likely to involve tension.

The repressing of adventitious detail, the concentration on one single line of event, and the elimination of contemporary local color—with the exception of the beaux who want to tell without having kissed—undoubtedly further increase the tension of Pope's poem. There is no loose lumber left lying around this temple.

Paradoxically, Chaucer's loose lumber achieves an effect comparable to Pope's tidying up. Chaucer is continually dragging into the *House of Fame* chunks of scientific speculation, history, mythology, moral generalizations, etc. He takes fifty-eight lines, for instance, to catalogue the musicians of all climes and ages who haunt Fame's castle (III, 1201–1258). The reader comes to expect these digressions and to delight in them. They enrich the texture and slightly delay the onward movement of the narrative.

Both poems profit from the moral tension generated by the displaying of the whimsical and transient nature of fame. In Chaucer, however, as far as can be surmised from the unfinished state of the poem, this emphasis is incidental. In Pope's poem this moral aspect is primary. Every element in the poem leads up to the speaker's placing himself, in the last line, on the side of the angels:

Oh grant an honest Fame, or grant me none!

Allied to the moral significance—in fact, to a large extent the means by which it is conveyed—is the allegory which plays a considerable part in both poems. Every event or scenic feature is of interest not only for itself but for what it signalizes on another plane. The allegory converts the poems into, at least, two-ring circuses. Pope's allegory tends to be channeled in its implications; it is limited and directed with a special purpose in view—the reinforcement of the central emphasis of the poem. Chaucer leaves his allegory freer to suggest tangentials. The difference between the two poets in this respect can be seen in their handling of heat-and-cold symbolism with reference to the duration of fame. Chaucer:

> Tho saugh I al the half ygrave
> With famous folkes names fele,
> That had iben in mochel wele,
> And her fames wide yblowe.
> But wel unnethes koude I knowe
> Any lettres for to rede
> Hir names by; for, out of drede,
> They were almost ofthowed so
> That of the lettres oon or two
> Was molte away of every name,
> So unfamous was woxe hir fame.
> But men seyn, "What may ever laste?"
> Thoo gan I in myn herte caste
> That they were molte awey with hete,
> And not awey with stormes bete.
> For on that other syde I say

Of this hil, that northward lay,
How hit was writen ful of names
Of folkes that hadden grete fames
Of olde tyme, and yet they were
As fresh as men had writen hem here
The selve day ryght, or that houre
That I upon him gan to poure.
But wel I wiste what yt made;
Hyt was conserved with the shade
Of a castel that stood on high—
Al this wrytinge that I sigh—
And stood eke on so cold a place
That hete myghte hit not deface.
(III, 1136–1164)

Pope:

High on a Rock of Ice the Structure lay,
Steep its Ascent, and slipp'ry was the Way;
The wond'rous Rock like Parian Marble shone,
And seem'd to distant Sight of solid Stone.
Inscriptions here of various Names I view'd,
The greater Part by hostile Time subdu'd;
Yet wide was spread their Fame in Ages past,
And Poets once had promis'd they should last.
Some fresh ingrav'd appear'd of Wits renown'd;
I look'd again, nor cou'd their Trace be found.
Criticks I saw, that other Names deface,
And fix their own with Labour in their place:
Their own like others soon their Place resign'd,
Or disappear'd, and left the first behind.
Nor was the Work impair'd by Storms alone,
But felt th' Approaches of too warm a Sun;
For Fame, impatient of Extreams, decays
Not more by Envy than Excess of Praise.
Yet Part no Injuries of Heav'n cou'd feel,
Like Crystal faithful to th' graving Steel:
The Rock's high Summit, in the Temple's Shade,
Nor Heat could melt, nor beating Storm invade.
There Names inscrib'd unnumber'd Ages past
From Time's first Birth, with Time it self shall last;
These ever new, nor subject to Decays,
Spread, and grow brighter with the Length of Days.
(27–52)

Chaucer's poem emphasizes constantly the psychological effect of the action on the narrator. This continual interaction between character and event is not present in Pope's poem. One result of this is that Chaucer's narrator is more intimately characterized. His own comments help characterize him. Pope's speaker, except for his declaration about fame at the end, stands aloof from the vision; he is more of a spectator than a participant. The relation of both speakers to their subject matter is productive of tension, but tension of a different quality in each case. The reader comes to expect a homely, often humorous garrulity in Chaucer's speaker. He is a clerk, a man who delights in reading; yet he is no novice in the art of living with others. Human frailties do not surprise him; neither have they embittered him. He looks at life ironically but easily. Pope's speaker is an earnest young poet with a systematic mind. He approaches his subject—and every glancing facet of his subject—with the universal norm in mind. The consciousness that he is dealing in universal norms gives him an almost dogmatic assurance, but he keeps his utterances on a rather courtly plane. His irony is sharp, the situations to which he applies it precisely observed, and his manner of delivering it formal, not casual. He communicates a sense of onward drive and of the tension associated with ceremonial pronouncements ex cathedra.

Both speakers clearly delight in describing for the sake of description, painting verbal pictures with a relish for scenic detail, whether natural or human, that suggests the Flemish masters. Pope's poem preserves the sensation frequently experienced in reading Chaucer that one is watching a *tableau vivant*. Frozen for a moment into a careful pictorial composition, it suddenly moves, dissolves, and progresses along a story line, only to form new *tableaux vivants* further ahead. But the scenic qualities that catch the eye of Chaucer's narrator are strangeness and Gothic gorgeousness, together with a homely reality often intruded into these. Pope's speaker stresses Palladian regularity, elegance, and appropriateness. The interest in his scenes lies not in their unusualness but in the pat way they satisfy normalized anticipation.

In Pope a dramatic personal relationship exists only between the goddess and her suppliants and between the speaker and his audience. The latter relationship becomes especially salient when the speaker makes his moral affirmation at the close. In Chaucer, aside from these two relationships, there are others: notably between the speaker and the eagle, the goddess and Eolus. To express these relations Chaucer uses, in addition to action and description, a highly colored, folksy conversation which helps to individualize the characters.

For the tension arising from interaction of many different characters Pope substitutes a tension gained by focusing on just a few relationships. The anonymity and colorlessness of the "One" in "One came, methought, and whisper'd in my Ear" (498) is no doubt purposeful. The conversations between Pope's suppliants and the goddess are homogeneous in style, and the style does not vary from that which prevails in the nonconversational context. The tension in Pope's conversations resides precisely in the fact that he does *not* reproduce the flavor of actual speech nor adapt the words to express the character's difference from others. It lies in his making each character give voice, in an ordered and verbally unforgettable way, to the universalized position he represents.

Pope and Chaucer follow much the same line of event in conducting the scene between Fame and her petitioners. The ruling passion of the goddess is stressed as a combination of caprice, inconsistency, and illogicality; and the complete irrationality of her behavior is demonstrated in instance after instance. Even when the good are rewarded with good fame and the bad with bad fame, it is the result of whim rather than of an attempt to do justice.

The strategy of Pope's poem, however, is to conduct the inquiry into Fame's unpredictable nature in a controlled, logical manner. The illogic of the goddess's judgments fight against the methodical way in which they are presented to the reader.

Not only are Fame's decisions irrational. She is also depicted as unreliable where time and duration are concerned, as at once fleeting and permanent. This is symbolized by the "Rock of Ice" on which her temple stands. Here, as we have seen, some names have "felt th' Approaches of too warm a Sun"; others remain, like ice in Zembla, unaffected:

> So Zembla's Rocks (the beauteous Work of Frost)
> Rise white in Air, and glitter o'er the Coast;
> Pale Suns, unfelt, at distance roll away,
> And on th' impassive Ice the Lightnings play:
> Eternal Snows the growing Mass supply,
> Till the bright Mountains prop th' incumbent Sky:
> As Atlas fix'd, each hoary Pile appears,
> The gather'd Winter of a thousand Years. (53–60)

This paradox of melting and not melting, fleeting and not fleeting—which Pope stresses more than Chaucer—fights against the logical process of the inquiry and the firmly controlled couplets in which this analysis of the uncontrolled and the illogical proceeds.

In this connection the controversial house of Rumor, sometimes said to detract from the unity of the poem, is seen to function logically. It stresses Fame's transience as Zembla's rocks stress her permanence.

As has been observed, Pope did not hesitate to make sweeping changes in Chaucer's unfinished original in order to secure for his own poem unassailable logic and tightness of design. If Chaucer's whirling house of Rumor had been in Pope's eyes a distraction and a superfluity, it too would have vanished. But Rumor represents only an intensification of the brief duration and fickleness of Fame herself. Rumor is another aspect of the same goddess. The ceaselessly whirling little house is appropriately and with climactic effect reserved for the end. Furthermore, the contrast is made stronger between unstable earthly Fame, who throughout the poem is dramatically analyzed in all her imperfections, and the heavenly fame, both just and enduring, which Pope turns to and apostrophizes in the closing lines.

As a whole, Pope's poetry achieves and maintains a high level of tension. Because of the care he gave to minute questions of finish, his mature works contain very few passages where tension —though it is often varied in quality—is relaxed in degree.

8

Tonal Variation

As Pope matured poetically he used tonal variation with increasing rhetorical emphasis, precision of effect, and complexity. The classic pastoral is one of the few genres in which tonal variation is not a desideratum. Uniformity of tone is one of pastoral's conventional assets. As mentioned previously, with the possible exception of Thyrsis' final speech in *Winter*, Pope carefully excludes from these poems any allusions to unpastoral material or attitudes. Even though *Summer* treats of unrequited love, *Autumn* of perjured love, and *Winter* of grief for the dead, these emotions are successfully tranquilized by the pastoral mode. The pervading equanimity and remoteness of the genre are not disrupted.

But *Windsor Forest*, a comparatively early poem with a relatively confined framework, already possesses considerable tonal range. Its basic tone is that of calm local description:

> Here waving groves a chequered scene display,
> And part admit, and part exclude the day. (17–18)

With this tone as an abiding referent Pope makes sallies into the following variety of tones:
The paradoxical and ironic:

> The swain with tears his frustrate labour yields,
> And famished dies amidst his ripened fields.
> What wonder then, a beast or subject slain
> Were equal crimes in a despotic reign?
> Both doomed alike, for sportive Tyrants bled,

136

But while the subject starved, the beast was fed.

(55–60)

The gorgeous and opulent:

The silver eel, in shining volumes rolled,
The yellow carp, in scales bedropped with gold.

(143–144)

The Homeric:

See the bold youth strain up the threat'ning steep,
Rush through the thickets, down the valleys sweep,
Hang o'er their coursers' heads with eager speed,
And earth rolls back beneath the flying steed.

(155–158)

The calm prophetic:

Hail, sacred Peace! hail, long-expected days,
That Thames's glory to the stars shall raise!

(355–356)

The rhapsodic:

I see, I see, where two fair cities bend
Their ample bow, a new Whitehall ascend!

(379–380)

And the denunciatory prophetic:

There Faction roar, Rebellion bite her chain,
And gasping Furies thirst for blood in vain.

(421–422)

Windsor Forest, however, does not exhibit any tonal divergencies as wide as is the case in later works. Nor is transition from one tone to another sudden or shocking to the degree found in later poems. Notable is the absence of humorous and low tones, and especially the absence of that obliquity which is as characteristic of the mature Pope as the organ tone is of Milton.

Especially interesting in view of later practice are several passages where Pope blends two or more different tones. In these lines, for example, the tones of dramatic action, gorgeous description, and elegy are fused:

See! from the brake the whirring pheasant springs,

137

And mounts exulting on triumphant wings:
Short is his joy; he feels the fiery wound,
Flutters in blood, and panting beats the ground.
Ah! what avail his glossy, varying dyes,
His purple crest, and scarlet-circled eyes,
The vivid green his shining plumes unfold,
His painted wings, and breast that flames with gold?

(111–118)

Blending of tones is not peculiar to Pope. There is no major English poet in whose work it does not occur, to a greater or less degree. But peculiar to Pope is the extent to which in his mature poems this fusing of tones is found in connection with oblique communication. Many passages already cited, particularly from *The Rape of the Lock* and the *Dunciad*, exemplify this.

A basic function of tonal variation, especially in longer poems, is the prevention of monotony. If Pope had produced in *Windsor Forest*'s four hundred and thirty-four lines nothing but unrelieved description of landscape, he would have been, like his own Dunces, "Sleepless himself to give his readers sleep."

Shifts from one tone to another keep the attention alerted. This is true even when the shifts are not extreme, as in the following shift from prophetic calm to prophetic rhapsody in the *Messiah*:

The smiling infant in his hand shall take
The crested basilisk and speckled snake,
Pleased the green lustre of the scales survey,
And with their forky tongues shall innocently play.
Rise, crowned with light, imperial Salem, rise!
Exalt thy towery head, and lift thy eyes!   (81–86)

When the shifts are between tones widely contrasted, the effect is one of shock. In the following lines from *Moral Essay* III the whole point of the passage turns upon the shocking contrast between epic, or the elevated sensuous, tone and the low or contemporary. Pope is envisioning what would happen if there were no paper money:

His Grace will game: to White's a Bull be led,
With spurning heels and with a butting head.
To White's be carried, as to ancient games,

Fair Coursers, Vases, and alluring Dames.
Shall then Uxorio, if the stakes he sweep,
Bear home six Whores, and make his Lady weep?
Or soft Adonis, so perfum'd and fine,
Drive to St. James's a whole herd of swine?

(55–62)

This effect is particularly well dramatized and explicitly recognized in the text in these lines from Dialogue II, *Epilogue to the Satires*:

F. And how did, pray, the Florid Youth offend,
Whose Speech you took, and gave it to a Friend?
P. Faith it imports not much from whom it came;
Whoever borrow'd, could not be to blame,
Since the whole House did afterwards the same:
Let Courtly Wits to Wits afford supply,
As Hog to Hog in Huts of Westphaly;
If one, thro' Nature's Bounty or his Lord's,
Has what the frugal, dirty soil affords,
From him the next receives it, thick or thin,
As pure a Mess almost as it came in;
The blessed Benefit, not there confin'd,
Drops to the third who nuzzles close behind;
From tail to mouth, they feed, and they carouse;
The last, full fairly gives it to the House.
F. This filthy simile, this beastly Line,
Quite turns my Stomach—
P. So does Flatt'ry mine.

(166–183)

The pervasive tone of this Dialogue, though not high, is elevated in comparison with this passage's drop into the stye. The method is dramatic, and the Friend's natural objection to the revolting comparison is cleverly used to cap the argument.

Humor is often a concomitant of this shift from high to low tone, as exemplified in the descriptions of the urination contest and Jove on the privy-seat discussed previously.

Another secondary effect of such shifting is its indication of a worldly conversational mobility in the dramatic speaker—a facility and assurance in handling various spheres and assuming the attitudes appropriate to each. The speaker of the *Essay on Criticism* illustrates this especially well.

Within a poem, tone often has a function which may be called ritualistic. A shift of tone serves notice of what the reader may expect to follow. It establishes a mood and sets up expectations. In the First Book of the *Dunciad* up through line 35 the reader is aware that he may expect mock-heroic humor; but he is not yet apprised of the depths to which the art of sinking will be carried. After the lines—

> One Cell there is, conceal'd from vulgar eye,
> The Cave of Poverty and Poetry.
> Keen, hollow winds howl thro' the bleak recess—

the next verse comes as a perceptible shock and as a warning of what lies ahead—

> Emblem of Music caus'd by Emptiness.   (I, 33-36)

Because this line can be interpreted in two ways, and because the preceding verses have not prepared the reader for cloacal comparisons, his reaction is likely to be somewhat delayed—but all the more effective. From this point on he will be alert for double meanings on this level.

Elizabethan dramatists used comic subplots or episodes such as the porter's knocking on the gate in *Macbeth* for the double purpose of relieving tragic emphasis and commenting on the tragedy by adding perspective. Pope achieves similar results by using different tones to analyze the same action or concept. Take, for example, a concept of much importance in Pope's view of human nature, the dangers of "reas'ning Pride." To cite only three tonal approaches out of many, all three from the opening of Epistle II of the *Essay on Man*, there is first the quiet and straightforward tone of

> Know then thyself, presume not God to scan;
> The proper study of Mankind is Man.   (II, 1-2)

This is followed by the ironic injunction,

> Go, wond'rous creature! mount where Science guides,
> Go, measure earth, weigh air, and state the tides.
>   (II, 19-20)

By the end of the passage the tone has risen to one of violent denunciation:

> Go, teach Eternal Wisdom how to rule—
> Then drop into thyself, and be a fool!
>
> (II, 29–30)

Associated with this are the cognitive functions of tonal variation. Tone, after all, cannot be completely distinguished from content. Tone is not only how a thing is said but also in part what is said. Tone thus may either confirm the syntactical statement of the text or fight against it. For example, tone straightforwardly confirms the compliment to Martha Blount in these lines from *Moral Essay* II:

> Ah Friend! to dazzle let the Vain design,
> To raise the Thought and touch the Heart, be thine!
> That Charm shall grow, while what fatigues the Ring
> Flaunts and goes down, an unregarded thing. (249–252)

Later in the same passage, tone adds a qualifying element which almost undermines the compliment:

> Let Fops or Fortune fly which way they will;
> Disdains all loss of Tickets, or Codille;
> Spleen, Vapours, or Small-pox, above them all,
> And Mistress of herself, tho' China fall. (265–268)

The undermining effect, however, is necessary to an accurate, convincing, and not one-sidedly sentimental portrayal of the character of the eighteenth-century Englishwoman. Besides, there is a sense in which the four lines above are not disparagement but real praise.

Dunces may try all tones and fail in all. A minor poet excels in at least one tone. But with the possible exception of the short lyric, Pope excelled in all he attempted; and the range of tones he attempted is comparable to Virgil's, or Spenser's, or Milton's. Some of the stops on the organ Pope either could not or did not choose to pull. But a poet who has handled successfully the wide variety of tones exemplified in Pope's works as a whole cannot justly be accused of narrowness of scope or of lacking the comprehensive comment on life expected of a major poet.

9

Narrative Elements

WHETHER Pope is using a short narrative to serve the strategy
of a particular poem or a long narrative as his primary organizing
element, he displays a keen perception of the demands, uses, and
conduct of fiction. And he satisfies these demands in ways consonant with his general poetic practice and outlook. Little attention has been focused on Pope's use of narrative, perhaps because
his excellence has been taken for granted. Yet, removing this element from his work would leave a very big gap indeed. Of all
Pope's major poems only the *Essay on Man* neither tells a story
in the conventional sense nor contains brief, interpolated stories;
and even the *Essay on Man* owes some of its success to elements
usually associated with narrative.

For the long narrative, Pope's chief master was Homer; for
the short anecdote introduced in a non-narrative context, Horace.
The narrative bases of *The Rape of the Lock* and the *Dunciad*
are Homer in reverse. The remainder of Pope's narratives, with a
few minor exceptions, are brief inserted *exempla* of the Horatian
type. Except for the metamorphosis of Lodona in *Windsor Forest*, all of Pope's narratives, long or short, are saliently moral. Most
frequently the moral is conveyed in the satiric mode.

The single narrative in the *Essay on Criticism*, the story of Don
Quixote's encounter with the Aristotelian bard, is introduced
largely to lend variety to an essay composed for the most part of
information and precepts. The story is preceded by these lines
of general instruction:

> Most Critics, fond of some subservient art,
> Still make the Whole depend upon a Part:
> They talk of principles, but notions prize,
> And all to one loved Folly sacrifice. (II, 263-266)

In relation to these introductory lines, the narrative functions somewhat like the *exemplum* in a medieval sermon. In a fictional mode it particularizes and dramatizes the general principle of right conduct being urged:

> Once on a time, La Mancha's Knight, they say,
> A certain bard encount'ring on the way,
> Discoursed in terms as just, with looks as sage,
> As e'er could Dennis of the Grecian stage;
> Concluding all were desperate sots and fools,
> Who durst depart from Aristotle's rules.
> Our Author, happy in a judge so nice,
> Produced his Play, and begged the Knight's advice;
> Made him observe the subject, and the plot,
> The manners, passions, unities; what not?
> All which, exact to rule, were brought about,
> Were but a Combat in the lists left out.
> "What! leave the Combat out?" exclaims the Knight:
> Yes, or we must renounce the Stagirite.
> "Not so by Heaven" (he answers in a rage),
> "Knights, squires, and steeds, must enter on the stage."
> So vast a throng the stage can ne'er contain.
> "Then build a new, or act it in a plain." (II, 267-284)

The tone is consonant with the over-all tone of the *Essay*: common sense easily and somewhat ironically dispensed. Colloquialisms, characteristic of the *Essay* throughout, aid in achieving this easiness. The colloquial exaggeration of "desperate sots and fools" is particularly happy.

In contrast to the coolness and good sense of the narrator (not, for very good reasons, identifiable with the "certain bard"), the Knight's partiality and undue warmth are conspicuous. His general identification with John Dennis further places him in the opposite camp from the poised and urbane speaker. Even the double spondee in "Knights, squires, *and* steeds" stresses the Knight's folly.

Not all the irony is directed against the Knight. A subtler portion falls to the bard who servilely follows a mechanical interpretation of Aristotle. This irony that cuts both ways has already been noted as especially favored by Pope. He demonstrates its usefulness in narrative, not only for characterization but for achieving a compression that produces tension and a sense of dramatic immediacy. In a very short compass of verses this double-edged weapon points up the ironical contrast and at the same time the ironical similarity between Knight and bard.

Immediately after this narrative the precept is repeated from a slightly different angle. The story is thus framed in the precept it illustrates. Both forms of the precept extend their caveats from the purely literary problem to life in general, and the story itself illustrates the extension.

A comparable extension is obtained in Pope's one brief narrative which is not notably moralizing: the myth of the chaste Lodona pursued by Pan, violated, and then at her supplication to Diana, transformed into a "soft, silver stream." This slight but charming and smoothly executed tale owes its inclusion in *Windsor Forest* partly to the need of the topographical poem for variety and partly to the fact that one of the conventional ways to secure this variety was to tell a tale. But Lodona's metamorphosis is also an imitation of Ovid and, as such, is conceived within the framework of classical mythology. Pope's myth, in a sense containing Greece and Rome, thus extends the shadow of Windsor Forest historically, geographically, and intellectually. Still, the general effect of the Lodona legend is decorative, not didactic.

In the *Pastorals*, as might be expected, Pope subordinates narrative to the over-all purpose of pastoral, which is communication of the sense that whatever happens is a part of the great tranquilizing framework of natural order. The narrative element has slight salience and is strongly predetermined by tradition. It tends to be as static as is consistent with any narrative at all. Conflicts and violence are minimized. Characterization is slight and conventional. Shepherd swains, if old, are wise and garrulous; if young, musical and in love. Shepherdesses are always youthful and desirable, varied perhaps as scornful, perjured, or faithful. Many words are expended on setting, but the settings are not individualized. References to setting, however frequent, are always to the generalized pastoral landscape with its recurrent processes. Suspense exists, but on a subdued level. The climax, such as it is, is reached somewhat before the end to permit its being followed by the conventional quiet close. Among the four *Pastorals*, Pope varies the conduct of the narrative somewhat. He uses a mixture of third person narration with dialogue in *Spring*, a simulated third person opening followed by most of the poem in the first person in *Summer*, the omniscient narrator approach in *Autumn*, and in *Winter* pure dialogue. It is a way of getting a little rhetorical variety into a genre which does not permit exciting and agitating modes of obtaining variety.

In contrast, Pope's use of the first person—Eloisa speaking for herself—in *Eloisa to Abelard* is his prime means of putting into this poem all the psychological excitement possible. There are two stories in *Eloisa to Abelard*. One is the tale of what happened to the lovers, seen through Eloisa's present psychological state. The other is the story of Eloisa's inner conflict between love and duty and its ultimate foreseen resolution, the despairing resolution of death. Though the forsaken woman lamenting her woes is a convention of the heroic epistle, it is unusual for Pope to be writing in a first person other than the man-of-the-world first person of the epistles and satires. In Eloisa, moreover, he is using the interior consciousness of a woman.

In her consciousness Abelard—though the idea of him is always present—is seen only in glimpses and from the outside. His portrayal is conventional; his character does not develop. Eloisa herself is presented in detail and with great psychological acuteness. She remains, nevertheless, a type rather than an individual. No matter how much detail is given on her inner life, nor how intimate, these details are always those which would be true of any intelligent, passionate woman in such a situation. In allowing Eloisa to characterize herself Pope is aiming, as he always did in characterization, at universal truth rather than delineation of personal peculiarities.

In presenting Eloisa's chief inner conflict, Pope uses setting in an especially significant way. The gloomy convent and its melancholy environs have a Gothic counterpart in Eloisa's mind. Interiorized, the setting becomes an important part of Eloisa's dilemma. Her outer prison symbolizes the inner prison created by her acquiescence, against the grain of her own personal make-up and best interests, in the demands of a morbid asceticism. Her mental attitude toward the situation, and not the situation itself, is her real tragedy. After Abelard's misadventure, a sensible woman with Eloisa's temperament would perhaps have waited a decent interval, found a suitable mate, married, and brought up a family. This would scarcely have been a Romantic course, but would certainly have been a sane one. The setting, then, is in a manner of speaking an exteriorization of the tragedy-making element in Eloisa's mind. As such it deserves the special emphasis Pope gives it.

Still, the purpose of the poem is not to exhibit the unfortunate results of a medieval delusion on the part of the heroine but to show, granting that delusion, how hard emotionally she finds it to accept the only way of life left open to her. The climax of the poem is not a climax of event but of feeling. Pope's method is simply to increase the fires till at the point of highest agony Eloisa can see no end but death.

The Rape of the Lock also places a great deal of stress on setting. Morbid setting, such as the Cave of Spleen and the psychological frustrations (mainly sexual) it represents, plays an important part. Prudery, its cause and consequences, is one of the pitfalls of the belle's world. But most attention is given to setting of another type: descriptions of Belinda's boudoir, her toilet table, the card table, the coffee service, wigs, sword knots, snuff boxes, silver watches, and clouded canes. For this there are two main reasons. One is the importance the poem's theme gives to appearances. Sir Plume's "nice Conduct of a clouded Cane" is not mentioned just for itself but for the distorted sense of values it conveys. Then, too, all the elegant little objects and ways are described as if they were portentous. This underlines another aspect of the theme mentioned previously—that to the belles and beaux little things seem big and big things little. In addition, so much description of the elegant appurtenances of the fashionable world adds to the poem's decorative beauty.

The marvel of this narrative is that so slight an actual episode as Lord Petre's snipping a lock of Arabella Fermor's hair could become the organizing mechanism of so rich a construct as the five-canto form of *The Rape of the Lock*. Pope's ability to make the little contain the big and a part suggest the whole is nowhere better shown. Nowhere else does he use quite the same method of starting with such trifling actions as "The young people went for an outing on the river, played cards, and drank coffee" and concreting around them a wealth of beauty and significance. Moreover, the concretions—for example, the Sylphs—do not remain tangential. They are integrated into the narrative. The very high degree of narrative integration is one of the excellences of this poem. What Pope said of the universe in the *Essay on Man* may be said of the story of Belinda's lock: "Nothing is foreign; parts relate to whole" (III, 21).

In both *The Rape of the Lock* and the *Dunciad* the groundwork of the narrative is contemporary actuality with an epic overlay. Both poems, in a sense, contain two narratives proceeding at the same time. It is as if Homer and the eighteenth century, having joined hands, went walking down the same path. But the actuality of the *Dunciad* is from a far more rough-and-tumble sphere than is that of *The Rape of the Lock*. This has its effect upon each poem's epic *Doppel-gänger*. In one poem Homer's games become cards played on a velvet-covered table; in the other, contests in urination and sewer-diving.

But the satire of Belinda's foibles and the satire directed against the vagaries of Dulness are alike in that the surface fun conceals a latent seriousness. In addition to the epic story (in reverse) and the actual story, a third story is going on in each poem—a weighty one where the issues are as real as the eventual death of even the most glittering belle or the downfall of the most brilliant civilization. Pope's ability to work on several levels at once, even in narrative, is a way he achieves his characteristic packed but terse style.

Setting is just as functional in the *Dunciad*; but instead of the boudoir and Hampton Court we have the pillory, the privy, and Fleet Ditch. In both poems setting is treated with epic elevation. The boudoir becomes a temple, the privy Jove's judgment seat. The difference is that, given the theme of *The Rape*, the boudoir is, as we have seen, in a sense really sacred; whereas the throne of Dulness is not truly a throne in any positive interpretation. The poems are alike, however, in that out of settings not usually thought of as beautiful Pope has produced beauty. A puddle of spilled lotion becomes a lake in the infernal landscape; a smoking cup of coffee becomes surf dashing against the China coast. In the *Dunciad* fools pressing around the goddess Dulness are compared to bees conglobed, orb in orb, around their queen; a crowd nodding as dull works are read is a forest of softly waving pine trees.

Characterization in the *Dunciad* is related with special intimacy to theme. The purpose of the poem is to strike a blow for intelligence and civilization by exhibiting pert fools in all their foolery. Consequently, characters are immediately divided into two camps, fools and wise men, though the latter are present mostly by implication. The fools are further divided into terrestrial and celestial. Most of the terrestrial fools bear actual names or pseudonyms which can be assigned with some certainty. But the aspects of Cibber, Curll, Eliza, or Aristarchus presented are those which, however distinguishing for the individual, function chiefly to signalize some type. The use of actual names or readily identifiable pseudonyms heightens both the tension and, in the heroic context, the comic contrast. At the same time the reader's awareness that Aristarchus is not just Bentley but the everlasting type of the narrow-souled pedagogue gives universal validity to the particular.

The subject matter, the triumph of Dulness, produces a narrative line of special interest. Overtly, the movement from a partial prevalence of dulness to the closing line where universal darkness covers all, is comic. From the standpoint of the dull, this is a happy ending. Actually, the narrative movement is tragic. The overt comic movement and the latent tragic movement interplay to create a double line of suspense which does not reach its climax till the very last verse.

But this is only the suspense of the narrative line. The greatest interest of the poem does not lie in the resolution of the main narrative line, which is a foregone conclusion and in a sense present throughout the poem. The interest chiefly lies in the cleverness with which each episode or incident adapts the heroic model to the satirizing of a particular kind of dulness. The end—the triumph of Dulness—is important in the way that Aeneas' eventual founding of Rome is important; but the principal interest of the *Dunciad* as of the *Aeneid* is not the destination but the journey.

Much the same may be said of the suspense strategy in *Moral Essay* II, "Of the Characters of Women." The major interest is not in Pope's thesis, "Most women have no characters at all." Nor is it in the turn of the poem from negative examples to the one positive exception. It lies in the individual negative portraits, the "characters."

Not only in this *Essay*, but in the satires and epistles as a whole Pope's portraits often tremble on the verge of narrative. Some portraits—those of Sporus and Atticus in the *Epistle to Dr. Arbuthnot*, for instance—qualify as pure portraits, though their function in the poem is comparable to that of interpolated anecdotes. Other portraits—such as, in *Moral Essay* IV, those of Villario, Sabinus and his son, and the prodigal depicted in the opening lines—are closer to true narrative. The portrait of the prodigal, for example, hints, especially in the last lines, at something that might make a plot for a novel:

> 'Tis strange the Miser should his Cares employ
> To gain those Riches he can ne'er enjoy:
> Is it less strange the Prodigal should wast

His wealth, to purchase what he ne'er can taste?
Not for himself he sees, or hears, or eats;
Artists must choose his Pictures, Music, Meats:
He buys for Topham, Drawings and Designs;
For Pembroke Statues, dirty Gods, and Coins;
Rare monkish manuscripts for Hearne alone,
And Books for Mead, and Butterflies for Sloane.
Think we all these are for himself? no more
Than his fine Wife, alas! or finer Whore.

(1–12)

The triumph of the scarlet woman and her effect on beholders at the close of Dialogue I, *Epilogue to the Satires* has kinetic elements, even a conflict of a kind, if what goes on between Juggernaut and his victims may be called a conflict. These lines from the same Dialogue

Shall Ward draw Contracts with a Statesman's skill?
Or Japhet pocket, like His Grace, a Will?
Is it for Bond or Peter (paltry Things!)
To pay their Debts or keep their Faith like Kings?

(119–122)

are typical of the very brief glancing portraits, containing germs of stories, which are sown liberally throughout Pope's work.

The *Epistle to Dr. Arbuthnot* opens, literally, with a bang: good John is instructed to shut the door in the faces of a swarm of poetasters. Such an opening is effective because, as in most good stories, it plunges the reader *in medias res*. The order to take violent action comes first. The following tirade gradually reveals the source of conflict.

This tirade slips constantly into illustrative anecdotes which have in common the emotional mode which introduces them—a mode of high but consciously comic indignation. The effect is that, in contrast to the explicit and even abrupt way the tale of Balaam is introduced in *Moral Essay* III, these anecdotes seem to tumble out without forethought, one after another; and all reinforce the main thesis—that the speaker himself is a good poet and a moral man, whereas his opponents are bad poets with spotted souls and venal quills. The anecdote of the unsuccessful play-

wright, for instance, points the moral, confirms the character of
the speaker, and, in addition, amuses:

> Bless me! a Packet.—"'Tis a stranger sues,
> A Virgin Tragedy, an Orphan Muse."
> If I dislike it, "Furies, death and rage!"
> If I approve, "Commend it to the stage."
> There (thank my Stars) my whole Commission ends,
> The Play'rs and I are, luckily, no friends.
> Fir'd that the House reject him, "'Sdeath, I'll print it
> And shame the Fools—your Int'rest, Sir, with Lintot."
> Lintot, dull rogue! will think your price too much:
> "Not, Sir, if you revise it and retouch."
> All my demurrs but double his attacks,
> At last he whispers, "Do, and we go snacks."
> Glad of a quarrel, strait I clap the door,
> Sir, let me see your works and you no more.   (55–68)

Here too we find portraits that are semi-narrative, such as that
of Bufo, the fatuous patron who, after long dealing with flatter-
ing scribblers, experiences an epiphany. He waxes cunning in
his purse if not in his literary discriminations. The post-epiphany
Bufo,

> . . . grown more frugal in his riper days,
> . . . pay'd some Bards with Port, and some with Praise,
> To some a dry Rehearsal was assign'd,
> And others (harder still) he pay'd in kind.   (241–244)

As usual in the satires and epistles, this poem is full of brief story-
germs, such as the couplet,

> Poor Cornus sees his frantic Wife elope,
> And curses Wit, and Poetry, and Pope.   (25–26)

The most important story in the *Epistle to Dr. Arbuthnot*,
from the standpoint of strategy, is perhaps the least interesting
from the standpoint of entertainment. It is the autobiography of
the good man, the poem's speaker: "How good I have been—and
my parents too." However indispensable to the poem it is to
establish this, mere goodness is apt to make a dull tale. Like the
portrait of the Man of Ross in *Moral Essay* III, it risks pious
fatuity. Pope has several devices for minimizing this danger. One

of them is to interrupt the tale of virtue with the anecdote of prating Balbus, the portraits of the indiscreet patron and Sporus, an epigram, or a series of epigrams. The speaker's humility and patience, for instance, are commended not directly but indirectly in the satiric mode:

> So humble, he has knock'd at Tibbald's door,
> Has drunk with Cibber, nay has rym'd for Moore.
> Full ten years slander'd, did he once reply?
> Three thousand Suns went down on Welstead's Lye!
> To please a Mistress, One aspers'd his life;
> He lash'd him not, but let her be his Wife.   (372–377)

With this background, the reader is better prepared to accept both the brief portrait of the good father who "walk'd innoxious thro' his Age," knowing "No Language, but the Language of the Heart," and the sentimental but functional portrait of the good mother who "thought no Wife a Whore."

Pope's procedure in the *Epistle to Dr. Arbuthnot* (and in *Moral Essay* II as well) of reserving to the end his portraits of the good and his perorations on virtue is reversed in *Moral Essay* III—and with reason. *Moral Essay* III concludes with the tale of Balaam, one of Pope's choice short narratives. Would it have been better to close this poem with the positive portrait of how the Man of Ross sensibly, charitably, and piously disposed of his wealth rather than with the story of a man who, after getting his money dishonorably and misspending it, could only "curse God and die"?

Concerning a poem primarily didactic these questions may properly be asked: Which would leave the stronger impression? Which would be more likely to motivate right conduct? The example of the Man of Ross is unique in the poem. All the other examples illustrate the improper use of riches. All the others too, including the story of Balaam, are complexly presented; ironic double meanings are common. But the lines on the Man of Ross are straightforward eulogy.

For an answer to the question of Pope's placement of this story, one must first look closely at the story itself—the tale, condensed

into a fast-paced sixty-four lines, of how the Devil corrupted
Balaam and his entire family through ill-gotten and ill-used
riches. In the opening verses Pope states that Balaam was "a plain
good man" and that the Devil was piqued at beholding "such
saintship." Pope is, of course, being ironic. Balaam is by no means
a good man corrupted by wealth but a man who has been bad
from the beginning. If the fruits of his evil character are at first
small, it is only because they grow in a scant soil. His ruling passion is very early made clear:

> . . . his gains were sure,
> His givings rare, save farthings to the poor.
> (347–348)

No saint is described here; rather, a sinner lacking opportunity.

Opportunity comes. A storm caused by the Prince of the Air
not only kills Balaam's father (from whom he presumably in-
herits) but casts two richly laden ships against his Cornish lands.
With this extra capital Balaam is fairly started on his career. The
drowning of his father and the two shipwrecks which "bless the
lucky shore" are recounted, from Balaam's point of view, as
windfalls. Balaam voices no concern for his father's death or for
the souls probably lost on the ships. Besides, it was common
rumor in Pope's day that not all Cornish shipwrecks were owing
to the Devil and the deep blue sea, unaided by man's contrivances
ashore.

In the next propitious incident Balaam is shown unequivocally
at fault:

> Asleep and naked as an Indian lay,
> An honest factor stole a Gem away:
> He pledg'd it to the knight; the knight had wit,
> So kept the Diamond, and the rogue was bit.
> Some scruple rose, but this eas'd his thought,
> "I'll now give six-pence where I gave a groat,
> "Where once I went to church I'll now go twice—
> "And am so clear too of all other vice."
> (361–368)

The factor is as "honest" as Sir Balaam is "good" and "plain."

And certainly Sir Balaam is not a rogue!—he merely has "wit." Especially significant is the knight's method of compounding for his guilt: the payment of money and bodily presence in church. His financial atonement, however, is not even to be munificent; that would run counter to his ruling passion. Where formerly he gave a groat, Balaam will now bestow sixpence.

His "And am so clear too of all other vice" may be read in two ways: The affair of the stolen diamond is the only sin I have upon my conscience; or, by giving sixpence and attending church twice as often I can clear myself of any other sins I have committed or may in the future commit. Both meanings are consonant with Balaam's close, calculating character. Ironically, these calculations are not his salvation but his damnation.

After his "good old Lady" has "catch'd a cold" and died, a "Nymph of Quality" marries the widower. But it is hardly likely that she "admires our Knight," city-bred as he is; not him, but his "abundant show'r of Cent. per Cent." His money, Pope hints, buys him cuckoldism. His money buys his son a "gay Commission"; the son drinks, whores, and dies in a duel. Balaam's money can also be blamed for the fact that his daughter marries a nobleman who has a venereal disease. The climax comes swiftly:

> My Lady falls to play; so bad her chance,
> He must repair it; takes a bribe from France;
> The House impeach him; Coningsby harangues;
> The Court forsake him, and Sir Balaam hangs. (395–398)

And the dénouement does not linger:

> Wife, son, and daughter, Satan, are thy own,
> His wealth, yet dearer, forfeit to the Crown:
> The Devil and the King divide the prize,
> And sad Sir Balaam curses God and dies. (399–402)

Since there was a prize of wealth forfeit to the Crown, the implication is perhaps that taking the French bribe was not strictly a necessity. Perhaps Sir Balaam, grown ripe in corruption, could not resist another windfall, even though it bore the name of treason. His lady's bad luck at gambling may merely have afforded him a rationalization.

At the beginning of the narrative Pope stated that Balaam was being tempted

> . . . like good Job of old:
> But Satan now is wiser than of yore,
> And tempts by making rich, not making poor.
>
> (350–352)

In the concluding passage this ironical analogy with Job is completed. London-bred Balaam, who had no ass to speak and chide him on the way, has taken literally the advice of Job's wife: "Curse God and die." His ruling passion is with him to the end. Clearly, Sir Balaam is "sad" not so much at leaving life or at having misspent his life—he never perceives that—but at being divided by an unbridgeable gulf from his wealth.

The strategy of the poem made it necessary for Pope to illustrate also the utilization of wealth in a manner that would be acceptable to God and for the benefit of man. But leaving the portrait of the Man of Ross as the final impression would have changed the statement of the poem. If not logically, yet rhetorically it would have become "Though some people abuse wealth, this is what a good man does with it." As it actually stands the poem states "Most people, with a very rare exception such as the saintlike man of Ross, led by their various ruling passions, misuse riches in a variety of ways, sometimes even to their own damnation and that of their families, here and hereafter."

In spite, then, of the seemingly casual way the story of Sir Balaam is introduced—"But you are tir'd—I'll tell a tale. 'Agreed.' "—the effect is finely calculated. The fall of such a sinner as "great Villiers," expiring "in the worst inn's worst room," was meteoric, extraorbital, something to be wondered at. But Balaam, the "dull cit" whose soul was in his counting-house; who dealt sharply and sometimes more than sharply six days of the week, making feebler and feebler attempts to balance his accounts with God on Sundays; Sir Balaam, who bought his way into St. James' to the temporal and spiritual ruin of himself and his children—this was, as riches go, a common phenomenon. If all were not as conspicuously "successful" as Sir Balaam, there were many little Balaams who succeeded in proportion to their gains.

This concentrating of a widespread manner of misusing money, dire in its effects on both the individual and family life, into a tale about one familiar City figure—as familiar as his "chirping pint" and the life glimpsed in "lo! two puddings smok'd upon the board"—this is the true and not fortuitous climax of *Moral Essay* III.

The poem begins discursively, with Pope and Bathurst commenting familiarly in the mode of random after-dinner conversation on the proper use of riches. It progresses, not in one straight line of logical, sequent development, but by a series of incursions into the subject from different points. Gradually, as these incursions develop various angles of the topic, knowledge of it is deepened, interest quickened, and appreciation of its moral urgency intensified. The story of Sir Balaam draws all the points together in the pleasing and emphatic mode of fictional particular.

Moral Essay I uses a similar pattern, reserving its three brilliant *exempla* for the end. All three illustrate the persistence of the ruling passion—a "love to parts" which has in one way or another destroyed the individual—even in death. All three depict stock characters—the glutton, the vain woman of fashion, the miser—and with only the minimum necessary indication of time and setting. In all three it is on the management of dialogue that much of the effectiveness of the anecdotes depends.

The first arraigns the glutton:

> A salmon's belly, Helluo, was thy fate,
> The doctor call'd, declares all help too late.
> Mercy! cries Helluo, mercy on my soul!
> Is there no hope? Alas!—then bring the jowl.
> (234–237)

The story is not, of course, original with Pope. What his version aims at is obviously, to paraphrase, "what oft was told but ne'er so well." The first verse, in the mock-heroic mode, presents Helluo as a kind of epic hero making his exit on the windy plains of Troy. At the same time, he is clearly a bathetic Jonah-in-reverse, the epic whale shrunk to a salmon. The death of a human being as the direct result of deliberate persistence in a mortal sin is not ordinarily funny. But the tone of the opening line alerts the reader to expect a comic element in this particular case. The second verse moves the action along and sets the stage for the climax. Then Helluo speaks—and we know from Pope's comments in the Preface to the *Iliad* how keenly he appreciated Homer's use of dialogue for characterization. These two lines of dialogue stigmatize Helluo as the glutton to outdo all gluttons.

"Mercy! mercy on my soul!" he cries. This is a conventional deathbed exclamation. But for a man whose consuming interest has been in supplying, not his spiritual part, but his belly, the plea carries at once special pathos and special irony. "Is there no hope? Alas!" seems to be moving toward a serious climax. "Then bring the jowl" not only has the happiness of a surprise ending— we might have expected "Then bring the priest"—but it closes the anecdote firmly, in spite of tragic overtones, in the comic mode.

Pope's anecdote of the female materialist who in the pride of her flesh objected to being buried in a woolen shroud, as English law required, is, with the exception of one explicatory line, entirely dialogue:

> "Odious! in woolen! 'twould a Saint provoke,
> (Were the last words that poor Narcissa spoke)
> No, let a charming Chintz, and Brussels lace
> Wrap my cold limbs, and shade my lifeless face:
> One would not, sure, be frightful when one's dead—
> And—Betty—give this Cheek a little Red." (242–247)

The adjectives "odious" and "frightful" are, in the context, slang; they are the feminine equivalent of Sir Plume's slang in *The Rape of the Lock*. Like most slang, Narcissa's is overemphatic. Pope uses this overemphasis to indicate Narcissa's feminine lack of perspective. "Frightful" has, besides, a telling double meaning. Narcissa's conventional, religion-based expression, "'twould a Saint provoke," illuminates, like Helluo's, a spiritual defect. She is clearly no saint. Dying saints are portrayed as concerned with very different matters from charming chintzes and rouge.

Still, Narcissa's speech reveals that she is not so unequivocally a sinner as Helluo. The lack of proportion in her outlook she could not altogether have escaped, short of becoming psychologically unsexed. Her misuse of "odious" and "frightful," reflecting as it does her participation in a perennial female attitude, is not her invention. She is merely using contemporary slang. Narcissa, however, is an extreme case of personal vanity, and Pope makes his moral plain enough. As was his habit, though, when dealing with feminine offenders, he qualifies his rebuke. Narcissa's foibles, like Belinda's, are viewed with a certain indulgence.

Pope has been accused of an uncavalier attitude toward women; but he often, as here, manifests a sympathetic understanding of the special difficulties of their role. He realizes that if women wish to achieve self-fulfillment in ways sanctioned by society, they are constrained to pay disproportionate attention to appearances in general and to personal appearance in particular—"Pow'r all their end, but Beauty all the means." If they go to excess, like Narcissa, it is an excess of "virtue" in a feminine sense. It is an excess fostered by society's attitude toward women and the resultant emphases in the training of women. By the tone of this anecdote Pope hints that the fair scholars in the school of appearances are at least not as culpable as the forgers and swindlers he really excoriates.

In both the preceding *exempla* Pope has used dialogue as the vehicle of suspense. In the story of old Euclio on his deathbed this is his main reliance:

> "I give and I devise, (old Euclio said,
> And sigh'd) "My lands and tenements to Ned."
> Your money, Sir; "My money, Sir, what all?
> Why,—if I must—(then wept) I give it Paul."
> The Manor, Sir?—"The Manor! hold," he cry'd,
> "Not that,—I cannot part with that"—and dy'd.
> (256–261)

The dialogue builds steadily toward a climax capped by the speaker's death. Questions and answers are felicitously devised to demonstrate Euclio's obsession with his properties and at the same time to move the story toward its climax, which is essentially the same climax, at once comic and tragic, as in the other two.

It was not by accident that Pope gave two of his satires the title "Dialogue." Others, called "epistles," have a dialogue element, since the speaker imagines the comments or questions of the person addressed and replies to them. As in any fictional construct, this imparts immediacy and suspense. In addition, Pope uses the colloquial situation to help set the easy, conversational tone which is his preference in satire. Even the *Essay on Man* would lose not a little if it were presented simply as an impersonal treatise instead of as an epistle addressed to "my St. John." St. John expands, of course, to man in general. "Know then thyself" is not addressed to Bolingbroke alone. Still, particularization does its work. The warmth, the easy friendliness, the perennial interest of the personal, are there.

In all Pope's narratives, and in every element of his narratives, one emphasis is constant. It is a thematic emphasis in which Good Sense is always the hero and its opposite the villain. Good Sense always has the last word and generally speaks it with his tongue in his cheek. Whether foolish women are fighting a foolish war with foolish men in *The Rape of the Lock*, or massed fools are moving with fatal cocksureness against the citadels of Sense in the *Dunciad*, or Helluo calls for the jowl that will write *finis* to himself and his gluttony—Good Sense, somewhat like Umbriel perched on the sconce's height, sits above the fray, observing it and drawing conclusions of use to all men. For it is the property of Good Sense, which implies poise and self-possession, to be at the same time a fighter and an integrated observer of the war.

Pope can thus in his narratives be at once passionate and detached, general yet particular. The stance seems ideally suited to his purpose, the besetting Augustan purpose—*Utile dulci*.

10

Genre

O<small>F ALL</small> the traditional factors which shaped Pope's career as
a poet, probably none was more powerful than the neoclassical
concept of genre. One of the most illuminating aspects of his
poetic practice is the way he adapts his style to various genres
and yet contrives to remain recognizably Pope.

Pope's attitude toward genre was of a piece with his attitude
toward the Rules. Conformity of subject matter and style to
genre requirements was, in fact, one of the Rules. Hence, the
maintenance of stylistic decorum in a genre is a part of Pope's
concept of "Nature methodised"; and by his adherence to decorum he succeeded in rooting his conception soundly in both the
historical and the metaphysical approaches to genre.

Pope tells us in the *Essay on Criticism* that an inspired poet,
confident of his powers, may on occasion stretch any Rule and,
by implication, any genre to achieve his poetic purpose. Yet
Pope's own performance—not to mention the hedging manner in
which he conveys the precept—makes clear that he was governed
in this, as in most other matters, by the doctrine of the *via media*.
He was not disposed to imitate his predecessors in a poetic kind
with tame slavishness. Neither was he about to let his invention
run wild, ignoring both precedent and natural fitness.

Pope began his official career as decorum for that "genre" of
human being, the poet, demanded: He published a set of pastorals.
A poet as audience-conscious as Pope was all his life could hardly
have failed to be aware that his classically educated readers would

appreciate the traditionalism and modest propriety of this beginning.

The "Discourse on Pastoral Poetry" which he later placed at
the head of his pastorals merits careful attention in this respect.
It reveals the scrupulousness of his preparation for writing in this
genre and his unremitting awareness of genre decorums.

An Augustan reader expected that a serious poet before trying
a new "kind" would thoroughly familiarize himself with its tradition. The poet would read and meditate on the most notable
poems in the genre. He would become conversant with the best
criticism on these poems and with the theory of the genre. Finally, when he came to select his own subject and determine his own
particular variant of approach and tone, he would do so with one
eye fixed on the historical decorum and the other on the metaphysical decorum of the kind. How thoroughly Pope prepared
to meet such expectations is clear from his close analysis of pastoral, part of which is as follows:

A Pastoral is an imitation of the action of a shepherd or one
considered under that character. The form of this imitation is
dramatic, or narrative, or mixed of both: the fable simple, the
manners not too polite nor too rustic: the thoughts are plain, yet
admit a little quickness or passion but that short and flowing: the
expression humble, yet as pure as the language will afford; neat,
but not florid; easy, and yet lively. In short, the fable, manners,
thoughts, and expressions are full of the greatest simplicity in
nature. . . . Pastoral is the image of what they call the golden
age: so that we are not to describe our shepherds as shepherds
at this day really are, but as they may be conceived then to have
been when the best of men followed that employment. . . .

We must therefore use some illusion to render a pastoral delightful; and this consists in exposing the best side only of a
shepherd's life, and in concealing its miseries. Nor is it enough to
introduce shepherds discoursing together in a natural way; but
a regard must be had to the subject; that it contain some particular beauty in itself, and that it be different in every eclogue.
Besides, a designed scene or prospect is to be presented to our
view, which should likewise have its variety. This variety is obtained, in a great degree, by frequent comparisons, drawn from
the most agreeable objects of the country; by interrogations to

things inanimate; by beautiful digressions, but those short; sometimes by insisting a little on circumstances; and lastly, by elegant turns on the words, which render the numbers extremely sweet and pleasing. As for the numbers themselves, though they are properly of the heroic measure, they should be the smoothest, the most easy and flowing imaginable.

Characteristically, Pope the moralist then reminds us that pastoral must in addition "by giving us an esteem for the virtues of a former age . . . recommend them to the present." Toward the conclusion of this "Discourse," after considering the merits and shortcomings of some noted predecessors, he points out the ways in which he has altered Spenser's treatment of the seasonal motif:

. . . the several times of the day are observed, the rural employments in each season or time of day, and the rural scenes or places proper to such employments, not without some regard to the several ages of man, and the different passions proper to each age.

Incidentally, Pope's alterations are designed, typically for him, to pack much meaning into a small compass, to make a single device serve more than one purpose.

Not only for the *Pastorals*, but for all the other principal genres Pope wrote in, we have his pronouncements in prose or verse, and sometimes in both, on what he conceived to be the nature and requirements of those genres. No one after reading his preface to the *Iliad* can have any doubt about Pope's grasp of the decorum of the epic, for instance—not to mention the example immediately following. The "Recipe to Make an Epic Poem" in the *Peri Bathous* has been acknowledged a good recipe for a mock epic. And Pope gave frequent voice to his theory of satire; the *Epistle to Dr. Arbuthnot* is, of course, the *locus classicus*.

For Pope, however, critical theory was only a beginning. The significant question is, How did his painstaking preliminary studies and his evident desire not to violate the basic decorums of a genre influence his practice? How do Pope's *idées maîtresses* change in presentation from genre to genre? How does his style reflect genre demands and yet remain throughout all genres definitely his own?

If we consider one of the most pervasive ideas in Pope's verse—the *via media*—how, specifically, does its presentation alter with genre?

To begin, as Pope did, with the *Pastorals*, the concept of moderation is first of all implicit in the genre, which forbids extremes of any kind. Passion, for example, must be muted or tranquilized. In *Spring* Daphnis and Strephon contest musically about the merits of their respective mistresses; they do not fight to the death. Alexis in *Summer* "pines in hopeless love"; but how moderately and how musically he pines! Even in *Autumn* when Aegon threatens that "one leap from yonder cliff" will end his pains, is his threat to be taken seriously? He *sings* it in company with another singing shepherd. The poem closes, not with Aegon's plunging off the cliff and his remains being collected by his horrified companion, but with a quiet description of a sunset and the ending of the shepherds' songs. *Winter* is a lament for a dead shepherdess. But how quickly the lament, always decorous, measured even in its hyperbole, turns to the consolation: "Daphne, our Goddess, and our Grief no more!"

In contrast, the heroic epistle has no such restraints on the depiction of emotion. A prime purpose of *Eloisa to Abelard* is to convey a picture of emotions at their highest pitch. Yet Eloisa, even while she raves, is aware that her unconquered passion for Abelard is off-center. By rebuking herself she keeps present in the poem a consciousness of the golden mean in conduct which she, to her agony, cannot attain. It is worth noting how simply, in accordance with genre expectations, the unrequited love of Alexis and the betrayed love of Aegon are presented, in comparison with the complex and subtly reasoned analysis Eloisa makes of her passion.

The *Essay on Criticism* is permeated with advice on applying the *via media* to writing in particular and to general conduct as well. In contrast to the exclusion of extremes and the tranquilizing *tableaux vivants* of the *Pastorals*, moderation is recommended in the *Essay* chiefly by direct precept followed by examples.

After his celebrated admonition to "Avoid Extremes," Pope gives, among other examples, the following:

Some foreign writers, some our own despise;
The Ancients only, or the Moderns prize.
Thus Wit, like Faith, by each man is applied
To one small sect, and all are damned beside.   (II, 394–397)

The examples, far from precious, are apt to be plain, dry, down-to-earth, or even sordid. There is no attempt, as in the *Pastorals*, to commend the *via media* by exclusion of the vulgar and unpleasant. In this *Essay* Pope deliberately uses unsavory matters to make his points.

The prevailing level of style too is medium—neither a high nor a low but a middle flight. The diction and tone are for the most part those of ordinary conversation. A short narrative, that of La Mancha's Knight, is used to enforce the precept of "nothing too much"—in this case too great a fondness for tourneys. Pope's favorite device, the set portrait, is used to instruct the critic in the specific ways he should observe the golden mean (III, 631–642). But in keeping with the conversational decorum of this type of didactic poem, Pope is careful to introduce this set portrait in an easy, casual way with the question "But where's the man, who counsel can bestow . . ."

The *via media* is commended in many of the same ways in the *Essay on Man*; and this is to be expected since they are both didactic poems. Still, there are signal differences. Some of these emerge if the portrait of the ideal critic is compared with the celebrated portrait of generic man at the beginning of Epistle II. When Pope describes man as

Sole judge of Truth, in endless Error hurl'd:
The glory, jest, and riddle of the world,   (II, 17–18)

it is immediately apparent that the stylistic level is different from that of the passage from the *Essay on Criticism* just cited. This stylistic difference reflects the fact that, however desirable good literary critics may be in society, good men—that is, men who know themselves—are even more important. A good critic is a desideratum, but man himself is a mystery. And man's middle nature is not the sort of mystery a human being can sit down and fold his hands about. Man has to live with the mystery of himself. Hence the urgency, hence the sublimity, hence the satire of Pope's portrait of generic man. The *Essay on Man* is didactic, but its didacticism is not that which advises turnip-planting in the dark of the moon or moderation in judging literature. It is more like the didacticism of a Lucretius speaking of first and last things.

In what way does *The Rape of the Lock* counsel the golden mean? Pope says he added Clarissa's speech "to open more clearly the Moral of the Poem." Belinda, whose conduct Clarissa reproves, has throughout the poem shown herself excessively concerned with appearance. She has even implied that she would prefer the loss of her chastity to the loss of her conspicuous lock. Clarissa tries—ostensibly only, for it was she who lent the Baron the fatal shears—to give Belinda a truer sense of values by ringing changes on the theme, "Charms strike the Sight, but Merit wins the Soul."

In keeping with the basic strategy of the poem, however, this advice is undercut in two ways. First, Clarissa's treachery has made her motives suspect. Second, in the fashionable feminine world, as we have stressed before, appearance sometimes really is more significant than actuality. The result is the paradox that Belinda is, and yet is not, a wanderer from the *via media*. This is the technique we would expect from a variant of mock-heroic that consistently cuts both ways.

In *Moral Essay* II Pope, again dealing with the feminine world in a genre which permits mockery, again undercuts his recommendation of the golden mean. But the undercutting in this instance is not bound up with an organizing narrative or with the deliberate inversions of mock-heroic. It is done with a mixture of portraits and general observations, the portraits predominating. All the portraits except the concluding one exhibit various forms of reprehensible or silly feminine conduct; they are of women who have gone to extremes in allowing secondary attributes of their sex, such as the decorativeness or the love of pleasure, to dominate their lives. Pope comments on the results of these vagaries:

> Yet, mark the fate of a whole Sex of Queens!
> Pow'r all their end, but Beauty all the means.
> In Youth they conquer with so wild a rage,
> As leaves them scarce a Subject in their Age:
> . . . .
> See how the World its Veterans rewards!
> A Youth of frolicks, an old Age of Cards,
> Fair to no purpose, artful to no end,
> Young without Lovers, old without a Friend.   (219–246)

Then comes the portrait of the ideal woman (lines 257–268). Without sacrificing feminine charm and the self-effacing, submissive qualities considered appropriate to her sex, she nevertheless shows sense, good humor, and a sturdy moral character. It is a special and somewhat paradoxical *via media* that Pope advocates for women. As desirable as he represents it to be, he presents it with a humor especially germane to the subject and to the bantering approach of this epistle.

The fundamental method by which satire encourages the *via media* is the castigation of deviations. Pope's chief means of castigation are portrait, precept, and brief narratives. Balancing the negative portraits and narrative examples are positive ones either commending others or establishing the good faith and moral competency of the satirist.

In almost every satire Pope uses a mixture of these means. In Satire II of Horace's Second Book, for example, he first employs plain precept:

> 'Tis yet in vain, I own, to keep a pother
> About one Vice, and fall into the other:
> Between Excess and Famine lies a mean,
> Plain, but not sordid, tho' not splendid, clean.   (45–48)

He follows this with the portrait of Avidien and his wife, who are too miserly to nourish themselves appropriately. This rhetorical process is then repeated in curtailed form by a couplet precept succeeded by glancing couplet portraits depicting the two extremes:

> He knows to live, who keeps the middle state,
> And neither leans on this side, nor on that:
> Nor stops, for one bad Cork, his Butler's pay,
> Swears, like Albutius, a good Cook away;
> Nor lets, like Naevius, ev'ry error pass,
> The musty wine, foul cloth, or greasy glass.
>
> (61–66)

The negative picture having been drawn, Pope follows it with the positive side, again utilizing both precept and example, in the passage beginning "Now hear what blessings Temperance can bring." Towards the close of the epistle two additional positive portraits are added—that of Bethel, to whom the epistle is addressed, and the speaker's self-portrait, in the following lines:

> Content with little, I can piddle here
> On Brocoli and mutton, round the year;
> But ancient friends, (tho' poor, or out of play)
> That touch my Bell, I cannot turn away.
> 'Tis true, no Turbots dignify my boards,
> But gudgeons, flounders, what my Thames affords.
> To Hounslow-heath I point, and Bansted-down,
> Thence comes your mutton, and these chicks my own:
> From yon old wallnut-tree a show'r shall fall;
> And grapes, long lingring on my only wall,
> And figs, from standard and Espalier join:
> The dev'l is in you if you cannot dine.
> Then chearful healths (your Mistress shall have place)
> And, what's more rare, a Poet shall say Grace. (137–150)

The Sixth Epistle of Horace's First Book is professedly devoted to hammering in the maxim "Nil admirari." Its advice to follow the *via media* is based first on religio-philosophic grounds:

> This Vault of Air, this congregated Ball,
> Self-centered Sun, and Stars that rise and fall,
> There are, my Friend! whose philosophic eyes
> Look thro', and trust the Ruler with his Skies. (5–8)

This technique of an inflated style immediately utilized to make a satiric point in humbler lines, is used frequently throughout the poem. It discourages excess in the heaping up of wealth, for instance:

Advance thy golden Mountain to the skies;
On the broad base of fifty thousand rise.

(73–74)

Again, the plain didactic style is used—this time contrasted with
a more complex utterance involving paradox:

Whether we dread, or whether we desire,
In either case, believe me, we admire;
Whether we joy or grieve, the same the curse,
Surpriz'd at better, or surpriz'd at worse.
Thus good, or bad, to one extreme betray
Th' unbalanc'd Mind, and snatch the Man away;
For Vertue's self may too much Zeal be had;
The worst of Madmen is a Saint run mad.   (20–27)

A similar use of contrast occurs in the lines below from the same
poem. General reference is followed and pointed by specific, personal reference. Exotic geographical and mythological references
are juxtaposed with contemporary topical references:

Or shall we ev'ry Decency confound,
Thro' Taverns, Stews, and Bagnios take our round,
Go dine with Chartres, in each Vice outdo
K—l's lewd Cargo, or Ty—y's Crew,
From Latian Syrens, French Circaean Feasts,
Return well travell'd, and transform'd to Beasts.   (118–123)

This consistent utilitarian alternation of styles and reference
areas in itself silently suggests a kind of *via media* obtained by inclusion of opposites—a stylistic balancing of the scales. Only a
genre permitting down-to-earth references, such as satire, lends
itself to this rhetorical process of a streak of fat and a streak of
lean.

The same technique is a stylistic mainstay in *The Rape of the
Lock* and the *Dunciad*. But the narrative and the consistent angle
of narration requisite in mock-heroic tend to produce a blending
of the streaks rather than methodical alternation. Mock-heroic,
in fact, demands that both contrasting elements be present at
once—either low matter in a high style or high matter in a low
style.

In Book I of the *Dunciad*, for example, Pope describes his starveling writer sacrificing to Dulness as if he were an epic hero sacrificing to an Olympic god:

> . . . twelve volumes, twelve of amplest size,
> Redeem'd from tapers and defrauded pies,
> Inspir'd he seizes: These an altar raise:
> A hecatomb of pure, unsully'd lays
> That altar crowns: A folio Common-place
> Founds the whole pile, of all his works the base:
> Quartos, octavos shape the less'ning pyre;
> A twisted Birth-day Ode completes the spire.
>
> (I, 155–162)

A good writer might well lay the fruit of his labors before deity and ask for divine guidance. For a literary dunce—and more, a plagiarist—to do this is a deviation from good sense, a kind of *hubris* sure to call down Olympian, and Popian, thunders. The same is true of Belinda's treating her lock, her toilet, and her chastity as sacred. Pope's presentation of Belinda's *hubris*, however, is two-edged. Her toilet, her lock, and certainly her chastity are, as we have observed, in a sense really sacred.

The epic proper paradoxically presents the *via media* by first of all not presenting it. Subject matter, narrative, characters, and language constantly remind the reader that the actions portrayed are those of gods and heroes, not those of common men. This is not to say that the epic overtly discourages heroic virtues. Hector's might and manliness, Agamemnon's kingliness, Ajax's force, Ulysses' subtlety, Nestor's experienced wisdom, Achilles' strength and swiftness—all these the *Iliad* tacitly recommends for imitation. At the same time, the special distinction of these chiefs and the wide gap between them and ordinary mortals is stressed continually. The deduction is that for an ordinary man, without Ajax's ponderous strength, to attempt singlehanded combat with Hector is to invite disaster. Epic, like pastoral, is a special realm, an imitable realm perhaps, but one inhabited by fire-eating heroes and "asbestos" gods, a realm where ordinary mortals get their throats scorched.

What Pope accomplished for Homer in this respect was to provide in English the equivalent of the distancing obtained in

Homer's Greek. The English of Pope's *Iliad* is, of course, no more the English of the slum denizens Hogarth drew than the language of *Paradise Lost* is the language John Bunyan heard in Bedford jail. To achieve his special purpose in the epic, Pope could not use the language of the coffee house or of a fashionable lady's boudoir. Within limits he could, and did, vary the level of his style, but the style at no time descends to the colloquial and vulgar.

In this connection, a particularly fortunate comparison is possible between Pope's straight rendition of Sarpedon's speech to Glaucus in Book XII of the *Iliad* and his imitation of this in Clarissa's admonitions to Belinda. Sarpedon says,

> Why boast we, Glaucus! our extended reign,
> Where Xanthus' streams enrich the Lycian plain,
> Our numerous herds that range the fruitful field,
> And hills where vines their purple harvest yield,
> Our foaming bowls with purer nectar crown'd,
> Our feasts enhanc'd with music's sprightly sound?
> Why on these shores are we with joy survey'd,
> Admired as heroes, and as Gods obey'd
> Unless great acts superior merit prove,
> And vindicate the bounteous Powers above?
> 'Tis ours, the dignity they give to grace;
> The first in valour, as the first in place:
> That when, with wond'ring eyes, our martial bands
> Behold our deeds transcending our commands,
> Such, they may cry, deserve the sov'reign state,
> Whom those that envy dare not imitate!
> Could all our care elude the gloomy grave,
> Which claims no less the fearful than the brave,
> For lust of fame I should not vainly dare
> In fighting fields, nor urge thy soul to war.
> But since, alas! ignoble age must come,
> Disease, and death's inexorable doom;
> The life which others pay, let us bestow,
> And give to Fame what we to Nature owe;
> Brave tho' we fall, and honour'd if we live,
> Or let us glory gain, or glory give!   (XII, 371–396)

Clarissa begins,

Say, why are Beauties prais'd and honour'd most,
The wise Man's Passion, and the vain Man's Toast?
Why deck'd with all that Land and Sea afford,
Why Angels call'd, and Angel-like ador'd?
Why round our Coaches crowd the white-glov'd Beaus,
Why bows the Side-box from its inmost Rows?
How vain are all these Glories, all our Pains,
Unless good Sense preserve what Beauty gains:
That Men may say, when we the Front-box grace,
Behold the first in Virtue, as in Face!   (V, 9–18)*

The basic contrast is, of course, between masculine and feminine viewpoints. But a further distinction must be made. Sarpedon is discussing the highest matters with which men are concerned: the brevity of human life, the relationships of deity to man and of man to deity, individual material and moral differences, the calamities or riddles of war and disease, the felt necessity of morally significant action. All these matters affect women too, but they are not her special realm. Woman's special realm may certainly be presented in epic—the wifehood and motherhood of Andromache, for instance. And in a sense this straight version of woman's special role is present in Clarissa's speech; but how conditioned it is by the presentation! Clarissa is only seemingly concerned with the impeccable moral that feminine charms strike the sight but merit, in the case of wives and mothers, wins the soul. One of her actual motives in the narrative is to criticize by implication Belinda's lack of good humor about the theft of her lock. Clarissa's concern is primarily with the secondary, the more frivolous, aspects of the feminine role, with the realm of make-up, curls, and gray hair. The true *via media* for a woman is not to neglect either but still to see primary things as primary and secondary things as secondary. The *via media* for a hero is not to assume the rashness in battle advisable only for an immortal, nor yet through excessive fear of death to lose the glory possible to a brave but sensible man. Epic being epic, however, if the hero errs, it must be on the side of contempt of death.

Sarpedon's speech makes a serious use of religion. He implies

* For lines 19–34 of this speech see pp. 126–27.

that kings are kings by the grace of God and have a duty to fill their places to the glory of God. Clarissa makes no actual use of religious sentiment, though she uses several terms with religious associations—angel, grace, saint, soul, glories, sin. But who are her angels? Belles. What is their cardinal sin? Using make-up.

Sarpedon is seriously concerned with "Disease and death's inexorable doom." Clarissa mentions a single disease, smallpox, which was serious enough in her century but especially dreaded by fashionable ladies because it often marred beauty of face. As for old age and death, Clarissa merely wants in a somewhat ostrich-like fashion to chase the one away and not to go to the other still a spinster. The imitation of Sarpedon's specific locutions—sometimes even including their alliteration and rime—points up these differences in outlook. The same thing is true of the diction. Sarpedon does not use slang expressions or colloquialisms, which represent our *via media* in daily speech. His consistently elevated diction, of course, suggests by exclusion the difference between heroic diction and the language of ordinary life.

Yet, a typically Popian complex of rhetorical usages is present in both selections: parallelism, antithesis, paradox, chiasmus, epigrammatism, and the readily detachable yet linked couplet. The difference lies in the use to which these devices are put. In the one passage they are all placed at the service of Sarpedon's exhortation to bravery on the field of battle. In the other they point up the differences between what is really significant for women and what seems to be significant in the fashionable world: "Behold the first in Virtue, as in Face!" The double meaning of "Face" here is noteworthy; it refers to both physical countenance and social poise, and has an overtone which suggests that the appearance is different from the reality.

The presence or absence of double meanings and the way, when present, they are used often points up differences in genres. For example, in this speech of Sarpedon's and throughout the *Iliad* double meanings are rare. When they occur they are apt to be, not humorous or satiric but serious in a non-oblique way, as in Jove's use of "trembling":

Ye strive in vain! if I but stretch this hand,
I heave the Gods, the Ocean, and the Land;
I fix the chain to great Olympus' height,
And the vast world hangs trembling in my sight!
(VIII, 29–32)

The pastoral poems too, as might be expected from the fact that the genre, like epic, is removed from the complexities and contradictions of daily life, make infrequent use of terms with double meanings. The simplicity demanded by pastoral is an additional reason for their scarcity. Where they occur, they often animate natural objects, raising them in the scale of life, sometimes to the human level, as, for example, "blushing" in "The dawn now blushing on the mountain's side" (*Spring*, 21), or "breathe" and "murmur" in

The birds shall cease to tune their evening song,
The winds to breathe, the waving woods to move,
And streams to murmur, e'er I cease to love.
(*Autumn*, 40–42)

But these double meanings associated with personification are conventional and unobtrusive. An especially interesting and somewhat different pastoral double meaning is the use of "betray" in these lines from *Windsor Forest*:

Before his lord the ready spaniel bounds,
Panting with hope, he tries the furrowed grounds;
But when the tainted gales the game *betray*,
Couched close he lies, and meditates the prey.
(99–102)

The scent borne by the winds reveals the presence of game to the hunter. At the same time, the treacherous winds *betray* the animals. This particular double meaning helps to convey one of the principal insights of this poem—that there is a case to be made for both the hunter and the hunted. The reader is made to enter imaginatively into the sentiments of both.

Windsor Forest also contains an especially interesting use of a conventional series of double meanings promoting the *rapprochement* of volitional and and nonvolitional beings on the Great

Scale. Here they explain with particular felicity the metamorphosis of the violated virgin Lodona into a stream:

> . . . *melting* as in tears she lay,
> In a soft, silver stream *dissolved* away.
> The silver stream her virgin *coldness* keeps,
> For ever *murmurs*, and for ever *weeps*.* (203–206)

A touch of humor, rare in the double meaning found in the pastorals, occurs in this poem's descriptions of the river Mole behaving like the animal of that name: for example in, "sullen Mole, that hides his diving flood." Milton, of course, had made the same joke in *At a Vacation Exercise in the College*; he refers to "sullen Mole that runneth underneath."

Words are always used with double meaning in an extended metaphor. Extended metaphors are infrequent in pastorals, but the *Messiah* contains one utilizing a floral analogy especially appropriate for pastoral:

> From Jesse's *root* behold a *branch* arise,
> Whose sacred *flower* with fragrance fills the skies.
> (9–10)

Finally the pastorals contain an occasional unemphatic double meaning derived from etymology, as this in *Summer*:

> That flute is mine which Colin's tuneful breath
> *Inspired* when living . . . (39–40)

or these in *Windsor Forest*:

> Bids his free soul *expatiate* in the skies,
> Amid her kindred stars *familiar* roam . . . (254–255)

An especially beautiful pastoral double meaning which fits into no classification but is felicitous for the genre is this use in *Spring* of "whitening." The vale is pictured as being whitened at the same time by the rising sun and the sheep:

> Soon as the flocks shook off the nightly dews,
> Two Swains, whom Love kept wakeful, and the Muse,
> Poured o'er the *whitening* vale their fleecy care.
> (17–19)

---

* Italics in this and the succeeding quotations from the *Pastorals* are mine.

Double meanings are more salient in the didactic epistles. Most of the outstanding double meanings in the *Essay on Criticism* are in their immediate effect ironic and in their cumulative effect enlightening about the principal concerns of the poem. Of these, undoubtedly the most celebrated is the multiple play on the word "wit." A few examples of this follow:

> In search of wit these lose their common sense.
>
> (I,28)

> Some, to whom Heaven in wit has been profuse,
> Want as much more, to turn it to its use;
> For wit and judgment often are at strife,
> Though meant each other's aid, like man and wife.
>
> (I, 80–83)

> If Faith itself has diff'rent dresses worn,
> What wonder modes in Wit should take their turn?
> Oft, leaving what is natural and fit,
> The current folly proves the ready Wit.   (II, 446–449)

> Jilts ruled the state, and statesmen farces writ;
> Nay wits had pensions, and young Lords had wit.
>
> (II, 538–539)

"Nature" runs a close second, of course, to "wit." Indeed, the chief point the *Essay* makes is that true wit and nature are one. Such terms with multiple meanings as Pope uses in the pastoral poems are mainly designed to please without interrupting the surface limpidity and simplicity of pastoral. In a didactic poem like the *Essay on Criticism* the chief function of the *doubles entendres* is to teach. The better to accomplish this, they are often used in such a way as to call attention to themselves. In the example below, for instance, rhyme is the attention-getting device. This is true both of the double meanings bound up with the central theme and those used incidentally in illustration of it, as is "sleep" in these lines:

> If crystal streams "with pleasing murmurs creep,"
> The reader's threatened (not in vain) with "sleep"
>
> (II, 352–353)

And "following" in these:

Then Criticism the Muses' handmaid proved,
To dress her charms, and make her more beloved:
But following Wits from that intention strayed,
Who could not win the mistress, wooed the maid.

(I, 102–105)

The *Essay on Man* continues the multiple use of Wit and Nature and adds to these such key words as "reason," "passion," "happiness," and "self-love." Pope's purpose is to teach a special interpretation of these terms, different from the popular interpretation. The whole of Epistle IV, for example, turns largely on the double meaning of "happiness"—happiness as it is popularly conceived contrasted with happiness as Pope wishes the reader to see it. His strategy in the opening lines is at first to seem to use the term in its popular acceptation, then gradually to question this concept and to begin, riddlingly, to supplant it with his own:

Oh HAPPINESS! our being's end and aim!
Good, Pleasure, Ease, Content! whate'er thy name:
That something still which prompts th' eternal sigh,
For which we bear to live, or dare to die,
Which still so near us, yet beyond us lies,
O'erlook'd, seen double, by the fool, and wise.
Plant of celestial seed! if dropt below,
Say, in what mortal soil thou deign'st to grow?
Fair op'ning to some Court's propitious shine,
Or deep with di'monds in the flaming mine?
Twin'd with the wreaths Parnassian laurels yield,
Or reap'd in iron harvests of the field?
Where grows?—where grows it not?—If vain our toil,
We ought to blame the culture, not the soil:
Fix'd to no spot is Happiness sincere,
'Tis no where to be found, or ev'ry where.   (IV, 1–16)

There is a second type of double meaning in the *Essay on Man*, a type more incidentally used than such a key word as "happiness." This usage may, in fact, be compared with Milton's occasional puns in *Paradise Lost*. In the following couplet "diff'rence" is such a pun, employed with the effect of paradox. With characteristic economy Pope has tied in the pun on "diff'rence" with the double meaning of "happiness":

But mutual wants this Happiness increase,
All Nature's diff'rence keeps all Nature's peace.

(IV, 55-56)

The same is true of "common" in

Heav'n breathes thro' ev'ry member of the whole
One common blessing, as one common soul.   (IV, 61-62)

Some of the incidental double meanings in satiric passages of
the *Essay on Man* are used in a way that becomes a mainstay of
the satiric epistles proper, for instance, "ribbands" and "yellow
dirt" in these lines:

To sigh for ribbands if thou art so silly,
Mark how they grace Lord Umbra, or Sir Billy:
Is yellow dirt the passion of thy life?
Look but on Gripus, or on Gripus' wife.   (IV, 277-280)

A particularly striking double meaning, neither a key word
nor yet incidental, is the pun on "standing" in the following
couplet:

Great standing miracle! that Heav'n assign'd
Its only thinking thing this turn of mind.

(III, 77-78)

The reference is both abstract and concrete. That man himself
is a miracle standing upright on two legs, a mystery, is one of
the central emphases of the poem. The mystery is, of course, also
"standing" in the sense of established, enduring, always present.

As the satiric element in a genre increases, so, quite properly,
do Pope's double meanings. The satiric epistles are thickly studded
with them. The lines at the beginning of *Moral Essay IV* (5-12)
depicting the Prodigal turn entirely upon a double meaning and
contain other double meanings incidentally. When Pope says the
wealthy man without taste does not see, hear, or eat for himself,
he is using "sees," "hears," and "eats" in a double sense. By doing
so he creates a paradox comparable to the Biblical allusions to
those who have eyes and see not and those who have ears and
hear not. Interestingly enough, the central double meaning in this
passage turns upon the preposition "for." The wealthy Prodigal

sees "for" Topham and the other connoisseurs mentioned. He buys "dirty"—a pun in itself— gods "for" Pembroke. He even keeps a "fine Wife" and "finer Whore" (note the incidental pun on "fine") "for" other men. The serious moral issue involved in this points to a double meaning underlying the whole passage: that a person who cannot see clearly to judge art, for instance, and who makes wealth a substitute for artistic discrimination, is also liable to be blind in more important concerns, such as choosing a wife or—and here the irony doubles back on itself—even choosing a whore.

This inability to see clearly also besets the celebrated Timon whose villa exhibits the kind of greatness that consists only in size. Timon sees falsely when his building suggests a town, his pond an ocean, and his parterre a down (lines 99–126).

Incidentally, the controversy that arose about the identity of Timon points to a type of double meaning found especially in the satires. Pope's appreciation of this effect is shown in these lines from the First Satire of Book II of Horace. The interlocutor says,

> A hundred smart in Timon and in Balaam:
> The fewer still you name, you wound the more;
> Bond is but one, but Harpax is a Score. (42–44)

In addition, the fictitious names of persons satirized are often in themselves *doubles entendres*; for example, Sappho, Gripus, Umbra, Sir Plume, Sporus.

A considerable number of the significant double meanings in the satires are based on religion or, at least, religious terminology —perhaps because religion provides a traditional accepted norm of conduct, and the ironic use of religious terms and concepts quickly and effectively conveys a satiric point. These range from short echoes of Biblical passages such as "For not in Chariots Peter puts his trust" in the imitation of Donne's Second Satire (the Biblical echo is not present in Donne) to a passage like the following from the *Epilogue to the Satires*, Dialogue I, based primarily on the general Christian concept of heaven:

> But let all Satire in all Changes spare
> Immortal S—k, and grave De—re!

Silent and soft, as Saints remove to Heav'n,
All Tyes dissolv'd, and ev'ry Sin forgiv'n,
These, may some gentle, ministerial Wing
Receive, and place for ever near a King!
There, where no Passion, Pride, or Shame transport,
Lull'd with the sweet Nepenthe of a Court;
There, where no Father's, Brother's, Friend's Disgrace
Once break their Rest, or stir them from their Place;
But past the Sense of human Miseries,
All Tears are wip'd forever from all Eyes;
No Cheek is known to blush, no Heart to throb,
Save when they lose a Question, or a Job. (91–104)

An interesting group of double meanings is connected with
dialogue situations in the satires. These double meanings arise
from the different interpretations put upon words by the two
persons concerned. In the First Satire of Horace's Second Book,
for example, the poet and his interlocutor clearly hold different
theories of satire, as is apparent in the friend's warning:

Alas young Man! your Days can ne'er be long,
In Flow'r of Age you perish for a Song! (101–102)

The poet's conception is certainly not that satire is a mere song.
He answers (note the additional *doubles entendres* in "point" and
"Front") in this way:

What? arm'd for Virtue when I point the Pen,
Brand the bold Front of shameless, guilty Men,
Dash the proud Gamester in his gilded Car,
Bare the mean Heart that lurks beneath a Star;

. . . .

Hear this, and tremble! you, who 'scape the Laws.
Yes, while I live, no rich or noble knave
Shall walk the World, in credit, to his grave.
(105–120)

In *Epilogue to the Satires*, Dialogue I, *doubles entendres* arising throughout the poem from the different concepts of satire
held by the poet and his friend are especially salient. In fact, this
double meaning provides the basic strategy of the poem. It is by
affecting momentarily to accept the courtier's moral standards

and ideas of satire that Pope obtains the double satire of such a passage as this:

> Virtue, I grant you, is an empty boast;
> But shall the Dignity of Vice be lost?
> Ye Gods! shall Cibber's Son, without rebuke
> Swear like a Lord? or a Rich out-whore a Duke?
> A Fav'rite's Porter with his Master vie,
> Be brib'd as often, and as often lie?   (113–118)

Double meanings are frequent in the satires, but they are the essence of the mock epics. Double meaning is the medium in which from start to finish mock epic moves. In a general sense, every line of the *Dunciad* and *The Rape of the Lock* is part of the double meaning inseparable from the genre—the double meaning resulting from treating low matter in a high style.

Aside from this, individual double meanings are more thickly sown than in any other genre in which Pope wrote. Of this individual type is "magnify," to be taken both ironically and literally, in these lines from the *Dunciad* addressed to the creator of Brobdignag:

> Whether thou chuse Cervantes' serious air,
> Or laugh and shake in Rab'lais' easy chair,
> Or praise the Court, or magnify Mankind . . . (I, 21–23)

Most of the individual *doubles entendres* of the *Dunciad* are directly concerned with the ironic elevation of Dulness, the "cloud-compelling Queen," who beholds such "miracles" as these, wrought by dull writers. The locution makes them seem true wonders; common sense knows them for mistakes:

> How Tragedy and Comedy embrace;
> How Farce and Epic get a jumbled race;
> How Time himself stands still at her command,
> Realms shift their place, and Ocean turns to land.
> Here gay Description Aegypt glads with show'rs,
> Or gives to Zembla fruits, to Barca flow'rs;
> Glitt'ring with ice here hoary hills are seen,
> There painted valleys of eternal green,
> In cold December fragrant chaplets blow,
> And heavy harvests nod beneath the snow.   (I, 69–78)

Other miracles are produced by the chefs whom dull, gluttonous nobles treat as if they were priests of a sacred mystery (Pope is resorting again to religion as a norm for satire):

> On some, a Priest succinct in amice white
> Attends; all flesh is nothing in his sight!
> Beeves, at his touch, at once to jelly turn,
> And the huge Boar is shrunk into an Urn:
> The board with specious miracles he loads,
> Turns Hares to Larks, and Pigeons into Toads.
>
> (IV, 549-554)

Scatological double meanings are frequent; and of course they are functional in a genre whose business it is to deal with base matter in a lofty style. Book II, devoted to the heroic games played before the Queen whose "head a cloud conceal'd,/ In broad effulgence all below reveal'd" is particularly rich in this kind. Typical is the *double entendre* extending throughout the following passage in which "from ambrosia, Jove retires for ease":

> There in his seat two spacious vents appear,
> On this he sits, to that he leans his ear,
> And hears the various vows of fond mankind;
> Some beg an eastern, some a western wind:
> All vain petitions, mounting to the sky,
> With reams abundant this abode supply;
> Amus'd he reads, and then returns the bills,
> Sign'd with that Ichor which from Gods distils.
> In office here fair Cloacina stands . . .
>
> (II, 85-93)

In *The Rape of the Lock* the chief pervasive *double entendre* is that the frivolous feminine matters treated are of the highest importance—as, of course, in a way they are. Once again Pope uses religious terminology to reinforce a fundamental *double entendre*, notably in the description of the "sacred rites" of Belinda's toilet. Religious echoes also play their part in stressing the false sense of values held by the belle:

> The skilful Nymph reviews her Force with Care;
> Let Spades be Trumps! she said, and Trumps they were.
>
> (III, 45-46)

Scatological *doubles entendres* are present, but they are more delicately put than in the *Dunciad*, as befits a mock epic primarily for ladies. Yet there is no mistaking the fact that the rape of Belinda's lock is throughout symbolic of a real violation of chastity. Thalestris' speech, for instance, plainly indicates this:

> Gods! shall the Ravisher display your Hair,
> While the Fops envy, and the Ladies stare!
> Honour forbid! at whose unrival'd Shrine
> Ease, Pleasure, Virtue, All, our Sex resign.
> Methinks already I your Tears survey,
> Already hear the horrid things they say,
> Already see you a degraded Toast,
> And all your Honour in a Whisper lost!
> How shall I, then, your helpless Fame defend?
> 'Twill then be Infamy to seem your Friend!
> And shall this Prize, th' inestimable Prize,
> Expos'd thro' Crystal to the gazing Eyes,
> And heighten'd by the Diamond's circling Rays,
> On that Rapacious Hand for ever blaze?
> Sooner shall Grass in Hide-Park Circus grow,
> And Wits take Lodgings in the Sound of Bow;
> Sooner let Earth, Air, Sea, to Chaos fall,
> Men, Monkies, Lap-dogs, Parrots, perish all!
>   (IV, 103–120)

Particularly felicitous in its application of epic terminology is this couplet describing the war of the beaux and belles:

> No common Weapons in their Hands are found,
> Like Gods they fight, nor dread a mortal Wound.
>   (V, 43–44)

Or the epic-based *doubles entendres* of the Baron to Belinda in

> Boast not my Fall, (he cry'd) insulting Foe!
> Thou by some other shalt be laid as low.   (V, 97–98)

It is the repetition of happy instances like these that helps make *The Rape of the Lock* so delightful a mockery of the epic. Pope lets no opportunity slip. At every point of the poem he is conscious of the demands of the genre and alert to adapt his particular subject matter to them.

Throughout his verse, whatever the idea, whatever the stylistic trait, Pope uniformly exhibits a nicety of judgment and a happiness of invention, in adapting ideas and rhetorical devices to a genre, that makes it possible to suggest that he himself is the great ideal he draws in the *Essay on Criticism*. What Pope's verse would have been like had he lived in such an age as ours, careless or scornful of fixed genre requirements, is hard to imagine. His verse is penetrated through and through, down to the least epithet, with awareness of the genre in which he is writing. The concept of the *via media* and the use of double meanings are only two of scores of ideas and techniques which Pope deftly adapts to the genre in hand. The chains of genre did not encumber him. Much of the beauty of his dance derives from the very limitations the chains imposed.

11

Imitation

IF IN its physiological aspect Pope's life was one long disease, in its poetical aspect it was one long imitation. The entire corpus of Pope's works may, in a sense, be placed under the heading of imitation. It is merely a question of degree.

"My first taking to imitating," he told Spence, "was not out of vanity, but humility: I saw how defective my own things were; and endeavoured to mend my manner, by copying good strokes from others." *

Humility, aside from being good common sense, was part of the public decorum of a young poet. The Augustan audience expected the young poet to defer to tradition, to measure himself against it, and to be always aware how unlikely it was that everybody was out of step but Joe. Pope voices his consciousness of this attitude in, among other places, the *Essay on Criticism*:

Hail, Bards triumphant! born in happier days;
Immortal heirs of universal praise!
. . . .
Oh may some spark of your celestial fire,
The last, the meanest of your sons inspire,
(That on weak wings, from far, pursues your flights;
Glows while he reads, but trembles as he writes)
To teach vain Wits a science little known,
T'admire superior sense, and doubt their own!

(I, 189–200)

* Joseph Spence, *Anecdotes, Observations, and Characters of Books and Men*, edited by S. W. Singer (London: W. H. Carpenter, 1820), p. 193.

It is a commonplace that the maxims of the *Essay on Criticism* apply not only to critics but to writers in general. For Pope the art of writing was, rightly understood, the art of imitating. Consequently, the *Essay on Criticism* may be read, to some extent, as a manual on how to imitate.

Closely related to this *Essay*'s recommendation of humility is the advice, "Be sure yourself and your own reach to know" (I, 48). One of the chief complaints of the nineteenth and early twentieth centuries against Pope was that he did not know his own limitations. Well equipped to be the English Horace, it was generally felt, he unwisely aspired to be the English Homer too.

"Imitate" and "Follow Nature" doubtless seemed incompatible commands to Romantic ears. Yet Pope's prime caution for the successful imitator was "Follow Nature." What he meant is clear from his account of Virgil:

> When first young Maro in his boundless mind
> A work t' outlast immortal Rome designed,
> Perhaps he seemed above the critic's law,
> And but from Nature's fountains scorned to draw:
> But when t' examine ev'ry part he came,
> Nature and Homer were, he found, the same.   (I, 130–135)

From this identification of Nature with the practice of the best classical writers Pope derived another principle, especially applicable to the imitator:

> Know well each ANCIENT's proper character;
> His fable, subject, scope in every page;
> Religion, Country, genius of his Age.   (I, 119–121)

Pope's praise of Roscommon, for instance, was that

> To him the wit of Greece and Rome was known,
> And every author's merit, but his own.   (III, 727–728)

That Pope followed his own advice in this respect is evident, to cite an instance in this same *Essay*, from his characterizations of classic critics in the third epistle. Horace, for example, whom he is actually imitating throughout the poem, he describes as follows:

> Horace still charms with graceful negligence,

And without method talks us into sense,
Will, like a friend, familiarly convey
The truest notions in the easiest way.
He, who supreme in judgment, as in wit,
Might boldly censure, as he boldly writ,
Yet judged with coolness, though he sung with fire;
His Precepts teach but what his works inspire.

(III, 653–660)

The charge that the *Essay on Criticism* is itself an imitation—
a composite of other writers' sentiments assembled in the Horatian mode—Pope would readily have admitted. He made no attempt, here or elsewhere, to conceal his poetic borrowings and
imitations, whether in subject matter or style. In a number of
cases he supplied identifying footnotes or otherwise called attention to the imitations. Plainly, he expected the educated reader
to be aware of many more. Both to Pope and to his Augustan
audience fire-new critical precepts originated by one poet, and
a young poet at that, would have been suspect.

Besides traditionalism, this attitude implies that the poet and his
verse are community-centered, not self-centered. The fact that
Pope imitated, rather than originated in the Romantic sense,
shows how strongly he felt himself to be a part of a tradition and
a community and not by any means, as a poet, spontaneously
generated or self-sufficient. Moreover, Pope could rely upon the
fact that the community to which he addressed his verse was
sophisticated in a way different from the way of a Romantic
audience. His imitations, in both large and small units, were considerably affected by the background and expectations of his
audience. In a manner of speaking, the Romantic audience showed
up in naked majesty and rather resented anyone—such as an
avowed imitator—who didn't. Pope's audience wore clothes and
carried a great deal of literary baggage. It behooved a poet who
addressed them to do the same.

All of Pope's imitations—which is to say, in a liberal sense, all
his poems—are enriched by the reader's knowledge of the material he imitated. Nevertheless, even such close imitations as
those of Donne and Horace are understandable and enjoyable

without reference to the related poems. Pope's poems, however imitative, achieve completeness in themselves. They are equivalents of, not commentaries on, the poems to which they are related.

The boundary between translation and imitation in Pope is not always easy to define. Certainly his renderings of Statius, Ovid, and Homer are properly called translations, though not in any belittling sense. Fable and most of the detail are taken from the original; the language is Pope's own. In his versions of the *Wife of Bath* and *January and May* the correspondence between the earlier poems and Pope's is looser. In the *Temple of Fame* it is so loose that Pope's poem may reasonably be called an imitation.

The following poems are neither translations nor yet imitations in the same degree as, for example, the poems labeled "Imitations of Horace": the *Pastorals*, *Eloisa to Abelard*, the *Essay on Criticism*, the *Essay on Man*, the *Moral Essays*, *The Rape of the Lock*, and the *Dunciad*. Yet each of these, though it does not have a strict play-by-play relationship to another poem, leans upon many predecessors.

For Pope, writing in any historically established genre was, in a broad way, imitation. The imitation consisted, to begin with, of treating a circumscribed area of subject matter in a particular manner. Pope's indebtedness in this respect can hardly be overestimated, though it is not always possible, with the scholarly techniques available, to assess precisely what he owes to individual poems that preceded his own attempts in a kind.

Neither can the problem of small-unit imitations be settled with exactitude. Still, to accept only passages where Pope himself has indicated his source seems overly cautious. Both the theory of imitation current in Pope's lifetime and his own admissions point to extensive, conscious imitation. Given these conditions, it is possible to go too far in ignoring the weight of the parallels assiduously collected by editors from Pope's day to ours. The pitfall of relying solely on the parallelism of parallel passages ought to be constantly in mind, but the reader who discounts all the parallels en masse will probably emerge with a distorted picture of Pope's craftsmanship. It would be nothing short of miraculous, for example, if the passage from the *Dunciad*,

> Flow Welsted, flow! like thine inspirer, Beer,
> Tho' stale, not ripe; tho' thin, yet never clear;
> So sweetly mawkish, and so smoothly dull;
> Heady, not strong; o'erflowing, tho' not full,
>
> (III,169–172)

were not an imitation of Denham's celebrated lines from *Cooper's Hill*—lines the whole century imitated and which Pope imitates again elsewhere:

> O could I flow like thee, and make thy stream
> My great example, as it is my theme.
> Tho' deep, yet clear; tho' gentle, yet not dull;
> Strong, without rage; without o'erflowing, full.
>
> (188–191)

The fun of Pope's passage, in fact, depends largely upon the reader's recognizing the imitation.

Many of Pope's small-unit imitations, acknowledged and probable, have a humorous or satiric purpose. Characteristically he takes a passage or a phrase from a serious context—say *Paradise Lost* or the Bible—and places it in a frivolous or mocking context. Raymond D. Havens in *The Influence of Milton on English Poetry* has pointed out a number of Miltonic imitations which he considers probable. As for the Biblical echoes, here are a few of the more striking ones which have a satiric effect.

From *The Rape of the Lock*:

> Safe from the treach'rous Friend, the daring Spark,
> The Glance by Day, the Whisper in the Dark.   (I, 73–74)

From the *Dunciad*:

> Who hunger, and who thirst for scribling sake.   (I, 50)
>
> All my commands are easy, short, and full:
> My Sons! be proud, be selfish, and be dull.
>
> (IV, 581–582)

From the Imitation of Donne's Second Satire:

> For you, he walks the streets thro' rain or dust,
> For not in Chariots Peter puts his trust.   (73–74)

From Moral Essay III:

> Yet, to be just to these poor men of pelf,
> Each does but hate his Neighbour as himself.
>
> (109–110)

The satiric point is made by contrasting different realms of value, one of the realms being established by the reader's awareness of the imitation. A similar effect is obtained, particularly in *The Rape of the Lock* and the *Dunciad*, by imitations of language and event from epic sources. In *The Rape of the Lock* this epic imitation is heightened—as in Clarissa's speech based on Sarpedon's or Belinda's based on Achilles' lament for Patroclus—by the additional contrast between masculine and feminine realms.

Striking in Pope's mock epics is the number of occasions on which the imitation is not of a single passage or verse but is an overlay involving many predecessors. The descent of the gnome into the Cave of Spleen is a striking instance. Pope commonly utilizes in these cases details and phraseology taken not only from similar incidents in other poems but from dissimilar incidents where a phrase or detail can be fitted in to serve his turn. His immediate poetic problem seems to have acted somewhat as a catalyst to urge words and details from various sources into union.

Another group of small-unit imitations seems to have a confirmatory rather than a contrasting tonal purpose. Happiness of phrasing or line-formula was, of course, the crucial factor in their being chosen for imitation. Such are the imitations of Dryden's version of the *Aeneid* in Pope's *Iliad* and of *MacFlecknoe* and *The Dispensary* in the *Dunciad*.

Close examination of a reasonably long passage for acknowledged, probable, and possible imitations is an excellent way to gain insight into the pattern of Pope's imitation. Generations of editors have supplied the paraphernalia. But the reader interested in Pope's craftsmanship will go beyond the question of *what* he imitated to the more revealing questions of *why* and *with what result*.

Consider, for example, the opening sixty-four lines of the *Dunciad*. The controlling purpose of imitation throughout is patently to magnify Dulness. Pope lifts from other writers only what will bear directly upon this purpose. Then he alters and adapts these borrowings to fit his own context in such a way that there is an increment of meaning.

The editorial array of presumed sources given in the Twickenham edition for these lines indicates that Pope borrowed chiefly from other satiric poems confirmatory of his tone and from high-flown, serious poems where the borrowings provide humor by contrast. This, by the way, is a general and predictable principle of his imitating. *The Rape of the Lock*, the satires, epistles, and the *Essay on Man* and the *Essay on Criticism* as well, in their satiric passages, follow this dual pattern of confirmatory and contrast borrowing. The non-satiric poems, of course, rely mainly on confirmatory borrowing. *Eloisa to Abelard*, for instance, imitates chiefly Ovid, Crashaw, Milton's minor poems, the Dido episode from the *Aeneid*, and, of course, Hughes' prose version. The determining principle seems to have been selection of language which would vividly strike the reader's sensibility. Most of the probable imitations in *Eloisa to Abelard* are of passages and phrases where the utterance is strongly passionate.

To return to the beginning of the *Dunciad*, the first imitation is its parody of the epic opening. Pope's "Mighty Mother" in the first line is related to the Greco-Roman concept of the *Magna Mater*. Because of the fertility connotation the identification is especially felicitous for Dulness, who is to foster whole shoals of fools to spring up and possess the land. Only one word in the parodied epic statement of subject betrays that it is a parody, and that is "Smithfield" in line 2. If for "Smithfield" "tuneful" were substituted, there would be no parody; and the ambiguity of "Mighty Mother" and "Son" would not function mock-epically.

Next comes the parody of the epic invocation to the Muses. Pope's muses are British noblemen who have the means and the hereditary obligation to patronize the arts but lack discrimination. Their efforts are described in elevated language and epic locutions, as in line 4; but the high-sounding "Call'd to this work" is undercut by naming the first of the trio of callers, Dulness.

"Jove and Fate" then change their connotation too. The noblemen are called to be foolish patrons because God and Fate caused
them to be born noble, rich, and stupid.

In line 6, "Still Dunce the second reigns like Dunce the first,"
Pope has been thought to have imitated Dryden's line, "And Tom
the second reigns like Tom the first," which occurs in *To My
Dear Friend Mr. Congreve, on His Comedy Call'd The Double-
Dealer*. In this poem Dryden discusses, though very briefly, the
same basic matter as the *Dunciad*. Dryden's two Toms are Thomas Shadwell and Thomas Rymer, both of whom had received
literary distinctions from the Crown. Dryden's context also suggests Tom Fool. Imitating this line achieved more than the mere
addition of a clever locution to Pope's poem. To the educated
Augustan, familiar with Dryden, the line would recall the entire
poem. This recall would emphasize how long, historically, dunce
succeeding dunce on the literary throne had been a problem to
English poets, and it would thus give weight to Pope's attack.
Moreover, George II just having followed George I on the political throne, Pope's one barb struck against the house of Hanover as well.

With line 9 Pope begins a parody of the celestial histories and
the geneses of individual heroes common in epic. Pope employs
his Olympian references with discrimination. "Ere Pallas issu'd
from the Thund'rer's head" is not otiose. In lines 10 and 11 he
states that Dulness reigned universally only before Pallas, goddess
of wisdom, was born from the head of Zeus. The Augustan
reader, well-read in Continental and domestic classics, would be
reminded by line 12, which describes Dulness as the daughter
of "Chaos and eternal Night," of a number of references to the
ancient reign of Chaos and Night. Milton's is typical:

> . . . where eldest Night
> And Chaos, ancestors of Nature, hold
> Eternal anarchy . . . (*Paradise Lost*, II, 894–896)

The epic connotations of the reign of Chaos and old Night and
their production of appropriate progeny set Pope's genesis of
Dulness firmly in an epic context—undercut, of course, by what

Pope is really saying: that the owl-eyed goddess had a feather-headed father and a mother densely stupid and ignorant.

Line 14, "gross as her sire, and as her mother grave," is thought to be an imitation of Dryden's "Fam'd as his Sire, and as his Mother fair" (*Aeneid*, VII, 1044). If the reader feels the similarity, the effect is to suggest, as do so many of Pope's imitations in mock epic of epic lines, the discrepancy between an epic hero and the gross, heavy, busy goddess, whose personal character often seems to resemble a Mother Needham's.

Whether or not line 18, "For born a goddess, Dulness never dies," specifically imitates "With Godhead born, but curs'd that cannot die" in Garth's *The Dispensary* (I, 116), the immortality with which Pope credits Dulness does raise this mother of the prostituted arts and sciences to the company of the blessed whose deathlessness and changelessness Homer continually and poignantly contrasts with the brevity of human life.

Lines 19–28, addressed to Swift, imitate the epic invocation of a god by all his aliases and additions. Dean Swift has more than one aspect to his divinity—"Dean, Drapier, Bickerstaff, or Gulliver"—and more than one function. The contrast between Swift and real deity is emphasized throughout the passage by constant alternation of the realms of reference, from Wood's halfpence to the Age of Saturn. Finally, in lines 27–28 the goddess spreads her wings and hatches the age of fools, in lines that parody the often grotesque classical theogonies.

In lines 31–32 Cibber's relation to his "fam'd father" is treated like that of epic hero and father—Ulysses and Telemachus, for instance—the exploits of the father adding to the prestige of the son, here mockingly. The Cell in line 33, which is "conceal'd from vulgar eye," is reminiscent of the aristocratic arrangements of epic. The Cave in line 34 recalls how many epic caves and grots! And the allusion to the Proteus myth in lines 37–38 reinforces the Greco-Roman associations. Line 35, "Keen, hollow winds howl thro' the bleak recess," has been thought to echo Pope's own "The hollow winds thro' naked Temples roar" (*Windsor Forest*, 68). Pope has made more striking self-borrowings; but if this is a self-imitation, it simply represents his willingness to repeat a good epithet once found. Pope himself indicates that lines 37–44 are designed on Virgil's

> . . . Genus unde Latinum
> Albaniq; patres atq; altae moenia Romae.
> (*Aeneid*, I, 6–7)

Pope uses the formality of the repeated "hence" structure and the memory of Virgil's elevated subject matter to contrast humorously with the works of Grubstreet.

Line 45, "In clouded Majesty here Dulness shone," contains another of the small-unit imitations Pope himself pointed out: that of Milton's ". . . the Moon/ Rising in clouded Majesty . . ." (*Paradise Lost*, IV, 606–607). Pope makes a particularly clever adaptation of this. In his context the simple physical description alters to an apt image of the befogged, pretentious Dulness he is satirizing. In lines 45–54 the ostensibly dignified picture of a throne supported by the four cardinal virtues is undermined by the fact that the "virtues" are not truly Fortitude, Temperance, Prudence, and Justice but brazenness, want arising from stupid persistence without talent, fear of imprisonment for low reasons —debt, perhaps, or libel—and the temptation to mercenary writing.

For lines 47–48 Pope refers the reader to Horace's "Quem neq; pauperies, neq; mors, neq; vincula terrent" (Lib. II, Sat. vii, 84). The contrast between Horace's wise man who is ruler over himself, "sapiens, sibi qui imperiosus," and hence does not fear poverty, chains, and death and the presumptuous scribbler described in these lines as not deterred by hisses, blows, and loss of ears is ludicrous. Pope's fourth catastrophe here, "want . . . of ears," adds a characteristic doubleness. A presumptive poet would do well to be concerned if he wanted an ear for meter, for instance. "Want . . . of ears" might also mean an obstinate refusal to listen to Good Sense. The irony of the Biblical echo in line 50 has already been discussed in another connection. Line 52 resembles Pope's own "Returning Justic lift aloft her Scale" (*Messiah*, 18), but the resemblance is so little distinctive it seems doubtful that anyone except an analogue-hunting editor would observe

it. However, if a reader does associate the line with the coming
of the Messiah, what a contrast between that and a wretched
scribbler's weighing solid pudding against empty praise! Regardless of the tenuous connection with the *Messiah*, operative within
Pope's immediate text is the contrast between the lofty (at least
in one sense!) actions of Poetic Justice and the low seesawings
of the scribbler between truth and gold, pudding and praise.

Lines 55–58, describing the formless darkness out of which the
works of the dull are produced, may represent an interesting
combination of several sources. Pope himself vouches for the
first:

> Within the chambers of the Globe they spy
> The beds where sleeping Vegetables lie,
> 'Till the glad summons of a genial ray
> Unbinds the Glebe, and calls them out to day.
> (Garth, *The Dispensary*, VI, 44–47)

> Here his forsaken Seat old Chaos keeps;
> And undisturb'd by Form in Silence sleeps.
> (*Ibid.*, 113–114)

> The rising world of waters dark and deep
> (*Paradise Lost*, III, 11)

These Flowers as in their causes sleep.
(Carew, "Ask me no more where Jove bestows . . .")

The coincidences of rhyme between Pope's text and the suggested models are noteworthy; such coincidences occur rather
frequently in imitated passages. Whether they are accidental or
deliberately retained by Pope to help recall the original to the
reader can only be speculated on. However, his purposive use
of the contextual values of imitations makes deliberate retention
of rhymes seem probable.

Lines 61–62 seems a possible development of Parnell's pun on
"maggots" in "Here crawls a Preface on its half burn'd Maggots"
from *On Bishop Burnet's Being Set on Fire*. In any case, Pope's
maggots crawl from a well-prepared matrix "dark and deep"
where many other "nameless Somethings" have been spawned.
Line 63 has as its probable original Dryden's "And torture one

poor word Ten thousand ways" (*MacFlecknoe*, 208). Pope has turned the line to his purpose by presenting the making of a hundred puns on one word as a kind of miracle of Dulness. Line 64, "And ductile dulness new meanders take," Pope acknowledges to be modeled on Garth's "How ductile matter new meanders takes" (*The Dispensary*, I, 26). The change of only one word in Garth's line makes it especially apt for Pope's use. The dulness he is satirizing is precisely the pert, inventive, "meandering" kind. "Meander" has, besides, classical associations.

These comments do not, of course, cover all the possible imitations in the sixty-four lines. But they are at least indicative of the degree to which Pope imitated and the way he went about it.

The imitations of whole poems, labeled by Pope as such, are in a special category. The rest of this chapter is devoted to a discussion of two such imitations: the First Epistle of Horace's Second Book and Donne's Fourth Satire.

Pope's adaptation of the work of an English poet not more than a century removed from his own—a poet, moreover, with a distinctive style of his own—is especially instructive for what it reveals of Pope's own principles and practices.

Particularly significant are Pope's omissions. Inquiry into the reasons for specific omissions cannot be more than speculative, but when inquiry is made in the light of the canons of taste commonly accepted in Pope's generation and of his own habitual practice, probability, at least, can often be attained.

On occasion Pope was capable not only of homely but of obscene references and language. His imitation of Horace's *Sober Advice* is a sufficient example. Why, then, in imitating Donne's Fourth Satire does Pope shy away from certain material of this kind? He even omits "lustful" from Donne's catalogue (line 14) of typical court sins. Donne's "Who loveth whores, and who boys, and who goats" (line 114) he changes to "who sins with whom?" (line 134). Yet in this very poem Pope does not hesitate at the following allusions:

> Whose Place is quarter'd out, three Parts in four,
> And whether to a Bishop, or a Whore? (136–137)

He tells what Strumpet Places sells for Life,
What 'Squire his Lands, What Citizen his Wife?
(148–149)

One possible explanation is the recognition of a seemly improper
and an unseemly improper. Selling the favors of one's wife may
be highly improper in itself but, since it is apparently a common
fault in the relations between the city and the court, proper to
mention in a satire on court life. Pederasty and bestiality are in
a different category altogether. Pope did not "startle at the name"
of either whore or pederast—in the proper place. His use of scatological material is determined by propriety in the genre or variant of genre he is using. As for Donne's "lustful," Pope omitted
it probably for a slightly different reason. The other court sins
Donne mentions, such as vanity, falsity, or being in debt, are
especially applicable to courtiers; lust is not.

Pope's principle of suppressing the tangential doubtless also
played a part in his leaving out Donne's ". . . If strange meats
displease,/ Art can deceive, or hunger force my tast" (38–39).
This occurs in the passage satirizing the courtier's hypocritically
complimentary language. Pope may also have preferred to avoid
the homely digestive associations in his context. Pope's satire
against the court has a courtliness of its own, a light, playful,
elegant touch which would make the much more scabrous West-
phalian hog comparison, directed against the court in Dialogue II
of the *Epilogue to the Satires*, distinctly out of place in this poem.

Avoiding tangentiality may also have been a factor in Pope's
omission of Donne's account (lines 136–151) of the courtier's
borrowing a crown. It is not that the borrowing incident is un-
typical of court life or that it is involved in verbal witticisms of
the type Pope tends to suppress; but the incident is not as relevant to the special emphasis of Pope's satire on courtiers. The
passage with which Pope (174–179) replaces Donne's stresses the
necessity the courtier feels under of resorting to debasing flattery
and toadyism. Four lines (Donne, 138–141) of this omitted passage contain a religious metaphor which Pope probably preferred
to eliminate, as he eliminated or altered the tone of other refer-

ences of Donne's to religion. Pope's strategy in handling Donne's religious material is discussed further on.

Tangentiality was very likely again a determinant in Pope's two remaining sizable omissions (Donne, 192–196 and 241–243). In the first case, Donne's riddle of "Why good wits ne'er wear scarlet gowns" may have seemed to Pope farfetched in the context and Donne's lines explicatory of this riddling inquiry both somewhat entangled in what Addison would have called "false wit" and repetitive. Besides, any fairly close transfer of these lines would have come as an anticlimax to Pope's brilliant rendering of the "naval encounter" in his lines 226–235. This is not to disparage Donne's version. Here and elsewhere the two poets were aiming at and achieving different effects. In his presentation of the "naval encounter" between the Countess and Sir Fopling Pope flew so high and spread his wings to catch so many glancing lights that sudden descent to a more pedestrian level of satire would not have done.

Donne concludes his satire with these lines:

> . . . Although I yet
> (With Maccabees modesty) the known merit
> Of my work lessen, yet some wise men shall,
> I hope, esteem my Writs Canonical.   (241–244)

Pope leaves out Donne's withdrawal of his modest disclaimer and the reference to Maccabee but retains and develops the religious allusion of the final couplet:

> How'er, what's now *Apocrypha*, my Wit,
> In time to come, may pass for *Holy Writ*.
> (286–287)

Pope has focused upon an aspect of the situation, the tenor of the metaphor, which suggests a similarity permitting sharp antithesis in the metaphor's religious vehicle. In doing this, Pope extends the implications of the couplet backward, with the result that his immediately preceding passage becomes a significant and broad-reaching prophecy.

In view of Pope's steady effort to suppress or turn to the support of his centralized purpose all material in Donne which appeared to him tangential, it may at first seem contradictory to suggest that Pope's poem has greater scope. For one thing, his poem is longer; it has 287 lines, to Donne's 244. Some of these are freely added; some are detailed developments of Donne's suggestions.

A good example of an added verse which enlarges scope is line 43 in this passage:

> The suit, if by the fashion one might guess,
> Was velvet in the youth of good Queen Bess,
> But mere tuff-taffety what now remained;
> So Time, that changes all things, had ordain'd!
>
> (40–43)

Line 43, an epic echo, places the courtier's threadbare suit on the level of Nestor's youthful prowess—or even on the level of the suns of Belinda's eyes, destined to set.

After the courtier has praised linguists and hinted that he too is proficient, Pope inserts this couplet of psychological generalization which extends the application of the incident to all men:

> Thus others Talents having nicely shown,
> He came by sure Transition to his own. (80–81)

The same is true of the couplet Pope introduces into the description of the man who shows the royal tombs. He can, Pope says,

> . . . get by speaking Truth of Monarchs dead,
> What few can of the living, Ease and Bread.
>
> (106–107)

This generalization relates the incident to the central emphasis of Pope's poem—that the courtier, for all his corrupting endeavors, gains neither economic nor mental ease; but in addition it comments on the broader social situation which makes it impossible for any but fools and heroes to tell the truth about the living great.

These are only a few examples of a type of expansion which is Pope's constant habit throughout this adaptation. Whether in couplets, larger units such as the comparison of court and stage (Pope, 218–225), or merely in an epithet or phrase—as when Pope translates Donne's "He knows what Lady is not painted" (110) into "What Lady's Face is not a whited Wall?" (151)—

Pope is continually ringing in wider areas of human experiences and different realms of value to set off and enrich the theme from which he never deviates. Both Donne and Pope indulge in tangentials. Donne's tend to lead him down knotted byways which have their own interest and charm. Pope's byways all prove to be feeders back to the trunk line.

Pope's treatment of the earlier poet's puns is closely related to this. Pope often omits them when they seem to be merely expressions of verbal cleverness without semantic reverberation connected with the main theme. Such are his eliminations of "I shook like a spied Spie" (Donne, 237) and the pun on "suit" in Donne's "I had no suit there, nor new suit to show,/ Yet went to Court . . ." (7–8). Pope alters the "spied Spie" phrase to "And shake all o'er, like a discover'd Spy" (279). The "suit" pun he replaces with four examples of suits at court, two of which are especially meaningful in relation to other emphases in Pope's poem. In "I bought no new Benefice" Pope stresses the corruption of religion at court. The traffic in secular places, he implies, has become so commonly accepted as to seem the norm. By nonchalantly slipping religious places into the same category and affecting to assume that this is the norm with them too, Pope is indulging in one of his favorite ironic techniques.

The second especially interesting example replacing the pun on "suit" is "Had no new Verses . . . to show" (13). Pope, as was his custom in satire, puts considerable stress on the character and reactions of the dramatic speaker. Donne has only two references to his speaker's vocation as a satiric poet (160–165 and 239–244). Pope's poem has many such references. Donne's speaker is clearly a scholar, a reflective man, who on a rare emergence from his study observes the court with disapproval and expresses it directly. Pope's speaker is more audience-conscious. He courts the reader, in a good sense. Without for one moment abandoning his stance as "the Terror of this sinful Town" (196), Pope's speaker nevertheless bends in an easy, gracious way. With a manner engaging and often playful, he entices the reader into making a tour of that earthly hell, a court. If Pope's visitor never sets foot on the burning soil but remains inside the elaborate vehicle the poet supplies, the contrast is only the stronger between his painted chariot and the frying souls. Donne's speaker observes the court disease, produces a bitter pill, and says, "This will cure you; now swallow!" Pope's speaker with a smile proffers what seems to be a glittering rococo Easter egg of dyed spun sugar; but what ancient corruption within the shell!

Donne says

> . . . Low feare
> Becomes the guiltie, not th'accuser; Then,
> Shall I, nones slave, of high borne, or rais'd men
> Feare frowns; And, my Mistress Truth, betray thee
> For th'huffing braggart, puft Nobility?
> No, no . . . (160–165)

Pope's version is as follows:

> Base Fear becomes the Guilty, not the Free;
> Suits Tyrants, Plunderers, but suits not me.
> Shall I, the Terror of this sinful Town,
> Care, if a livery'd Lord or smile or frown?
> Who cannot flatter, and detest who can,
> Tremble before a noble Serving-Man?
> O my fair Mistress, Truth! Shall I quit thee,
> For huffing, braggart, puft Nobility? (194–201)

By replacing Donne's "accuser" with "Free" Pope gives the entire passage a different turn. Incidentally, the emphasis Pope gains for the important word "Free" by making it the end-rhyme may profitably be compared with the effect of Donne's use of the unimportant word "Then" (161) for his end-rhyme at this point. Pope, having emphasized "Free," in every subsequent line stresses that his speaker is free—free from sin, free from the necessity to flatter and be servile, free to detest and sear vice. Pope eliminates Donne's tangential emphasis that some men are born high and some raised to eminence. Pope prefers, by repeating the idea in "livery'd Lord" and "noble Serving-Man," to underline the fact that all courtiers, however highly placed, are slaves. Interestingly enough, except for smoothing the meter, Pope preserves intact Donne's felicitous description of the nobility in line 164.

In various ways Pope gets more dramatic immediacy into his version. This may be to some extent a result of the effort Pope's speaker makes to entertain the reader while instructing him. Donne describes his first sight of the courtier thus:

> . . . Towards me did runne
> A thing more strange, then on Niles slime . . .
> (17–18)

Here is Pope's description:

> Scarce was I enter'd, when behold! there came
> A Thing which Adam had been pos'd to name.
> (24–25)

Donne has

> One, to whom, the examining Justice sure would cry,
> Sir, by your priesthood tell me what you are.
> (28–29)

Pope replaces the otiose epithet "examining" with "wise," turning the Justice from a static figure into a "wise guy" who actually is duped by the courtier's appearance into thinking him a disguised priest. In fact, the courtier's appearance, Pope stresses, is so outlandish that a dignified magistrate jumps up from his chair:

> And the wise Justice starting from his chair
> Cry, by your Priesthood, tell me what you are?
> (36–37)

The contrast in dramatic immediacy is particularly striking in the scene describing the entrance of the ladies—the "naval encounter." Donne's lines are as follows:

> . . . Now,
> The Ladies come; As Pirats, which doe know
> That there came weak ships fraught with Cutchannel,
> The men board them; and praise, as they thinke, well,
> Their beauties; they the mens wits; Both are bought.
> (187–191)

These are Pope's:

> Painted for sight, and essenc'd for the smell,
> Like Frigates fraught with Spice and Cochine'l,
> Sail in the Ladies: How each Pyrate eyes

So weak a Vessel, and so rich a Prize!
Top-gallant he, and she in all her Trim,
He boarding her, she striking sail to him.
"Dear Countess! you have Charms all Hearts to hit!"
And "sweet Sir Fopling! you have so much wit!"
Such Wits and Beauties are not prais'd for nought,
For both the Beauty and the Wit are bought. (226–235)

The syntactic suspension in Pope's opening sentence is the vehicle
of a suspense in meaning. The exclamatory mode of the second
sentence increases the dramatic aspect. The individualization of
the encounter as between Sir Fopling and a countess, together
with the use of direct speech, also help. But the profoundest way
Pope heightens the dramatic suspense is by his extension of the
naval metaphor and his fusion of its every detail with the sexual
metaphor present in Donne but not developed.

Pope makes a sexual pun and rings in Biblical associations by
changing Donne's "ship" to "Vessel." In relation to this, the sexual
double meanings in "boarding" and "striking sail" become prominent. Then, in retrospect the first couplet fairly reeks of sexual
emphasis. All in all, the basic effect in Donne is of a social encounter; in Pope, of a sexual encounter.

Pictorial qualities too play a part in creating dramatic suspense;
Pope does not neglect these. The ladies do not merely enter in
his poem; they "sail in," "painted for sight." Each pirate "eyes"
them. The courtier is described as "top-gallant," the lady as being
"in all her Trim." This pictorialism is the source of an element
of sensuous beauty in Pope's adaptation which is not found, and
probably was not desired, in Donne's.

Important insights into the differences between Donne and
Pope in poetic approach can be reached by study of the metaphors alone. Above, we have seen Pope elaborate a metaphor of
Donne's which suited his purpose. On other occasions Pope eliminates, or condenses, or plays down Donne's metaphors. An interesting instance occurs toward the end, where Donne has

. . . Preachers which are
Seas of Wit and Arts, you can, then dare,
Drowne the sins of this place, for, for mee

> Which am but a scarce brook, it enough shall bee
> To wash the staines away.   (237–241)

Pope modifies it:

> Courts are too much for Wits so weak as mine;
> Charge them with Heav'n's Artill'ry, bold Divine!
> From such alone the Great Rebukes endure,
> Whose Satyr's sacred, and whose Rage secure.
> 'Tis mine to wash a few slight Stains; but theirs
> To deluge Sin, and drown a Court in Tears.   (280–285)

No doubt Pope felt that to call preachers "Seas of Wit and Arts" and a satiric poet a "scarce brook" was too eccentric. Yet he saw possibilities in the pervading body-of-water metaphor. Instead of preacherly seas drowning sin by virtue of the water's witty and artful properties, Pope directs a bold divine to open fire with Heaven's artillery. This change of metaphor gives him occasion to indite a two-edged couplet on the permitted—and generally ignored—invective power of the pulpit. Pope is then ready to use Donne's water imagery in a more conventionally acceptable because more natural form. Without implying that he is a "scarce brook," a poet can speak of washing away a few slight stains from court life. Sin may be deluged, as God deluged the sinful world of Noah. And such a court as has been pictured might well be drowned in tears of repentance.

This metaphor provides some light on the different treatment of religion in the two poems. Donne constantly applies religious metaphor, and nonreligious material as well, to the court and the speaker's reaction to it. Donne opens his poem with these lines:

> Well; I may now receive, and die. My sinne
> Indeed is great, but yet I have beene in
> A Purgatorie, such as fear'd hell is
> A recreation to, and scarse map of this.   (1–4)

Pope would not have objected to this metaphor as eccentric, but apparently he did object to its comparatively serious tone. Donne's lines have a grim humor of exaggeration. In his corresponding passage (1–8) Pope softens and lightens this. Donne's direct reference to taking the last sacrament becomes in Pope "I die in

Charity with Fool and Knave" (3). Pope is downright playful about purgatory. "I've had it here betimes," he informs us breezily. Donne's "fear'd Hell" becomes in Pope "the Poet's hell"—an ambiguous expression here, perhaps signifying Dante's inferno, or the stock hell complete with "Tortures, Fiends, and Flames" facilely conjured up in any poet's imagination, or even a special hell for poets, consisting of persecution by fools and knaves.

Where Donne uses religious humor of exaggeration without grimness, as in his outcry against being approached by the courtier

> . . . I whisper, God!
> How have I sinn'd, that thy wraths furious rod,
> This fellow chuseth me?" (49–51)

Pope makes his version still more colloquial and, by the addition of another artillery metaphor, downright comic:

> . . . I whisper, gracious God!
> What Sin of mine cou'd merit such a Rod?
> That all the Shot of Dulness now must be
> From this thy Blunderbuss discharg'd on me!
> (62–65)

Donne's courtier makes a passing reference to the linguistic ability of the Apostles:

> . . . Nay, your Apostles were
> Good pretty linguists, and so Panurge was;
> Yet a poore gentleman, all these may passe
> By travaile. (58–61)

Pope plays this up and, in conjunction with a completely changed application of Donne's "Yet a poore gentleman," takes advantage of the courtier's confused sense of values to use religious material, though in a playful manner, for serious satire:

> Why yes, 'tis granted, these indeed may pass
> Good common Linguists, and so Panurge was:
> Nay troth, th'Apostles, (tho' perhaps too rough)
> Had once a pretty Gift of Tongues enough.
> Yet these were all poor Gentlemen! I dare
> Affirm, 'twas Travel made them what they were.
> (74–79)

Pope also uses Donne's religious analogy in describing the courtier seen to

> call his clothes to shrift,
> Making them confesse not only mortall
> Great staines and holes in them; but veniall
> Feathers and dust, wherewith they fornicate.
>
> (200–203)

Pope omits the eccentric reference to feathers and dust clinging to clothes as fornication. He arranges the venial and mortal sartorial sins antithetically and in order of climax. The courtiers, Pope says,

> Adjust their Cloaths, and to Confession draw
> Those venial sins, an Atom, or a Straw:
> But oh! what Terrors must distract the Soul
> Convicted of that mortal Crime, a Hole! (242–245)

For all the fun he is having with the analogy, Pope is making a serious moral charge. He makes it in harmony with the playful surface tone he maintains in this poem.

These are only a few among scores of features of Pope's imitation of the Fourth Satire which might fruitfully be examined. But they indicate the trend of Pope's treatment of Donne's material.

In a sense, Pope's imitation of Donne's matter is also an imitation of Horace's manner. But nowhere, perhaps, does Pope's peculiar flavor as a satirist emerge more sharply than in a close imitation of a specific poem of Horace. Pope resembles Horace more than any of the other Roman satirists, but the ways in which he differs from Horace are the most revealing.

Horace addresses the First Epistle of his Second Book to Augustus Caesar in these terms:

> Cum tot sustineas & tanta negotia, solus;
> Res Italas armis tuteris, moribus ornes,
> Legibus emendes; in publica commoda peccem,
> Si longo sermone morer tua tempora, Caesar.
>
> (1–4)

The praise is straightforward; the statement stripped and businesslike. Here is Pope's equivalent, addressed to George II of Hanover ("Dunce the Second"):

> While You, great Patron of Mankind, sustain
> The balanc'd World, and open all the Main;
> Your Country, chief, in Arms abroad defend,
> At home, with Morals, Arts, and Laws amend;
> How shall the Muse, from such a Monarch, steal
> An hour, and not defraud the Publick Weal?
>
> (1-6)

The expansion is characteristic of Pope's treatment of Horace's poem throughout. Horace has 270 lines; Pope makes them 419. The different geniuses of Latin and English cannot be charged with any considerable portion of this. It is chiefly by investigating the various reasons for and effects of these expansions that some of the most striking differences between Pope and Horace are made evident.

Pope's apostrophe to George II is anything but businesslike. Horace's style suggests a soldier ready to advance who has thrown away all paraphernalia except what he needs for immediate, effective combat. Pope, gorgeously appareled, glittering over every inch like the "Birth-night Beau" he celebrates in *The Rape of the Lock*, advances with all the multivalences he can lay his hands on to a far different kind of combat.

Pope deliberately overdoes Horace's praise. In a pejorative sense Pope magnifies George II. The epithet "great Patron of Mankind" might truly have been applied to Augustus, and the emperor of Rome might well have been said to "sustain / The balanc'd World, and open all the Main." George II had conferred no fatherly benefits on the human race. England at that time was not a great world power comparable to imperial Rome. Pope is ironically striking at the king's unaggressive foreign policy. George had indeed recently been "in arms abroad"—the arms of his German mistress. His conduct in England gave little more satisfaction, at least to Pope and his friends. His aversion for literature was notorious. In the light of this, Pope's concluding question is purely ironic. It is notable that Pope uses the more alerting

form, that of the question. By making the Muse and not himself
the subject, Pope raises Horace's terse, factual statement to a more
pretentious plane. Finally, Pope alters the metaphor of Horace's
"in publica commoda peccem" to the more sensational one of
theft from the government.

Pope continues this heightening for the purpose of making
George II ridiculous. Horace has said briefly,

> Praesenti Tibi maturos largimur honores:
> Jurandasque tuum per nomen ponimus aras,
> Nil oriturum alias, nil ortum tale fatentes.
>
> (15–17)

Of these three lines, together with the suggestion in Horace's line
19, "Te nostris Ducibus, Te Graiis anteferendo," Pope makes
these:

> To Thee, the World its present homage pays,
> The Harvest early, but mature the Praise:
> Great Friend of LIBERTY! in Kings a Name
> Above all Greek, above all Roman Fame:
> Whose Word is Truth, as sacred and rever'd,
> As Heav'n's own Oracles from Altars heard.
> Wonder of Kings! like whom, to mortal eyes
> None e'er has risen, and none e'er shall rise.
>
> (23–30)

The whole world was not about to pay homage to any English
monarch—not even the world of George's own subjects. Pope
seizes on Horace's epithet "maturos," puns on it, adds a related
harvest metaphor, and produces the antithesis in line 24. "Great
friend of LIBERTY!" is Pope's gratuitous addition of praise suitable to a British monarch, if deserved. The British do not set
up altars to kings, living or dead; nor do they swear by them in
Horace's solemn sense. Pope deals deftly with the religious problem posed. In line 27 he employs a Biblical echo, "Whose Word
is Truth," to set George II egregiously in the Christian pantheon.
Line 28 completes the ironic deification with images from a realm
of religious reference not distinctively Christian, but rather
Greco-Roman.

In "Wonder of Kings" Pope is punning doubly. George is a

wonder among kings, and other kings wonder at his actions. Horace's praise in line 17 is credible. Augustus really was an outstanding ruler; there had been no other like him and probably would not be. Pope, adding the phrase "to mortal eyes," ostensibly continues his fiction of George II's divinity. The praise would be exaggerated even if George were Augustus' equal in mortal merit. Pope's lines 29–30, of course, actually convey that George was such a very bad king that the like of him had never been seen before and probably wouldn't be again.

In hit-and-run thrusts at other points in his poem Pope continues this ironic adaptation of Horace's praise of Augustus, but perhaps his most brilliant passage of this kind occurs toward the close. Horace, in lines 250–259, has told Augustus in substance that he regrets he hasn't the proper kind of poetic bent to celebrate his victorious wars and strong peace. Pope, using his customary puns and ambiguities, applies this satirically to George II:

> Oh! could I mount on the Maeonian wing,
> Your Arms, your Actions, your Repose to sing!
> What seas you travers'd! and what fields you fought!
> Your Country's Peace, how oft, how dearly bought!
> How barb'rous rage subsided at your word,
> And Nations wonder'd while they dropp'd the sword!
> How, when you nodded, o'er the land and deep,
> Peace stole her wing, and wrapt the world in sleep;
> Till Earth's extremes your mediation own,
> And Asia's Tyrants tremble at your Throne— (394–403)

Pope achieves here not merely telling satire, but beauty—a type of beauty not found in Horace's equivalent. In this passage, elsewhere in the poem, and in the other Horatian imitations, Pope actually does mount on the Maeonian wing. The verses, if taken for a moment unsatirically, are at the epic pitch of grandeur. Instead of George II bungling his foreign policy and allowing Walpole to bribe right and left for peace at any price, the reader can see a Zeus-like king at whose Olympian nod warring nations drop their swords and peace covers the globe.

Speaking of the poems of Livius, Horace says,

Inter quae verbum emicuit si forte decorum, &
Si versus paulo concinnior unus & alter;
Injuste totum ducit venditque poema. (73–75)

By dropping Horace's idea of selling the poem and introducing
several apt metaphors of his own, Pope converts these lines into
a passage of considerable pictorial beauty:

But for the Wits of either Charles's days,
The Mob of Gentlemen who wrote with Ease;
Sprat, Carew, Sedley, and a hundred more,
(Like twinkling Stars the Miscellanies o'er)
One Simile, that solitary shines
In the dry Desert of a thousand lines,
Or lengthen'd Thought that gleams thro' many a page,
Has sanctify'd whole Poems for an age. (107–114)

Pope uses a similar technique on Horace's

Urit enim fulgore suo qui praegravat artes
Infra se positas: extinctus amabitur idem. (13–14)

"Fulgore" was probably the germinal word for Pope's development of a solar metaphor to convey the idea that till they die,
great men who are truly patrons of mankind are regarded not
with admiration and gratitude but with envy:

Sure fate of all, beneath whose rising ray
Each Star of meaner merit fades away;
Oppress'd we feel the Beam directly beat,
Those Suns of Glory please not till they set.
(19–22)

Pope is more given to topical allusions of a nonliterary nature
than Horace. Horace below speaks in a general way of trades;
he does not name individual seamen, physicians, or carpenters or
events in which they figured:

Navem agere ignarus navis timet: abrotonum aegro
Non audet, nisi qui didicit, dare: quod medicorum est,
Promittunt Medici; tractant fabrilia fabri:
Scribimus indocti doctique poemata passim. (114–117)

Pope's equivalent is made of the stuff of current London conversation. Specific individuals are named to represent medicine and

carpentry. The English navy is let off; perhaps no suitable contemporary example of poor seamanship was available. Pope says,

> He serv'd a 'Prenticeship, who sets up shop;
> Ward try'd on Puppies, and the Poor, his Drop;
> Ev'n Radclife's Doctors travel first to France,
> Nor dare to practise till they've learn'd to dance.
> Who builds a Bridge that never drove a pyle?
> (Should Ripley venture, all the World would smile)
> But those who cannot write, and those who can,
> All ryme, and scrawl, and scribble, to a man.   (181–188)

Pope, of course, is at his usual work of introducing meaningful antitheses (as in line 182, where the antithesis is emphasized by alliteration), making pointed references and statements as much as he can, and getting in extra satiric thrusts (as at Radclife's medical traveling fellowships in line 183). The neutral "scribimus" Pope accommodates aptly to his own context as "scrawl" and "scribble."

Pope did not merely turn Horace into rhymed English, supplying British examples for Roman. He used even Horace as he used any grist that came to his poetic mill. He was not content merely to grind it to make bread, but he put much of it through a transforming process in his private poetic still. The examples discussed above are not exhaustive, but they do give some insight into the type of alteration Pope habitually made.

Recognition of the vast extent of Pope's imitations, large and small—and indeed most of Pope's lines have a literary ancestry comparable to the physiological ancestry of the individual—should not obscure for the reader the fact that Pope's poems are his own and no one else's. Once the extent to which Pope imitated and the creative acuteness with which he did so have been grasped, the next important step is to submerge this knowledge and look freshly at each poem as a poem.

Almost every line of Pope's comes trailing clouds of other poets' lines. Pope's peculiar excellence was his ability to condense these clouds into one sun-catching, brilliant drop, the aim he himself referred to as "What oft was thought, but ne'er so well expressed." The theory underlying this verse explains why Pope thought it no sin but only good sense to imitate.

12

The Approach to Correctible Evil

Pope's poetry deals with two kinds of experience which, from the standpoint of the individual, may be called evil: cosmic evil, about which man can do nothing except submit; and man-made evil, which is correctible by human endeavor. Pope's own basic attitude toward evil is conveniently summarized in these lines from the *Essay on Man*:

What makes all physical or moral ill?
There deviates Nature, and here wanders Will.
God sends not ill; if rightly understood,
Or partial Ill is universal Good,
Or Change admits, or Nature lets it fall;
Short, and but rare, till Man improv'd it all.
(IV, 111–116)

Concern for human wills that err in their attitude toward cosmic evil is the chief source of Pope's interest in it. His concern with morals is practical. For Pope, as for thinking men in all times, the prime human error from which all others stem is that of setting up feeble and fallacious mortal reason against a reality omnipotent, infallible, and immortal. This foolish attitude, whether called *hubris* or unchristian pride, is correctible.

Throughout his major poems Pope wars relentlessly against pride as well as against specific consequent aberrations of the human will. Each of his longer poems derives its deepest import from the castigation of some correctible evil. Even *Eloisa to Abelard*, which at first glance might seem to be a glorification of mad passion, is in effect a caveat against it. Who would suffer as

Eloisa suffers? Or as Abelard? Both early and late in Pope's verse, from *Windsor Forest* to the *Dunciad*, the reader is confronted with attacks, in one guise or another, on correctible evil.

The *Moral Essays* and the *Satires* are a veritable catalogue of sinners. Narcissa, Atossa, Sporus, Gripus, Atticus, Bufo, Sir Balaam, Sappho—all in his gallery of sinners, whether fictional or historical, are labeled and pinned wriggling to the wall of Pope's Inferno. Like Dante, Pope is careful to preserve the entertainment aspect of his excursion among sinners, though he of course does it in a very different way. The pity the reader feels, for example, at Dante's story of the tragic love of Francesca and Paolo and the horror excited by Ugolino's confession of cannibalism are unequivocal. But the pity and horror evoked by such a typical Popian sinner as Narcissa are conditioned by humor. Narcissa, though at the point of death, is anxious about having her cheeks rouged and her corpse tricked out in Brussels lace.

What is true of Pope's rhetorical approach to Narcissa is true generally of his approach to correctible evils. He constantly displays in this, as in other matters, his tendency to condition and qualify, to build richly and complexly rather than simply or thinly. This tendency, together with other aspects of his technique of dealing with correctible evil, is plainly visible even in so early a poem as *Windsor Forest*.

Inseparable from Pope's strategy in handling evil is the principle of antithesis. *Windsor Forest*, specifically, has a polar construction: Its positive pole represents peace, order, and unity; the negative pole, war, disorder, and disunity. And the desired mean is presented as a state

> Where order in variety we see,
> And where, though all things differ, all agree.
>
> (15–16)

Unlike later poems in this respect, *Windsor Forest* devotes by far the greater number of lines to idyllic scenes of the positive pole. Yet sufficient space to provide contrast is given negative scenes. After showing England under Queen Anne as a land of peace and plenty, Pope describes a condition of correctible evil prevailing under previous reigns. His comparison, he knows, is not dead history. For human beings, the threat of civilization slipping into chaos, and peace into war is always present. Turning from Anne's smiling fields, Pope says,

> Not thus the land appeared in ages past,
> A dreary desert, and a gloomy waste,
> To savage beasts and savage laws a prey,
> And kings more furious and severe than they.
>
> (43-46)

> In vain kind seasons swelled the teeming grain,
> Soft showers distilled, and suns grew warm in vain;
> The swain with tears his frustrate labour yields,
> And famished dies amidst his ripened fields.   (53-56)

> Awed by his Nobles, by his Commons curst,
> Th'Oppressor ruled tyrannic where he durst,
> Stretched o'er the Poor and Church his iron rod,
> And served alike his Vassals and his God.   (73-76)

The use of antithesis in these passages is primarily pictorial. But a simple pictorial antithesis was not enough for Pope. Following the Augustan precept to teach delightfully, he strove for variety within the antithesis. The pictorial effects are cinematic rather than static. Combined with the "before and after" pattern is a movie-like pattern of panoramic shots and close-ups. At one moment the camera shows a bird's-eye view of fruitful plain or devastated abbey; at the next it swoops close enough for the observer to see a peasant farmer robbed of his produce.

Non-pictorial antitheses in these passages are frequent. One in particular is characteristic of Pope's insight into correctible evil and his treatment of it. The Norman oppressor is said to have "served alike his Vassals and his God." The presumption is that man and God ought not to be served alike even in a favorable sense. But this tyrant did not seek to worship God or help man. What in his era was officially earmarked God's—the Church—he persecuted. God's human creatures he maltreated as if they were lower than beasts. In doing this he violated, in Pope's view, not only the spiritual hierarchy of being but the derived political hierarchy as well. He transgressed the decorum of a king, and in a manner un-kinged himself; for his bestial actions degraded him below his own subjects.

In the phrase "served alike his Vassals and his God" the reader is conscious of a temporary glimmer of complimentary meaning. It is of course illogical in the context. But the glimmer dazzles just long enough to make is necessary to re-examine the contextual meaning of "served alike." This is decidedly not "The conquerer served his vassals as if they were God," though syntactically, in isolation, and for a fruitful instant the words do convey that. The transient illogicality sharpens the contrast between what should be and what is.

Pope's approach to the correctible evil in this passage exhibits other factors typical of his approach throughout his verse. Aside from employing antithesis in a variety of ways, he paints a vivid and concrete but universalized picture. He mingles fictional personalities with historical. He uses plot or elements of it. He defines evil by reference to the Great Scale and its decorums. He maintains an urbane tone. Finally, he conditions all these factors by weaving them into a verbal and metaphysical net so fine it gives the effect of a smooth surface.

The ordering principle of the *Essay on Criticism* is also the polarity of good and evil. Here the specific polarity is good critic against bad. The literary apprentice is instructed to avoid the bad critic's faults by keeping constantly in mind the good critic's merits. Part III, for example, contains both an honor roll of critics from Horace to Walsh and a generalized portrait of the ideal critic. In accordance with the demands of urbanity, Pope does not have a formal "dishonor roll" of bad critics (though he consigns a few lines, in passing, to John Dennis). For the most part, however, the descriptions of bad critics are couched in the mode of fictional generalization, as in these lines:

> The bookful blockhead, ignorantly read,
> With loads of learnèd lumber in his head,
> With his own tongue still edifies his ears,
> And always list'ning to himself appears.

All books he reads, and all he reads assails,
From Dryden's Fables down to Durfey's Tales.
(III, 612–617)

The poem places particular emphasis on the critic's need for
urbanity, but it also stresses that, however sternly analytic his
method, the critic's manner must be conversational and easy.
Pope's own approach illustrates this. Part II, for instance, is an
itemized analysis of the pitfalls that beset critics. But in examining these, Pope is as careful to avoid monotony of approach as
Homer was when describing death after death in the *Iliad*. He
never forgets that his purpose is not only to explain but to entertain.

For example, he approaches pride, the first evil to which critics
are prone, by way of ironic humor:

Pride, where wit fails, steps in to our defence,
And fills up all the mighty Void of sense. (II, 209–210)

The evil of imperfect learning is presented in the sparkling paradox of drinking from the Pierian spring and then enlarged upon
in the Alpine image Dr. Johnson admired. The fallacy of judging
the whole by the part is approached in several different ways.
Pope begins by enumerating various kinds of partial criticism.
Next he introduces a brief narrative, that of the playwright and
La Mancha's Knight. Then, turning to critics concerned mainly
with the minutiae of versification, he adopts the amusing device
of illustrating with his own verse the points he is criticising:

These equal syllables alone require,
Though oft the ear the open vowels tire;
While expletives their feeble aid do join;
And ten low words oft creep in one dull line.
(II, 344–347)

This variation in approach is continued throughout Part II.
Clearly Pope is not content to fight the devil of bad criticism with
mere rhymed textbook maxims. His method of attack is Parnassian; all the colors of rhetoric are enlisted.

In *Moral Essay* I the correctible evils aimed at are chiefly these
two: haste and presumption in judging other human beings, and

failure to control passion to a worthy end. By means of a series of aphorisms and portraits Pope develops the theme that accurate knowledge of the motives of others is virtually unobtainable, and concludes with the following admonition:

> Know, GOD and NATURE only are the same:
> In Man, the judgment shoots at flying game.
>
> (95–96)

Passion, in the observer, the observed, or both, will always hinder exact knowledge.

But passion is not presented as an unqualified evil. Rather, like the alternation of night and day, Pope says, it must be accepted as a condition inseparable from man's estate. Passion becomes a definite evil only when uncontrolled by right reason. After repeatedly admonishing the reader that human nature cannot be accurately judged by man, Pope paradoxically but rightly assumes that human beings must attempt to judge one another. He further assumes that if they are sufficiently wary of the pitfalls pointed out, they may arrive at approximately correct estimates.

The aim of character analysis, he says, should be the discovery of the Ruling Passion. This, like passions in general, may be either good or bad. Some ruling passions, such as Wharton's lust for praise and Helluo's gluttony, are not restrained by reasonable ends and bring disaster. Others, such as Cobham's love of country, have rational aims and bring the rewards of virtue.

It is characteristic of Pope's method of dealing with undesirable moral traits that, though he gives a long catalogue of negative examples, the only positive one in this poem is Cobham's patriotism. This practice he specifically defends in Dialogue II of the *Epilogue to the Satires*:

> P. To find an honest man, I beat about,
> And love him, court him, praise him, in or out.
> F. Then why so few commended?
> P.   Not so fierce;
> Find you the Virtue, and I'll find the Verse.
>
> (102–105)

Pope here has metaphysical truth as well as rhetorical convention and satiric strategy on his side. Wise and virtuous men are scarcer than fools and villains. And satire cannot be an honor roll of the virtuous.

In *Moral Essay* I, as in some other poems where Pope adduces "virtuous examples," the lines on Cobham are in some degree undercut by satire. Pope's long-standing friendship with Cobham, the political circumstances surrounding the Viscount's inclusion in the poem, and the fact that it is dedicated to him—none of these necessarily means that a reference to Cobham will be pure praise. The verses about him, coming after a series of brief narratives portraying the persistence of vicious or absurd ruling passions in death, are

> And you! brave COBHAM, to the latest breath
> Shall feel your ruling passion strong in death:
> Such in those moments as in all the past,
> "Oh, save my Country, Heaven!" shall be your last.
> (262–265)

Politics is properly a concern of the living citizen, but a Christian reader would question whether the last moments of a dying man should not be employed in setting his spiritual house in order. Still to be concerned with the affairs of any particular earthly government would seem to smack more of passion than of reason. Nevertheless, love of country is undeniably a worthier passion than the miserly Euclio's solicitude for his possessions or the itch of the senile lecher who ". . . to his wench . . . crawls on knocking knees,/And envies every sparrow that he sees." Cobham does not die like a saint, with every mortal care transcended; but at least he dies in the grip of a good ruling passion.

The reluctance exhibited in this poem to portray specific persons as unqualifiedly virtuous is typical. Pope's regard for metaphysical truth as well as for practical, everyday realism prevented him from depicting any human being as faultless. Even his eulogy on Martha in *Moral Essay* II is amusingly undercut. She is the best of women, but still a woman, and as such only the "fairest of the spotted kind."

Practicality, or in the favored Augustan phrasing "good sense," is a distinctive mark of Pope's treatment of correctible evil. It is part of the decorum of the subject. And good sense is frequently used like a touchstone to distinguish good from evil.

In *Moral Essay* IV, for example, one of Pope's purposes is to identify correctible evil in the fields of architecture, interior decorating, and landscape gardening. Uniformly he exposes evil as defiance of good sense. Fools, he says, will

> Reverse your Ornaments, and hang them all
> On some patch'd dog-hole ek'd with ends of wall,
> Then clap four slices of Pilaster on't,
> That, lac'd with bits of rustic, makes a Front;
> Or call the winds thro' long Arcades to roar,
> Proud to catch cold at a Venetian door. (31–36)

Or in Timon's dining-room,

> The rich Buffet well-colour'd Serpents grace,
> And gaping Tritons spew to wash your face.
> Is this a dinner? This a Genial room?
> No, 'tis a Temple, and a Hecatomb. (153–156)

Religious principles, however, are invariably at the bottom of Pope's approach to correctible evil. St. Paul's admonition, "We are all members one of another," is good sense on the practical level. It also lends itself to a mystical approach to human evil. That a certain mysticism, traditional and taken for granted, underlies Pope's attitude toward the community repercussions of individual guilt is undeniable. Breaking the mystic union which exists between all members of the Great Scale wreaks havoc, corrupting religion and perverting polity. The Golden Age ended, says Pope in the *Essay on Man*, when man set himself up against both animal and man, inventing

> Th'enormous faith of many made for one;
> . . . .
> Altars grew marble then, and reek'd with gore:
> Then first the Flamen tasted living food;
> Next his grim idol smear'd with human blood;
> With Heav'n's own thunders shook the world below,
> And play'd the God an engine on his foe. (III, 242–268)

It is from this principle of the interdependence of all created beings that the *Dunciad* derives its most serious impact. Pert dullness, the evil it attacks, will not voluntarily confine itself to Bedlam. It walks abroad courting acceptance as wit until unmasked by true intelligence. The tone of an entire culture, Pope feels, is as surely lowered by the propagation of dull books and wrong-headed philosophies as it is by felonies condoned. Hence the Tibbalds and Cibbers, the misguided patrons, Grubstreet scribblers, pedantic schoolmen, freethinkers, and positivistic natural scientists are presented as not merely ridiculous but as a menace to civilization.

But Pope's presentation of the menace is not direct. Though he never allows the reader to lose sight of the current on which the Dunces are rushing toward chaos, he concentrates attention upon the fool's-gold structure on which they float. In order to destroy more thoroughly their real capacity for evil, he highlights their ridiculous aspect. The pert ecclesiastical dullard, John Henley, for example, is exhibited thus, functioning in his "gilt tub":

> Imbrown'd with native bronze, lo! Henley stands,
> Tuning his voice, and balancing his hands.
> How fluent nonsense trickles from his tongue!
> How sweet the periods, neither said, nor sung!
> Still break the benches, Henley! with thy strain,
> While Sherlock, Hare, and Gibson preach in vain.
> Oh great Restorer of the good old Stage,
> Preacher at once, and Zany of thy age!   (III, 199–206)

The loyalty of certain university professors to Dulness' throne is described in this manner:

> Prompt at the call, around the Goddess roll
> Broad hats, and hoods, and caps, a sable shoal:
> Thick and more thick the black blockade extends,
> A hundred head of Aristotle's friends.   (IV, 189–192)

The reader is left to draw his own conclusions about the seriousness of the threat when the professors, who should be leaders of thought, roll in a hooded, undistinguished herd like swine around Circe.

The nature of the evil again determines the strategy of the attack in *The Rape of the Lock*. The central problem in this poem is the inability to see clearly what things are of major importance and what minor. Closely connected with this is a failure to accept realities and a preference for appearance over realities.

Representative of both the matter and the method of the poem is this couplet:

> The hungry Judges soon the Sentence sign,
> And Wretches hang that Jury-men may Dine.
> (III, 21–22)

Judges and jurors are sacrificing a major concern, life or death for accused prisoners, in order not to be late for their dinners— a pat instance of the deadly nature of gluttony. And the Cave of Spleen, the underworld of this poem, is tenanted by men and women who were unable to come to terms with reality:

> Here living Teapots stand, one Arm held out,
> One bent; the Handle this, and that the Spout:
> A Pipkin there, like Homer's Tripod walks;
> Here sighs a Jar, and there a Goose-pye talks;
> Men prove with Child, as pow'rful Fancy works,
> And Maids turn'd Bottels, call aloud for Corks.
> (IV, 49–54)

Belinda herself is visited by spleen because of the prudish outcries she raises at the rape of her lock. And in her speech at the close of Canto IV she indicates a preference for appearance over reality when she implies that she would rather actually have lost her chastity—providing the loss were not apparent—than her conspicuous curl. Belinda doesn't see clearly.

Throughout this poem much attention is focused on what *is* seen, the ceremonies and elegant possessions of the fashionable world. Pope's manner of rebuking that world is seemly and ceremonious. Its real evil he approaches indirectly, urbanely, even playfully. The weapon he uses to encounter evil here is not the rapier of the *Satires* or the cudgel of the *Dunciad* but Belinda's bodkin. In the world of Hampton Court that little silver bodkin is a sufficient weapon.

The *Satires* proper, of course, constitute Pope's most direct attack on correctible evils. The vices and follies they censure are always with us; and Pope is not afraid to present them topically, in accordance with his mature habit of fearlessly naming names. Still, however lamentable the failing or sordid the crime, he is always careful to preserve the framework of conversational urbanity. The contrast between matter and manner sharpens the impact of what he says. Pope never relaxes "the strong Antipathy of Good to Bad"; occasionally he even rises to a tone of prophetic denunciation. But he invariably maintains rhetorical control, and his pervading approach is subtle and detached.

This very detachment in all its many guises imparts to Pope's lifelong campaign against correctible evils much of its power and brilliance. The persistence of that campaign leaves no doubt that it is a mainspring of his poetry. His shafts strike home because in his verse he is able to withdraw from the practical urgency of evil and to insinuate his attack under cover of a brilliant display of rhetoric and surface interests.

13

Pope's Poetic World

THROUGHOUT his work Pope's attention is firmly focused on man, generic man, as he is related to other men in human society, the world, and the universe. The direction of Pope's interest in man is not inward and exclusive, but outward and inclusive. And the movement of his poetry, to borrow his own metaphor in the *Essay on Man*, is like that of self-love (by which he means a natural and proper concern for directing one's self as a unit in society):

> Self-love but serves the virtuous mind to wake,
> As the small pebble stirs the peaceful lake;
> The centre mov'd, a circle strait succeeds,
> Another still, and still another spreads;
> Friend, parent, neighbour, first it will embrace,
> His country next, and next all human race,
> Wide and more wide, th'o'erflowings of the mind
> Take ev'ry creature in, of ev'ry kind;
> Earth smiles around, with boundless bounty blest,
> And Heav'n beholds its image in his breast.
>   (IV, 363–372)

This outgoing tendency, observable both in Pope's large and in his small rhetorical units, does not, as might be expected, lead to unsubstantiality and diffuseness. On the contrary, it actually sharpens the impact of the original "pebble." His habit of fixing whatever concept or object he is presenting in relation to other concepts and objects gives it a more unassailable communicative value, as, for example, does Eliot's fixation in *Gerontion* of

> . . . De Bailhache, Fresca, Mrs. Cammel, whirled
> Beyond the circuit of the shuddering Bear
> In fractured atoms. . . .

Pope's constant emphasis upon a total and universal frame of reference for particulars permits his poetry—and in the Popian world, man—to view reality with some steadiness and to view it whole. It is notably the goddess of dulness whom Pope makes express the opposite opinion:

> O! Would the Sons of Men once think their Eyes
> And Reason giv'n them but to study Flies!
> See Nature in some partial narrow shape,
> And let the Author of the Whole escape. (IV, 453–456)

And it is one of the devotees of dulness who, in a prayer to the goddess, gives explicit expression to the position of the sinning solipsist:

> Let others creep by timid steps, and slow,
> On plain Experience lay foundations low,
> By common sense to common knowledge bred,
> And last, to Nature's Cause thro' Nature led.
> All-seeing in thy mists, we want no guide,
> Mother of Arrogance, and Source of Pride!
> We nobly take the high Priori Road,
> And reason downward, till we doubt of God:
> Make Nature still encroach upon his plan;
> And shove him off as far as e'er we can:
> Thrust some Mechanic Cause into his place;
> Or bind in Matter, or diffuse in Space.
> Or, at one bound o'er-leaping all his laws,
> Make God Man's Image, Man the final Cause,
> Find Virtue local, all Relations scorn,
> See all in Self, and but for self be born:
> Of naught so certain as our Reason still,
> Of naught so doubtful as of Soul and Will.
> Oh hide the God still more! and make us see
> Such as Lucretius drew, a God like Thee:
> Wrapt up in Self . . . (IV, 465–485)

Dulness herself is made an archsolipsist; and the dull, scorning all outward guides, confident that they possess an infallible inner light, are shown ready to act without hesitation upon any hare-brained schemes that visit their heads—schemes uncorrected by humble measuring against standards outside themselves.

There is a significant difference, by the way, between the typical dullard of Pope's day and the twentieth-century solipsist as he is typified in Prufrock. The present-day dullard, feeling, for better or worse, that he has no guide but himself, yet doubts himself and is therefore inhibited from all effective action, whether wise or foolish.

"Reas'ning Pride" is one of the chief supports of this spiritual nearsightedness; hence in Pope's world, as in Greek and Christian theology, pride is a deadly sin. Pope inveighs against pride frequently, forcibly, and in a wide range of human concerns.

Closely allied to these attacks on pride is Pope's distrust of reason as an unqualified instrument for dealing with reality. In *Moral Essay* I he phrases it this way:

> Our depths who fathoms, or our shallows finds,
> Quick whirls, and shifting eddies, of our minds?
> On human actions reason though you can,
> It may be Reason, but it is not Man:
> His Principle of action once explore,
> That instant 'tis his Principle no more.
> Like following life through creatures you dissect,
> You lose it in the moment you detect.
> Yet more; the difference is as great between
> The optics seeing, as the object seen.
> All Manners take a tincture from our own;
> Or come discoloured through our Passions shown.
> Or Fancy's beam enlarges, multiplies,
> Contracts, inverts, and gives ten thousand dyes.
> Nor will Life's stream for Observation stay,
> It hurries all too fast to mark their way:
> In vain sedate reflections we would make,
> When half our knowledge we must snatch, not take.
> Oft, in the Passions' wild rotation tost,
> Our spring of action to ourselves is lost:
> Tired, not determined, to the last we yield,
> And what comes then is master of the field.   (23–44)

Even in poems where the fictional rather than the didactic element predominates, reason affords only feeble help—to Eloisa; for example, in reconciling herself to the realities of her situation. And Clarissa's reasoned speech in Canto V of *The Rape of the Lock* persuades no one:

> So spoke the Dame, but no Applause ensu'd;
> Belinda frown'd, Thalestris call'd her Prude.
> To Arms, to Arms! the fierce Virago cries,
> And swift as Lightning to the Combat flies.
>
> (V, 35-38)

The insufficiency of reason as a guide for comprehending the workings of providence, understanding human nature, or administering his own life, throws Pope's man back upon an acquiescence in "whatever is, is right," and ultimately upon an attitude of wonder in regarding the universe. The emphasis upon Pope as a poet of reason has been carried too far when it has led to the overlooking or slighting of this important element in his system.

The philosophy Pope was combating views reality as a mechanism which man now partially comprehends and will some day comprehend entirely. This view tends toward a homocentric universe, a universe in which man's attention is focused upon himself as the only knower and knowledgeable controller.

The viewing of reality as mystery—assuming that irresponsible enthusiasm is shunned—tends toward an abatement of man's preoccupation with himself. No longer the sole competent knowing and judging agent, he is thrown outward, away from himself, and toward the infinite. His individuality is seen in perspective, as part of a greater individuality; his "is-ness" as part of a greater "what is."

Connected with Pope's resultant stressing of the moral dangers of "spiritual incest" and "reas'ning Pride," is his well-known preference for the generic rather than the eccentric.* For Pope as

* The more common phrasing, "preference for the general over the particular," is misleading. It has engendered a misconception that Pope was deficient in particular observation and reference—a misconception which cannot consist with attentive reading of his works, whether his observation of human or nonhuman nature is in question.

for Dante, those closest to the Center (the non-solipsists) were the most blest, the most to be commended, and the most real.

But Pope did not, any more than Dante, deny the existence of eccentrics. In fact, Pope often describes his sinners with great vividness and homeliness of detail. Examples of this are such portraits as the celebrated ones of Atticus, Sporus, and Atossa, or his description of the wretched end of Lord Villiers in *Moral Essay* III:

> In the worst inn's worst room, with mat half-hung,
> The floors of plaister, and the walls of dung,
> On once a flock-bed, but repair'd with straw,
> With tape-ty'd curtains, never meant to draw,
> The George and Garter dangling from that bed
> Where tawdry yellow strove with dirty red,
> Great Villiers lies—alas! how chang'd . . .   (299–305)

The sordid details enhance the reader's aversion to this earthly hell and to the backslider inhabiting it, thereby increasing the attractiveness of such an individual as the Man of Ross, whose behavior is more in harmony with the divine plan, particularly as concerns the use of riches.

Riches, incidentally, whether hoarded or spent lavishly on personal whims, can, Pope points out in *Moral Essay* III, give rise to a very tangible sort of solipsism:

> Riches, like insects, when conceal'd they lie,
> Wait but for wings, and in their season, fly.
> Who sees pale Mammon pine against his store,
> Sees but a backward steward for the Poor;
> This year a Reservoir, to keep and spare,
> The next a Fountain, spouting thro' his Heir.
>
> (171–176)

Riches are mishandled when spent madly or hoarded, as madly, for the self. Their proper use is outgoing, with discretion such as the Man of Ross exemplifies.

In this respect, Pope's concern with the mean as preferable to the extreme in conduct—a concept especially well demonstrated in the *Essay on Criticism* and supported in all his works—is also related to his antipathy for solipsism. By following the *via media* the individual avoids the eccentric and approaches the generic, the norm in any realm of conduct. And the positive norm is the one most conscious of human society, most outgoing, most consonant with "the army of unalterable law." Pope's unremitting recommendation and display of such qualities as control and balance, qualities which tend to make the individual center-seeking rather than center-fleeing, confirm this viewpoint.

Since solipsism is a distortion of values resulting from failure to measure one's self and the world outside accurately in relation to each other, Pope is greatly concerned with an exact, a nice representation of values. Vagueness and nebulosity are no part of his poetic world, whether it is a matter of enunciating general principles or of searching for le mot juste.

Diction, metaphor, rhyme, and meter contribute to this precision; and all the elements are carefully controlled to that end. Pope as a craftsman is not content with near misses; nor will he tolerate superfluous shots. Though he is a master of multivalence, he handles both his technical resources and the stuff of poetry with a splendid economy.

He does not, for example, employ epithets in the somewhat loose and unessential way in which Yeats uses "white" in the following lines from Among School Children:

> I walk through the long schoolroom questioning:
> A kind old nun in a white hood replies.

It is not important to the total meaning of Yeats' poem whether that hood is white or gray; it is not even strictly necessary that the hood be mentioned. The same is true of the use of "white" in these lines from Auden's Doom is Dark:

> Doom is dark and deeper than any sea-dingle.
> Upon what man it fall
> In spring, day-wishing flowers appearing,
> Avalanche sliding, white snow from rock-face . . .

And it is true of the use of "dusty" in Hart Crane's At Melville's Tomb:

> Often beneath the wave, wide from this ledge
> The dice of drowned men's bones he saw bequeath

An embassy. Their numbers as he watched,
Beat on the dusty shore and were obscured.

Yeats' "white," Auden's "white," and Crane's "dusty"—the minute exactitudes conveyed by these adjectives, however true, are not indispensably pertinent. But John Crowe Ransom's "white" in *The Equilibrists* and Eliot's in *Ash Wednesday* function essentially, in somewhat the way Pope's epithets function. Pope dispenses with the truth of the photographic epithet in favor of a truth of stricter relevance to central meaning.

However clear and detailed an individual impression, it is impossible to have an accurate perception of values unless the perceptions have been formulated upon a basis of complete, not partial knowledge. The solipsist errs in part because he does not know or is not at the moment conscious of the whole truth. He perceives, perhaps, that Sir Isaac Newton has made some searching observations about natural science; and proceeds to an arrogant pride in human reason. Pope recalls to his mind the frailty of reason by re-establishing Newton's accomplishment in a universal context:

> Superior beings, when of late they saw
> A mortal Man unfold all Nature's law,
> Admir'd such wisdom in an earthly shape,
> And shew'd a NEWTON as we shew an Ape.
> (*Essay on Man*, II, 31–34)

It is a significant aspect of Pope's communication that no attempt is made to present a situation in the one-sided manner characteristic of pragmatic oratory. Pope's end is not action but contemplation. His practice, therefore, is not the suppression of all but some narrow part of the truth as an incitement to action along lines preconceived by the orator, but the presentation of all aspects, even to the point of paradox. Paradox, irony, and metaphor drawn from homely or unaesthetic realms are, as has been demonstrated, important in achieving this end.

Related to the effort to depict the whole truth and to avoid the suppression of incongruities is the fact that Pope has a clear preference for securing scope by oblique rather than by direct methods. Homer, Dante, and Milton deal overtly with themes of epic scope, in the main excluding or euphemizing nonheroic matter. Milton's warring angels do not, for instance, like the *Dunciad* Jove, take time out for latrine duty. Eve does not, like Silia in *Moral Essay* II, get a pimple on her nose after eating the forbidden apple.

Yet Pope, with the most unlikely subject matter—a dressing table, a card game, a coffee service—can open windows on a wider world. He can make little, ridiculous, and even sordid things convey portentous meanings. In an urbane, worldly-wise age, an age like the Augustan that strove for integration rather than separation, this was a more effective means of attaining scope than would have been a direct plunge into unrelieved heroic.

In this respect the twentieth century resembles the Augustan age; it distrusts the heroic. Prufrock's baldness and white flannel trousers function in this oblique way. Furthermore, for a poetry like Pope's, mainly cerebral in its approach to reality, this oblique method permits the inclusion of many enriching concrete details and provides that firm anchorage in the tangible facts of daily existence which makes possible, ultimately, Pope's convincing emphasis upon the nature of reality as mystery—as a whole transcending man's rational part.

In seeming contrast to these outward-going aspects of Pope's poetic world is the undeniable tightness and concentration of his verse, the packed and epigrammatic quality for which he is celebrated. But the contrast is altogether superficial. Actually, the centrifugal and centripetal elements reinforce each other and conduce to the same end.

Pope's packing of multiple meanings into epithets and metaphors results not in a solipsistic narrowing down but in an expansion of communication. The circumscribed form plays against the extending meaning. It is as if, when the pebble is cast into the pool, the ripples could go out in ever widening circles and still remain within the pebble.

Because Pope's statements and metaphors are valid on more

than one plane, they have the effect of drawing together the universe of cognition, of integrating it rather than permitting it to disintegrate into solipsistic fragments. The jaguar looks into the pool, not at his own image, but at an image of the complete universe, with himself in his proper place there; the whole brought within the focus of his own eyeball:

All forms that perish other forms supply,
(By turns we catch the vital breath, and die)
Like bubbles on the sea of Matter born,
They rise, they break, and to that sea return.
Nothing is foreign: Parts relate to whole;
One all-extending, all-preserving Soul
Connects each being, greatest with the least;
Made Beast in aid of Man, and Man of Beast;
All serv'd, all serving! nothing stands alone;
The chain holds on, and where it ends, unknown.

(*Essay on Man*, III, 17–26)

INDEX

Index

Addison, Joseph, 30, 197
Aesthetic distance, 10, 12, 88
Allegory, in *Temple of Fame*, 131-32
Ambiguity, *see* Multivalence
Ancients: imitation of, 23, 185-86; versus Moderns, 24, 40-41
Antithesis, 25, 60, 69, 90, 94, 101, 117, 125, 134, 172: effect of Pope's use of, 66; in *Pastorals*, 70, 71; in *Eloisa to Abelard*, 72, 73-74; in *The Rape of the Lock*, 74-75; in *Essay on Man*, 75-84 *passim*; in Imitation of Donne's *Fourth Satire*, 197, 205; in Imitation of First Epistle of Horace's Second Book, 207, 210; in *Windsor Forest*, 212-14
Arbuthnot, John, 4
Aristotle, 97, 123, 144
Auden, W. H., 125, 227-28

Bathurst, Allen, first Earl, 156
Beauty, 58, 104-6, 121-22, 147, 202, 208-9. *See also* Ugliness
Bentley, Richard, 18, 120, 148
Beowulf, 86, 125, 126
Biblical echoes, 86, 112, 118, 178-79, 188-89, 198, 207
Biographic fallacy, 7, 17-18
Blount, Martha, 141
Boethius, 81
Bolingbroke, Henry St. John, Viscount, 19, 159
Bridges, Robert, 91
Brooks, Cleanth, 5, 51, 74, 96
Browning, Robert, 9, 10
Bunyan, John, 19, 170

Carew, Thomas, 194
Chandos, Duke of, 18
Chaucer, Geoffrey, 105, 126, 187: use of tension compared to Pope's, 128-35
Cibber, Colley, 18, 38, 116-18, 120, 121, 128, 148, 192
Cobham, Richard Temple, Viscount, 216-17
Complexity, *see* Multivalence, Scope
Crane, Hart, 227-28
Crashaw, Richard, 190
Criticism, of Pope, 3-5, 15, 52, 125, 146, 185, 186
Curll, Edmund, 121, 148

Dante, 9, 20, 212, 226, 229
Decorum, 84, 123: of poet, 5, 55, 184; and irony, 38-42 *passim*, *Essay on Man*, 39, 61; *Moral Essay IV*, 39-42; and metaphor, 87, 91, 99; *Essay on Criticism*, 97; and genre, 99, 160, 161, 162; and Great Scale, 214
Denham, Sir John, 188
Dennis, John, 18, 143, 214
Dialogue, use of, 156, 157-59, 179-80
Dialogue I, *Epilogue to the Satires*, 61-63, 63-64, 127-28, 150, 178-80
Dialogue II, *Epilogue to the Satires*, 139, 216-17
Dickens, Charles, 32-33
Diction: *Essay on Criticism*, 21, 24, 26-27, 143, 164, 227-28; *Temple of Fame*, 134; *Moral Essay I*, 157; *Moral Essay II*, 157-58; *Iliad*, 169-70, 172; *The Rape of the Lock*, 172;

233